CHICKEN

OVER TWO HUNDRED RECIPES DEVOTED TO ONE GLORIOUS BIRD

CATHERINE PHIPPS

EBURY
PRESS

10 9 8 7 6 5 4 3 2 1

Ebury Press, an imprint of Ebury Publishing,
20 Vauxhall Bridge Road,
London, SW1V 2SA

Ebury Press is part of the Penguin Random House group
of companies whose addresses can be found at
global.penguinrandomhouse.com

First published by Ebury Press in 2015

www.eburypublishing.co.uk

A CIP catalogue record for this book is available from the British Library

Design: Will Webb
Photography: Andy Sewell
Food stylist: Ellie Jarvis, Stephanie Dellner and Tanya Sadourian
Stylist: Laura Fyfe

ISBN: 978 0 091 95972 2

Colour origination by Altaimage, London
Printed and bound in China by C&C Offset Printing Co. Ltd

Penguin Random House is committed to a sustainable future for our business, our readers and our planet. This book is made from Forest Stewardship Council® certified paper.

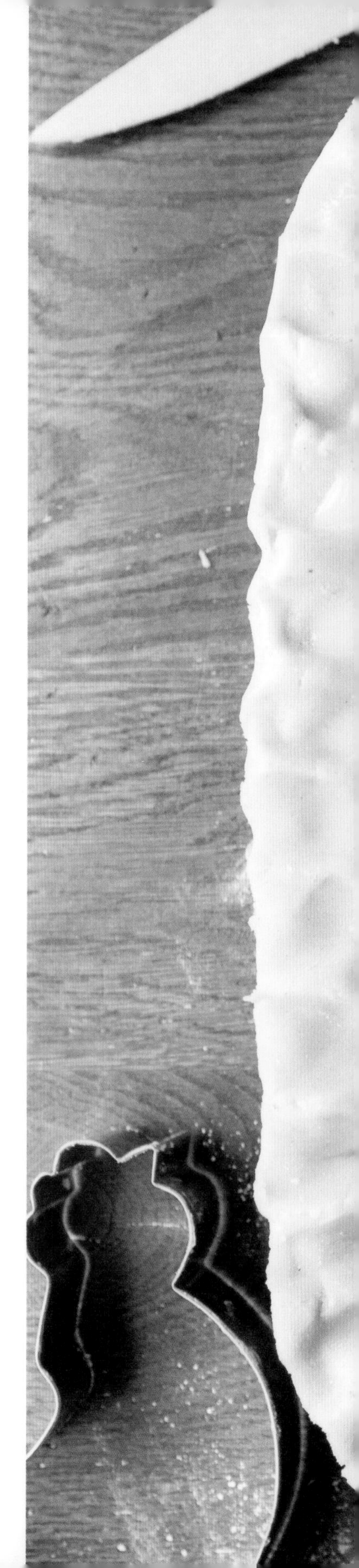

CONTENTS

INTRODUCTION

'Poultry is for the cook what canvas is to the painter.'
Brillat-Savarin

'Everyone loves chicken, right?'
Homer Simpson

I remember the first time I roasted a chicken. I was around seven or eight and my mother was ill and directed operations from the sofa. I cooked the whole meal: chicken smeared in butter on a bed of onions and thyme, roast potatoes, vegetables, even proper gravy. I don't remember much about eating it, but I do remember being proud of myself and feeling as though I'd 'saved' Sunday. Because in our house, a Sunday without a roast – especially a roast chicken – was no Sunday at all. Even now, it's my idea of home.

I may not remember sitting down to the meal, but I know exactly how it would have tasted, because I've been cooking it on a regular basis ever since. I love everything about the taste and texture of proper chicken, no other meat gives quite so much variety in both. There's that strong savoury quality, balanced by the merest hint of sweetness and – if decently reared with outdoor access – a touch of gaminess, too.
I especially love the crisp and sticky skin and the soft, tender texture of the brown meat, but even the slightly stringy breast meat is made worthwhile as it can have such an intensely umami quality it can make the mouth pucker and water.

A decent chicken has always been one of my favourite things to eat and I was taught from an early age to appreciate its usefulness in the kitchen. My parents believed strongly that I should understand the origins and value of the food we ate and my mother ensured I knew how to cook it. Chickens were the first animals we kept, for both eggs and meat. They were my responsibility as soon as I was deemed old enough and despite the fact that I loved the homely cluck the chickens made whilst they grubbed around the garden (I still love that sound and the feeling it evokes), I was also quite happy to eat them when the time came. And of course, that time did come with an inevitable regularity. Roasters – usually young cockerels – were allowed to strut around until fattened up (a bit older than spring chickens or poussins), then they were dispatched, along with any old and tired layers.

Our home-reared chickens were supplemented by birds from local producers: farmers' wives or retired farm labourers who raised small flocks for 'hen money' all year round, but especially at Christmas when we would eat cockerel rather than turkey. We knew where our chickens came from, what they had been fed, how they had been slaughtered, all things I do my best to find out about the chicken I eat today. And in this age when intensively farmed chicken is the norm and people are becoming more and more disconnected from their food, this can be hard to do. Hard, but not impossible and it needn't break the bank either.

Cooking and eating a whole chicken was an event, a special treat no matter how many times we ate it on a Sunday. But leftovers were extensive and old layers – the 'boiling fowls' – were also treated with respect. They were slowly and gently poached (boiling is a bit of a misnomer) to extract the full amount of flavour and goodness for nourishing broths, and to soften the perfectly edible but rather stringy meat. Stock from poaching or from saving up old carcasses was always plentiful, so the flavour of chicken was carried through into many of our meals.

I realise now that this way of cooking – using the complete chicken in as many ways as possible – has informed my whole approach to food. It was economical, being very nose to tail or beak to claw in this case. We didn't use the cockscomb or the feet (and I still don't today), but ate just about everything else. What this meant was that chicken could often be used to enhance, add depth to or transform an otherwise meatless meal, whether by frying in schmaltz (rendered chicken fat, as nutrient-rich and well-flavoured as duck or goose fat); using a well-balanced chicken stock, sometimes with some leftover meat, in a soup, stew, rice or pasta dish; or simply adding some shards of well-browned chicken skin as a garnish. Consequently I have never adopted the modern and deeply uneconomical way of buying chicken pieces (especially chicken breasts), but have always, even during my most impecunious periods, bought a whole bird and made it last at least a week, longer if I use the freezer. The recipes in the book reflect this.

I have always known that this is a very economical way of eating chicken, but it is only quite recently that I realised how traditional it is, too. While researching this book I found that, when looking specifically at British cookery books, before 1950 there are few chicken recipes beyond ways to roast, stew and occasionally grill. The other emphasis is on dishes using cooked chicken, i.e. leftovers. There are one or two dishes using chicken pieces, such as an early curry recipe in Eliza Acton's *Modern Cookery for Private Families*, but these are largely ancillary.

In the last 60 years or so, our culinary landscape has changed almost beyond recognition and the way we eat chicken is at the heart of this. We now eat more chicken than any other meat. This really took off in the 1950s, when two things happened. Firstly, chickens became widely available again after World War II and we started raising them intensively. Secondly, and more positively, this was when our outlook broadened. The world shrunk, we travelled more and we discovered new cuisines; the cookery book market, spearheaded by the Penguin list, expanded beyond recognition to accommodate this. We came to value chicken more for its versatility, for its ability to work with so many different flavours.

There are good and bad aspects to this. On the one hand, I love – and am still quite excited by – the universality of chicken. It is central to virtually every omnivorous culture and no other meat can claim this. It means that for those of us who always thirst for something new to try (and let's face it, the average Westerner is a culinary magpie, constantly wanting to be dazzled by the latest, just-discovered cuisine), chicken provides us with the way in, the point of familiarity in an otherwise strange new world. The downside is that chicken has become ubiquitous, most of us accepting the modern trope that it will work with everything. What is wrong with this is that instead of being valued for its flavour, chicken has been relegated to the position of flavour carrier. Homer Simpson may well say we all love chicken. Brillat-Savarin may also say it's a blank canvas. I say that many of us now treat it with indifference and throw anything at it, without discrimination. For me, this is completely missing the point of chicken; we may as well be eating soya chunks. I feel strongly that if I can't appreciate the pure chicken-ness of chicken in every meal in which it appears, I shouldn't be eating it at all.

This is not to say that I don't appreciate chicken's versatility. Of course I do, and this book is brimming with recipes I have adapted from other cuisines, particularly those that I am most familiar with, by way of travel and family connections. After all, a book based solely on British chicken cookery would be a slim book indeed. So, of course, I have paired chicken with a whole host of different ingredients, some quite classic, others tried by me along the way. I have also allowed chicken to take a supporting role in places, particularly among some of the soups and salads, to illustrate how well 'chicken economy' can work. However, whether it is adding depth or a background note, or is part of an ensemble, or is taking centre stage, the chicken flavour is always paramount. Nowhere will you find a dish where chicken has been added as an afterthought, a way of ticking the protein box.

This book celebrates everything that I think is good about chicken. As a home cook I value the fact that it helps me cook economically, that it is possibly the most useful ingredient I have in my kitchen, that it is so versatile. Most of all, I love that even after months and months of testing recipes – many, many more than appear in this book – my family still feel happy, contented, even lucky, when they sit down to any kind of chicken dinner.

1. CHICKEN BASICS

including: Stocks, Schmaltz, Salting & Smoking

This is the chapter which I hope will convince you that it is always worth buying a whole chicken, because if treated properly, it will give you so much more – both in the eating and in value for money – than a trayful of pieces ever could.

This is a book about celebrating chicken, so, when talking about how to buy it, I do not want to dwell too much on the horrors of the intensive farming of birds. If you want to read up on this, you can't do better than Hattie Ellis's book, *Planet Chicken*.

I will just say this: if you buy an intensively reared chicken – welfare issues aside – you are buying a product that has been developed with speed of growth in mind. The birds will be out of proportion, with breasts so large they will find it difficult to stand. They will be pumped full of antibiotics and growth hormones and fed a homogenous diet, which results in meat with little flavour and a flabby texture. This kind of chicken is a good flavour carrier, but that's all.

If you do want to buy what I consider to be a better chicken, there are lots of options. I have tried many different chickens, from the much-fêted Poulet en Bresse and Label Anglais to the free-range birds in the supermarkets. You can also buy chickens raised on a specific diet; I love corn-fed free-range chickens, particularly for the beautiful yellow fat that they render. I am not going to recommend any particular type and I will rarely, if ever, buy an expensive 'artisan' organic chicken. I can't afford to and I don't see enough of a difference in flavour to warrant the extra money. What I have done is find a happy medium, and look for free-range chickens that have good access to the outdoors and a varied diet. If you live in a rural area it is still possible to find lots of farms raising small flocks and selling at the farm gate, or in local markets or butchers. This is a case of seek and ye shall find. When I lived in Norfolk (until quite recently), I found a good supplier quickly by word of mouth and the prices were competitive. If you live in an urban area, you need to depend more on the middle man, usually the supermarket or your butcher. You can't really do better than cultivate a good, trustworthy butcher (again, word of mouth will help here), as he should be able to tell you everything you need to know about the chicken. There are other benefits: he should be able to provide you with chicken carcasses if you want to make stock. Mine sells trays of them for next to nothing and, if you poach them gently, you will find that you can take a surprising amount of meat off them, too, before making the stock.

It is not for me to tell you what kind of chicken to buy, but, please, if you usually buy intensively farmed chicken, perhaps you could try spending a bit more for just one week. Roast or poach it simply with little additional flavouring and see if you can tell the difference. You could make up for the extra outlay by eating more vegetarian meals that week, or using some of the leftovers in the way I describe below. I always supplement my chicken buying in this way, but, if you buy a whole bird this time and you usually buy chicken pieces, I expect you will immediately start saving money, simply because you can create so many extra meals out of the leftovers.

I mostly buy a whole bird and either cook it whole or joint it. I find that it usually costs around the same as buying three or four chicken breasts and is much more useful. I also buy large piles of wings and thighs always on the bone as it is much cheaper. If you want to fillet them, you can still use the bone for stock. I never buy chicken breasts; they are expensive, something I have always found odd as the meat on the rest of the bird has a much better flavour and texture.

Let me give you an example. My household consists of two adults and two children under 10. If I roast or poach a bird, I make sure I have enough cheaper side dishes (stuffing, potatoes or other carbohydrates, lots of vegetables), so a reasonable amount of chicken – usually breast meat and anything attached to the carcass – is left over. Then there will be enough meat left over for a couple of sandwiches (again bulked out with salad ingredients), or to add some flavour to a risotto, soup or pasta dish, or to shred into a salad, fritters or pasties. Then of course the stock can be used from the carcass. Contrast this with the purchase of four chicken breasts, which is both more expensive and leaves you with nothing.

Regardless of the type of chicken you buy, you need to check it for freshness. This isn't so easy if you are buying plastic-wrapped chicken from the supermarket, but is still possible. You want to make sure that the skin is pale and creamy (or yellow if corn-fed). It should look quite taut and dry – not wrinkly and flabby – and if it is sitting in a tray, look out for any liquid: anything very runny is fine, anything that looks thicker and tackier means the bird is probably past its prime. Look out, too, for discolouration. I have too often seen hock burns (bruises on the legs) on birds purported to be free-range. Birds do get grazes which can look similar but be aware.

To store chicken, remove any plastic wrapping and put the bird on a plate or a rack above a tray. Cover loosely with kitchen paper. Store it on the bottom shelf of the fridge, making sure it has enough air circulating round it and that it isn't touching anything else.

How to joint a chicken

How many pieces you joint your chicken into will depend entirely on what you want to do with the chicken pieces and how many people you are serving. I do six (breasts, whole legs, wings), or eight (the legs cut into thighs and drumsticks) or 10 (the breasts cut in half through the bone). The back does not form part of any of these joints, so you can save it for stock.

This method (see pages 12–13 for step photography) will also help you take out the oyster intact, which can be very useful if you want to use them separately in salad (see pages 196–197). Removing them is entirely optional, you can leave them attached to the leg joints if you prefer.

FIND AND REMOVE THE OYSTERS Put the chicken on a work surface, breast-side down (1). Cut off the parson's nose. Cut through the skin, right down the centre of the back, from one end to the other (2). Use your thumbs to feel for the oysters – you will find two bumps either side of the centre of the back, at the top of the thigh. Make a cut across the back, just below the oysters and peel back the skin. Work to loosen the oysters with your knife, then pop them out (3).

REMOVE THE LEGS Turn the chicken breast-side up. Pull one leg away from the body and cut between the leg and the rest of the body. Push the leg down to pop the ball of the thigh bone out of its socket (4), then cut through the rest of the sinews and skin. Repeat on the other side (5 and 6).

REMOVE THE BREASTS If you want fillets here, simply cut down the sides of the breast bone (7), following the contour of the rib cage, to cut through the meat as close to the ribs as you can until it comes clean away (8 and 9). For breasts on the bone, cut down the side of the breast bone as before, but, instead of continuing to cut the meat away from the rib cage, instead use poultry shears to cut through the rib cage (11 and 12). Turn the carcass over again and cut away where the breast is still attached to its side.

SEPARATE BREASTS FROM WINGS Feel where the wing joint attaches to the breast (this is the bone you will normally find attached the chicken breast when sold as a supreme) and cut through it (13 and 14).

SEPARATE THIGHS FROM DRUMSTICKS Put the leg skin-side down. You will see a line of fat; cut along this to expose the joint, then bend it back to pop the ball of the joint out of the socket (16 and 17). Trim through any flesh, sinews and skin.

HALVE THE BREAST PORTIONS Cut at an angle across the breast. Cut through the flesh with a knife and finish with poultry shears to cut the bones to give a cleaner cut.

How to spatchcock a chicken

Turn the chicken so it is breast-side down on a work surface, with the large cavity and the parson's nose facing you. Using poultry shears or sharp kitchen scissors, cut down each side of the parson's nose, all the way to the neck end, cutting through any bones you encounter on the way. You will be removing the backbone; how much of it depends on you, but try to cut close to either side of the backbone, as that way you will preserve the oyster on the leg.

When you have cut out the backbone, flip the chicken over on the work surface so it is breast-side up. Gently press down on the breast bone with the heel of your hand to flatten it.

How to butterfly a chicken breast

First, skin the breast (save the skin for cooking separately). Lay the chicken breast on the work surface skinned-side down. Remove the small fillet if it is still attached. Turn the chicken breast over again, then, with your non-cutting hand lying flat on the breast, cut horizontally through the breast from one side almost to the other side. Open the flesh out and lie it flat.

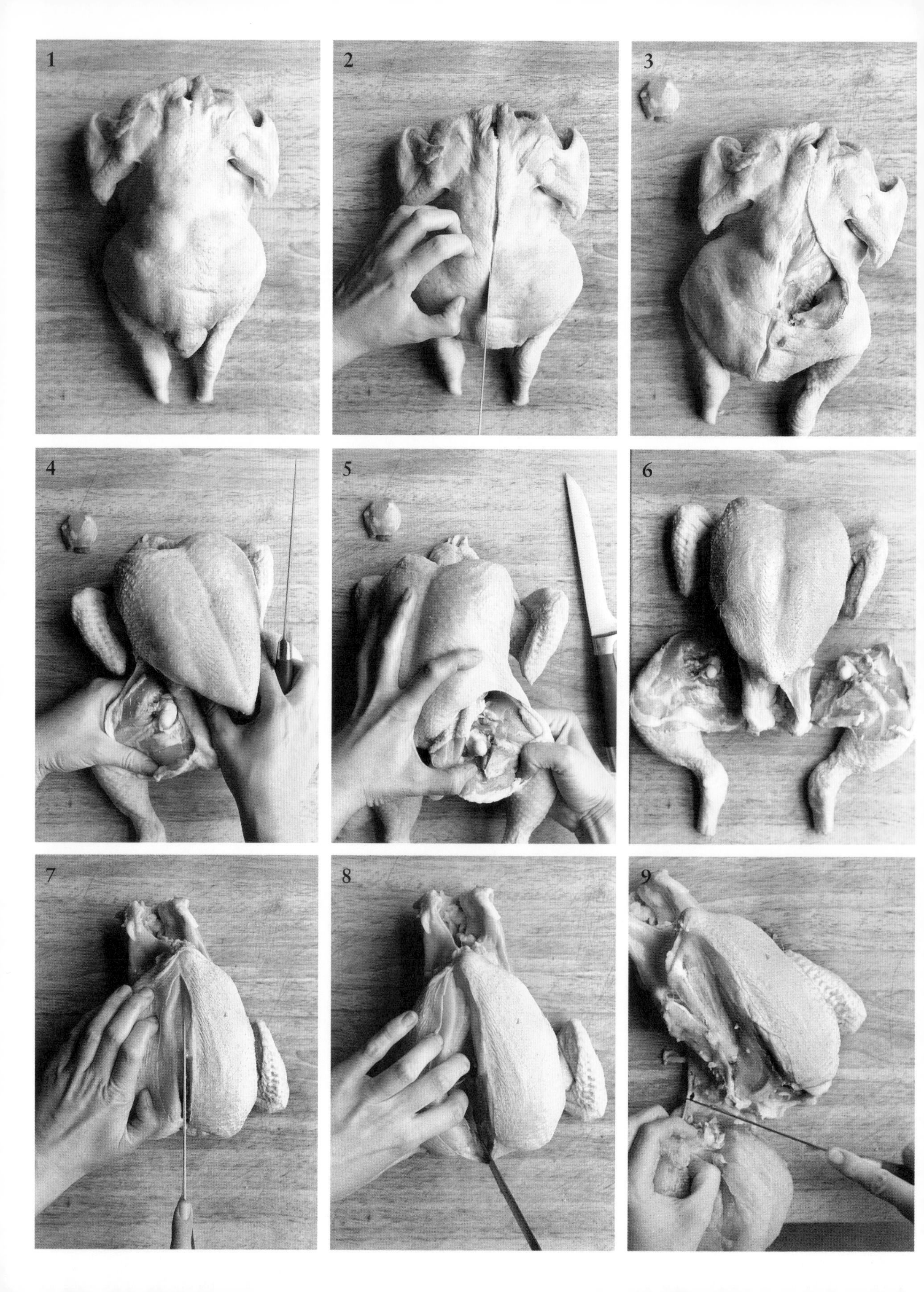
1
2
3
4
5
6
7
8
9

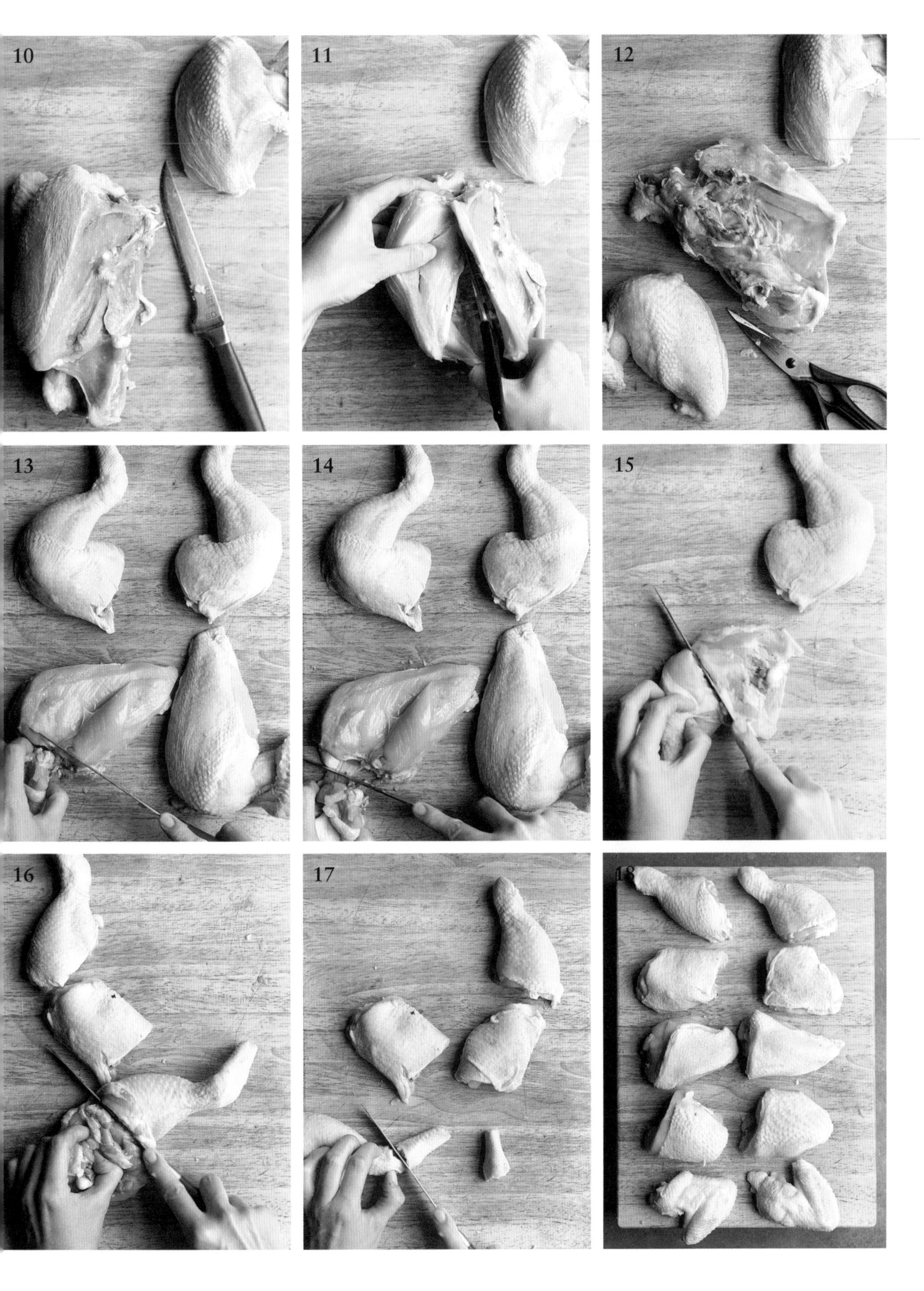
10
11
12
13
14
15
16
17
18

How to make a chicken escalope

Follow the instructions for butterflying a chicken breast on page 10. Put the opened-out chicken breast between two sheets of cling film and pound lightly but firmly with a meat mallet or a thick rolling pin until it is as thin as you can get it, with a vastly increased surface area. These will be large, so you can cut them into any size you want.

How to truss a chicken

Trussing is a very good idea for roasting, as compacting the bird together will help it cook more evenly, with the added bonus that the tops of the breasts will be protected from the heat a little by the legs. Most chickens come ready-trussed, but, if you need to untruss them for some reason – for instance, if you are pushing stuffing underneath the skin – it is useful to know how to do this. This is the most elegant way I know, as it follows the contours of the bird rather than having the string criss-cross over the breasts.

Take a long piece of kitchen string, around a metre in length.

Put the chicken breast-side up on a work surface, with the neck end facing away from you. Make sure the wings are tucked well in. Put the string under the bird at the cavity end, so the middle of it is just under the parson's nose. Bring the string up, hooking under and round the legs, then cross over. Pull tightly to pull the legs together and upwards so the tip of the legs are level with the tip of the breast bone. Pull the strings round the sides of the chicken to the neck end, crossing them over, then loop them underneath, pulling the wings tightly into the body. Flip the chicken upside down, then knot the ends of string as tightly as you can. If possible, tuck the ends of the legs under the skin attached to the end of the breast bone.

Remember to remove the string after the bird has rested.

STOCK

The single most useful thing you can make from the leftover carcass of a chicken is stock. Reduced down and seasoned, it's a meal in itself, before you even think of adding vegetables or carbohydrates. It is extremely versatile, as it has a good flavour but, unless you have reduced it down considerably, it is unlikely to overpower any dish you choose to use it in; it will simply enhance and give depth to what is already there. I use it for risotto, pasta sauces, soups or stews and keep a supply of reduced frozen stock cubes to add to anything I feel could do with a bit of extra help.

If you aren't used to using home-made chicken stock in your food, you will immediately notice the difference in flavour; most bought stocks are very heavily salted and often have a slightly unpleasant aftertaste. A home-made stock will taste fresher and puts you completely in control as to how you season and flavour a dish. And while a general-purpose stock is always useful to have, you can also tailor-make stocks for specific dishes, adding a subtle but significant layering of flavour to your food.

There are two main types of chicken stock and numerous ways to make them. The first is a white stock, which will have a milder flavour and is good for 'background noise'; you would use this for a mild vegetable or fish soup, or a risotto which needs savouriness, but not necessarily a pronounced chicken flavour. The second is a brown stock, which will have a more developed flavour and is a good basis for richer sauces, or anything where you want the chicken flavour to sing out.

Ingredients

THE CHICKEN

You can make a very good stock with just the debris from a single roast chicken, as long as you aren't precious about using all those bones that have been discarded at the table. This will make a good litre of stock which will be well flavoured enough to use for a risotto or soup. You can also save the bones from roast chicken until you have perhaps three carcasses' worth; this will give you a good amount of stock to play with and is definitely worth the wait. If you have the remains of a roast chicken, plus its carcass, that you're not sure you are going to use immediately, take all the meat off (store it separately) and freeze the carcass. That way you can ensure the carcass will be fresh. Otherwise make sure you use it within a couple of days and always smell for freshness; throw out anything you aren't completely sure about.

My preferred way of making chicken stock is with raw chicken backs and carcasses. If you are following my advice and buying predominantely whole chickens, you will have the chicken back and parts of the breast bone and ribs left over once you have jointed your chicken. This, along with any skin or fat, will make a very good flavoured, collagen-rich stock. The other way you can get hold of chicken backs for stock is by asking your butcher. I have often seen them sold for 50p a tray at farmer's markets, but a friendly butcher will give them to you for nothing. That's because he has to keep his customers happy by providing plenty of filleted chicken breasts and other chicken pieces and, usually, will have to pay to dispose of the rest of the chicken. There is an additional benefit from buying these: there is often a fair bit of meat on the backs. Once it is cooked and removed, you will be surprised at how much. I add this meat to risotto or pasta, use it in sandwiches, or even brown it to make a shorter version of *Pulled chicken* (see pages 232–234). You can use chicken backs to make either white or brown stock.

Whether you are using raw chicken backs or saved roasted carcasses, the stock will always benefit if you add a couple of wings, or some of the giblets, if you have them. I always add the neck if I have it, but avoid using the liver as it makes the stock bitter.

You can also make a good stock with just chicken wings. This is more expensive, obviously, but worth mentioning just in case you are desperate for home-made chicken stock and can't get hold of any backs. I also keep a bag in the freezer in which I keep wing tips, cut off before the wings are used elsewhere. They add a surprising amount of flavour to a stock.

If you want a rich, gelatinous stock without having to reduce it too much, you can add a pig's trotter. It will not give out much flavour, but the stock will set to a fairly firm jelly at room temperature.

In terms of quantities, I would say that 1kg of chicken bones and wings – in any of the forms above – will give you 1 litre of well-flavoured stock. Reducing the chicken-to-liquid ratio further will give you a much lighter stock which can be intensified through reduction, but it will not taste quite as good.

THE VEGETABLES

I always add at least a carrot, a couple of celery sticks, an onion and a leek to my stock, but there are plenty of other vegetables that will benefit it. Fennel trimmings and discarded sweetcorn cobs will add sweetness. Unassuming white or button mushrooms (even just their peelings) will add a good savoury flavour without making the stock murkily dark. Dried seaweed, used in moderation, will also give savouriness.

If you want to be very economical, keep a bag of vegetable trimmings in the freezer. I include onion skins (which add a rich, pleasant ochre colour), carrot peelings, seeds and skin from tomatoes and squashes... anything as long as it is in good condition (you don't want anything past its prime spoiling your stock). There is one other rule about which vegetables to add: you must never add anything starchy or anything likely to make it bitter. So no potatoes or brassicas and no bitter greens.

THE AROMATICS

The traditional additions to a general purpose chicken stock are simply a couple of bay leaves, some black peppercorns and perhaps a sprig of parsley. These give enough flavour without dominating any resultant dish. Other things I like to add include garlic, tarragon, fennel seeds and perhaps a paring of lemon zest. I am wary of anything else, including the woodier herbs such as thyme or rosemary, as I feel they can overpower. I never use chilli, and root ginger only rarely, as they give out too intense a flavour for my taste. White wine, sherry, vermouth, or a cider vinegar – all in small quantities – are very good things to add when making a brown stock, as you can use them instead of water to deglaze the roasting dish. They will add a touch of acidity and help the flavour along.

If I have earmarked my stock for a specific dish that contains specific aromatics, I may include them in the stock, too – in moderation – to help develop and layer the flavour. For example, for Caribbean dishes I will add that cuisine's consistent flavour note: allspice berries.

The methods

Regardless of what ingredients you are using, the method is basically the same. For a white stock, or a stock in which you are using pre-cooked carcasses, pull them apart into small pieces, so they will sit snugly in a saucepan. Cover with water. Do not use too big a saucepan here; you do not want your chicken floating around in a vast lake of water, or you will get very little flavour. Bring the stock to the boil and skim off any impurities: you will see a mushroom-coloured scum starting to collect. As soon as this turns white, you can stop skimming, then reduce the heat to the barest simmer (a gentle plup, plup, plup) and add the remaining ingredients. Simmer for as long as you can – at least two or three hours, preferably longer.

To make a good, brown stock with raw chicken carcasses, your best bet is to roast them first. Preheat the oven to 220°C/fan 200°C/425°F/gas mark 7. This time, cut up the chicken into pieces and put in a roasting tray with a sliced onion (no need to peel). Leave for 25 minutes, then transfer everything to your stockpot or saucepan. Deglaze the bottom of the roasting tray with a little water or other liquid, making sure you scrape up anything that is sticking, and pour the lot over the chicken. Proceed as above.

HOW TO MAKE STOCK IN A PRESSURE COOKER

The accepted wisdom about stock is that long and slow is the way to go, this leaves plenty of time for the chicken to give up all its flavour and for the connective tissue and collagen to be broken down into gelatine. However, you will get all this with a pressure cooker. Not only that, you will definitely get more depth of flavour, as the pressure will push flavour out of the chicken and vegetables and into the water, and, because the temperature is higher, it will kick-start the Maillard reaction. This is what happens when foods start to caramelise, so it will improve the flavour no end. This also means that, if you want to make a good brown stock without roasting the chicken carcasses first, you can do so.

To make your stock this way, simply follow the instructions above but, instead of using a stockpot, put everything in a pressure cooker. After you have added the vegetables and aromatics, put the lid on, bring up to high pressure, then reduce the heat. Cook at high pressure for 20 minutes for a light stock, or for 35 minutes for stock with more depth of flavour. Leave the pressure to drop naturally.

STRAINING, REDUCING, STORING

Once your stock has finished simmering, you need to strain it. For any stock that isn't going to be used as a consommé, either strain the liquid through a very fine mesh sieve, or line a colander with a layer of muslin and strain it through that. If you are not worried about your stock being slightly cloudy, you can press down on all the ingredients to extract as much flavour as possible. Let your stock cool to room temperature, then refrigerate it. You will probably find that it sets to a very soft jelly and that it will have a layer of fat on top. I recommend that you use the fat in place of the oil or butter you are going to use in your chicken recipe. Stock will keep for up to a week in the fridge.

If you have made a large amount of stock, or you know you aren't going to use it immediately, you can freeze it for around three months. Simply decant into an airtight container or, even better, zip lock bags which can be stored flat in the portion sizes you need. I usually do this in half-litre amounts.

If you want to optimise freezer space, you can reduce your stock down. Simply do this by putting the stock into a clean saucepan and keeping it at a rolling boil until it reduces. It is up to you by how much. I will normally reduce by about half and then dilute it when I come to use it. However, for some dishes, it is useful to keep some that is reduced further, to what is called a glace. This is stock reduced to the stage where it is taking on a slightly sticky, tacky quality. It has a very concentrated flavour and is very good added to sauces and gravies. It is best frozen in ice cube trays, as you will rarely need more than a cube at a time. Once it has frozen solid, turn the cubes out into a freezer bag or carton and use as instant flavour boosters.

REDUCING FURTHER: CHICKEN EXTRACT

You can reduce stock even further, up to and beyond the point when it is no longer liquid. One of the most useful things in my fridge is a smallish jam jar which contains three litres of stock, reduced to a paste. This is basically a kind of chicken Bovril (meat spread or extract), but with no added salt, or indeed any other additives. It will taste salty –

intensely savoury, actually – and it can be used for absolutely anything for which you would use stock or chicken broth. I dilute it with boiling water and drink it as chicken broth and I use teaspoons of it to enhance a lighter flavoured stock or water.

To make, simply take your stock slightly beyond the glace stage (see page 17). Keep a close eye on it at this point, because it can very easily burn. Reduce the heat a little and cook, stirring occasionally, until the glace is slightly thicker; tracing a wooden spoon along the bottom of the pan should leave a trail behind that doesn't immediately disappear. It will be fairly liquid but will set once it cools down. I have taken this too far before and ended up with a dense jelly firm enough to be sliced. Don't worry if this happens: you won't be able to spread it, but you will be able to use it in every other way and it will keep just as well. This paste will keep for at least three months in the fridge.

AND FURTHER STILL: CHICKEN BRITTLE AND POWDER

If you want to preserve the life of your chicken extract even further, you can dehydrate it. Instead of decanting your chicken paste into a jar, spread it thinly over a baking tray lined with non-stick baking parchment. Set your oven to its lowest temperature and put the baking tray inside, leaving the oven door slightly ajar. The chicken paste will gradually dehydrate; this will take anything from overnight to 24 hours. You will find that the edges dry out quite quickly and become brittle while the centre will remain quite tacky for much longer, a bit like fruit leather. Once the chicken extract is completely dry, you can either break it up into pieces and store (I must admit to liking these to crunch and suck on, like a very savoury boiled sweet), or simply put in a food processor or coffee grinder and blitz to a fine powder. You can store this in a jar, it doesn't have to be kept in the fridge and it will keep indefinitely. I hesitate to make the comparison – as it's so much better than anything you can buy – but it's basically the same principle behind making a stock cube or bouillon.

You don't just have to use this powder as reconstituted stock. The flavour is so good that it makes a brilliant seasoning. It can be mixed with herbs and spices and used to sprinkle over home-made crisps and chips, mixed with breadcrumbs as a gratin topping – there are lots of possibilities. I like the zestiness that comes from mixing it with lemon zest, black pepper and a pinch of citrus salt; the smokiness from hickory smoked salt and chipotle; and heat from Szechuan peppercorns.

One of the ingenious things about reducing stock is that the flavour intensifies and the stock, extract or powder will go much further. So 1 tsp of the chicken extract or powder will make around 500ml of well-flavoured stock, but add a little more for a strongly flavoured chicken drink.

How to clarify stock

You may want a particularly clear stock because you are using it to make a consommé or even an aspic-type jelly. There are two main ways to do this:

ICE FILTERING

This is my preferred method, as it is the most economical and simple to do as long as you have room in your fridge. It will result in a crystal-clear well-flavoured stock. The only downside is that this method does remove the gelatine so, if you want to set the stock, you will have to add it back, using commercial gelatine.

Freeze your stock. Line a colander or sieve with a double layer of muslin or cheesecloth and place over a bowl that is large enough to hold all the stock once it has melted. When the stock has frozen solid, put it in the colander and put everything in the fridge. Leave it to melt. This will take anything between one and two days. You will end up with a crystal-clear, extremely well-flavoured stock.

EGG FILTERING

I don't normally bother with this method, as it's much more fiddly, but it is useful if you don't have enough space in your fridge to ice filter. To clarify a litre of stock, make sure your stock is well-chilled so you can remove the fat from the top. Do so. Separate two eggs (reserve the yolks for another recipe). Whisk the egg whites lightly with a fork. Crush up the egg shells and add to the egg whites. Put the stock and the egg mixture into a saucepan and whisk together. Bring slowly to the boil, then simmer for 15 minutes. By this point, a crust of egg and impurities should have formed on top of the stock. Remove from the heat.

Line a colander or sieve with muslin. Break through the crust and remove it. Strain the stock through the muslin. You should end up with a beautifully clear stock.

RENDERED CHICKEN FAT (SCHMALTZ)

There are several chicken foodstuffs for which we can thank the Jewish community. The best-known is chicken soup, more of which in the next chapter. Another is schmaltz – or rendered chicken fat – itself an important component of the soup. This tastes as good as duck or goose fat and is just as useful. You can also almost – hallelujah – say it's good for you, thanks to the fact that it contains a fatty acid (palmitoleic acid) which is believed to boost the immune system, as well as oleic acid which can have a beneficial effect on cholesterol levels. Plus, if your chicken has been reared on a diet of grass, it will have a healthy ratio of omega 3 and 6 fatty acids, as well.

I love the stuff; I eat it as a slightly healthier and tastier version of smalec, the pork equivalent which I've loved since visiting Poland years ago, when I discovered how good it could be spread on rye bread, especially when flavoured with onions and peppered with tiny nuggets of crisp skin.

Originally, the kosher variety of schmaltz was typically rendered goose fat, presumably, as a goose gives a very generous yield of fat. Over time, chicken became more available than goose and took over. This leaves a slight problem these days as chickens – naturally leaner than those prolific fat producers, geese, ducks and pigs – have been bred to be even leaner. So acquiring enough fat to make rendering worthwhile requires patience, or at the very least a trip to an accommodating butcher. (If you don't have a butcher who will give you trays of chicken skin, save any uncooked chicken skin in the freezer until you have enough. There are plenty of recipes in this book which are made with skinless chicken, see especially the sections on poaching and curries, pages 45–56 and 132–147.) On a well-reared chicken, you will find fat just inside the neck cavity and under the skin. If your chicken has been corn-fed, this will often be a beautiful deep yellow, which will keep its colour during the rendering process and imbue anything you cook it with the same warm tone. Golden droplets of this fat on the top of a chicken soup are particularly fetching. Of course, most sensible cooks will use chicken fat regularly, as it will always render out a bit when you make stock or collect on top of gravy from the roast. I've always used this to roast or sauté potatoes and other vegetables (sautéed cabbage and onion in schmaltz with a bit of bacon is particularly good). But it has many other uses – you can even use it in place of butter or lard in baking.

How to make schmaltz (and, on the side, gribenes)

This is something to make when you have a few hours free and are happy to spend it pottering around the kitchen. Schmaltz is actually low-maintenance to make, as all it needs is an occasional stir during the rendering process, but you do need to keep a regular eye on it.

Collect an amount of chicken skin. I store mine in the freezer until I have enough. The secret to efficient rendering is to cut the chicken skin up into slices as thin as possible. It is much easier to do this when the skin is frozen. The best way to do this is to open-freeze it on a baking tray in strips, then decant into freezer bags, as, if it is frozen in a solid block, it will be harder to work with.

It's worth making a fair amount of this at once, I would say try to use at least 500g of skin. When you have sliced it finely, put it in an even layer in a wide frying pan. Add 100ml of water to help get it started. Bring it to the boil, then reduce the temperature to the lowest and cook very slowly until the skin is golden brown. Give it a stir every so often, to make sure it isn't catching on the pan or cooking too quickly; you don't want the fat to go dark, it needs to remain a light golden brown. This could take any time from 90 minutes to several hours.

When the skin is a golden brown, you can add a finely chopped onion if you like. This is traditional and entirely optional. I do both;. I like the slightly sweet caramelisation the onion adds to both the schmaltz and gribenes, but I like it in its pure form, too. At this point you can increase the heat very slightly and cook, keeping a close eye on it, until the skin and onion (if using) is a much deeper brown. The skin should be crisp and slightly sticky in places, just like the wings on a roast chicken.

Strain the fat (schmaltz) through a fine sieve. If you want it very clear, you can then strain it through cheesecloth or muslin (don't try use anything denser, it won't go through). Drain the oniony chicken skins (gribenes) on some kitchen paper, then keep in the fridge.

Flavoured schmaltz

As I mention above, it's traditional to add onion to schmaltz; this makes good sense as the sweetness does add an extra note to all that savouriness, while the burnished oniony nuggets in and amongst the gribenes are an added bonus. You can add any other flavours you like and I would say the same rule applies to schmaltz as to stock: if it is for general use you don't want to add anything too strongly flavoured, and if you are using it for baking – especially for baking anything sweet – I wouldn't add anything at all.

Smoked schmaltz

If you like smoky flavours, you can add them into schmaltz via smoked salt, but the best way is to smoke the chicken skin first. Smoked schmaltz smells wonderful when it is rendering down and has an excellent flavour. I don't add onion to this schmaltz as I find the flavour of smoke and browned onion don't work well together. Adding small amounts of herbs such as thyme works well, though. (See page 22 for instructions on how to smoke chicken skin.)

Making schmaltz and stock

If you want to make a lot of schmaltz at once, as well as stock, you can add lots of chicken skin/backs/wings to anything else you've put in a stockpot or pressure cooker and proceed as for stock. When it has simmered/pressure-cooked for the right amount of time, strain the whole lot through a sieve and cool it down. The liquid and fat will separate and you will be able simply to take off the top layer of fat to store.

There are advantages and a disadvantage to doing this. It's a quicker and more efficient way of rendering fat and you are killing two birds with one stone; you will also be making a particularly well-flavoured, collagen-rich stock. There is just one major disadvantage: no gribenes!

Using gribenes (and chicken skin)

People are funny about chicken skin. Of course it's higher in calories as, on a chicken and much other poultry, the fat sits just under the skin rather than being marbled throughout as in other meats. And there is no doubt that some dishes work better with skinned chicken; it makes perfect sense, for instance, if a chicken is going to be in a casserole with no hope of browning. However, when the skin is crisp and burnished brown, I don't think you can beat it. The flavour is robust and has pure essence of chicken, which can be added to all kinds of things.

You can use gribenes or crisped-up chicken skins in the same way you might use croutons, or lardons of bacon. They will add crisp, savoury hits to anything, so you can sprinkle them into soup (see page 28) and sandwiches (page 232) or over salads. I add gribenes to *Chopped Liver* (page 248) and combine them with breadcrumbs as a coating, or a topping for a gratin (page 181). So, if you are making *Chicken parmigiana* (see pages 120–122), consider adding to the chicken flavour with some blitzed crisp chicken skin mixed into the breadcrumb coating.

My favourite thing to do with crisp skin is to add it to a leek or chicory gratin. Cook the leeks or chicory slowly in butter with a splash of white wine, then caramelise the chicory with a little sugar, if you like. Coat thin slices of ham with mustard and use these to wrap up the leeks or chicory. Smother with béchamel, top with lots of cheese, then mix breadcrumbs with ground gribenes or crisp chicken skin and sprinkle over. Bake in a hot oven until brown and bubbling.

How to cook chicken skin

There are times when I will skin a chicken and don't have time to make proper schmaltz. In these instances, I will just roast or fry the skin much more quickly until the fat has rendered out and the skin is crisp and brown. Simply preheat the oven to around 220°C/fan 200°C/425°F/gas mark 7 and spread the chicken skin out on a baking tray. Roast for around 25 minutes until it is crisp and brown. This is not such a complete process as not all the fat will render out and what's left will be slightly darker, but it's a good compromise and is good if you are more concerned about crisp skin than the amount of fat you will be left with.

You can do this much more slowly and render out more of the fat if you like. This is a still a more convenient and slightly faster way of making schmaltz and gribenes as it's lower maintenance and you can get away with using larger pieces of chicken skin. Preheat the oven to 180°C/fan 160°C/350°F/ gas mark 4. Put the chicken skin over a rack, use a mesh cooling rack if you have one rather than one which has quite widely spaced parallel lines. Put on top of a roasting dish to catch any rendered fat, then roast in the oven for 1–1¼ hours until much of the fat has rendered out. Increase the oven temperature to 220°C/fan 200°C/425°F/ gas mark 7 for a further 5 minutes to brown.

You can also barbecue chicken skin (see page 26 for details).

'IMPROVING' CHICKEN

A well-reared chicken needs very little done to it. If you cook it properly, it should have an excellent flavour and texture. However, there is a school of thought that thinks chicken, like other 'drier' meats such as turkey and pork, will always benefit from brining. The reasons given are several: we are told the salt subtly enhances the flavour and helps tenderise the meat; further, that it will add water, via osmosis, some of which will remain even after cooking, thus resulting in moister meat. Brining is popular as a prelude to roasting and barbecuing, as it is commonly believed that chicken breasts will dry out before the rest of the bird has cooked through. I am not convinced. If you are buying a decent chicken, you shouldn't need to brine it. If you are buying a stringy old bird, well, the salt will soften the meat very slightly, but not nearly enough for you to want to bother roasting it. And if you're using anything less than a free-range bird, it will always have a pappy, flabby texture anyway and brining will only emphasise that.

I've experimented with brining over the years and have never found it to make any positive difference. So just to be sure I roasted a brined and a non-brined bird, side by side. Both birds cooked well but while the breast meat was very slightly moister on the brined bird, it also changed the texture for the worse. It was sponge-like and I swear the flavour wasn't as good. I came to the conclusion that brining is actually diluting flavour by adding water, which I really don't want. So no brining for me.

A better way to improve chicken: salting

This could not be simpler. The first thing I do when I buy chicken is take it out of any plastic and put it on a rack placed over a plate in the fridge. This will keep it fresher and will ensure that the skin will be firm and dry: perfect for roasting. I will usually do this overnight, or for most of the day if I buy it in the morning and want to eat it at night. To salt, all you have to do is sprinkle salt inside the cavity and over the skin and leave it to do its work. Do this from a height so you get an even spread, and use around 1 tbsp (I use finely crumbled-up sea salt). The initial effect of salting is to draw moisture out of the skin, but leave it alone and the liquid will be reabsorbed and the skin will dry out. This will result in slightly moister meat and a very slightly enhanced flavour. It doesn't make a huge difference to a decent bird but as I am drying out the chicken anyway there seems little point in missing out this step. You end up with a better texture and flavour than if you've brined.

Using flavoured salts

There are plenty of recipes throughout this book – spice mixes, rubs and so on – most of which have salt in them. You can use any of these in place of plain salt and they will start adding flavour to the surface of the chicken. You can also use flavoured or smoked salts, I particularly like hickory smoked salt or smoked sea salt.

'Lime washing'

This is a tip I picked up in the Caribbean and I do it with much of the meat and fish I cook. Many West Indians do this in the belief that rubbing citrus juice or vinegar into the meat will clean it and get rid of any unpleasant smells. I worked in a kitchen where this was done regularly and started doing it myself, purely because I noticed the difference it made to the flavour of the chicken: it seemed to intensify the savoury quality. Very simply, juice a lime or two, dilute with a splash of water (to prevent it immediately 'cooking' the top layer of the meat) and rub it all over the chicken. Pat dry, then salt as above.

Of course, you aren't really washing the chicken. And it's unnecessary to do so as cooking will kill the bacteria and washing it will just spread germs around your kitchen sink.

PRESERVING: CONFIT

The best way to preserve chicken, if you don't want to freeze it, is to confit it in the same way you would duck.

A jar of this in the fridge means you always have cooked chicken to hand, without the worry of it going off quickly. As long as you keep the chicken covered in fat, it will keep almost indefinitely. All you have to do is dig it out, wipe off most of the fat, heat up a frying pan and fry it until crisp.

Like gribenes, it is especially good in anything you would want crisp bacon on, particularly shredded into salads (try the *Salad of confit chicken, endive and pears*, see pages 205–207), or crisped up as a garnish for soups.

Secondly, there is the fat, which can be used for anything, but especially roasting potatoes. The best chicken to confit is leg meat, either whole or in pieces. The process is as follows:

3 tbsp sea salt
3 garlic cloves, finely sliced
1 tsp freshly ground black pepper
1 tsp dried thyme
finely grated zest of 1 unwaxed lemon
4 chicken legs
up to 500g schmaltz, duck or goose fat, or the equivalent in olive oil

Blitz together all the ingredients except the chicken legs and fat. Rub the salt mixture over the chicken legs, then put them in a container or bag and leave in the fridge overnight, but for no longer than 12 hours.

Preheat the oven to 140°C/fan 120°C/ 275°F/gas mark 1. Remove the chicken legs from the fridge and wipe off the salt mix (don't rinse the chicken). Put the chicken in a roasting dish; you want a snug fit here, because you don't want to have to use too much fat. If using fat, warm it in a saucepan to render it liquid, then pour it over the chicken, making sure the bird is completely submerged. If using oil, just pour it over the chicken to cover. Put the roasting dish over a medium heat until the fat is just starting to simmer, then cover the dish with foil or greaseproof paper and put it in the oven. Cook for about three hours, until the meat is tender and falling off the bone.

Remove the legs from the fat and put in a sterilised jar (I use a large Kilner or Le Parfait jar, the sort with a rubber seal). To sterilise, either put the jars and seals through the hottest cycle of your dishwasher, or wash them thoroughly in hot soapy water, rinse well, then leave to dry out in a low oven. Carefully pour off the fat from the roasting dish into the jar, making sure that any meat juices are left behind. Make sure that the chicken is well covered with the fat. Seal the jar. When the chicken has cooled to room temperature, transfer it to the fridge. To use, remove from the jar, scrape off any excess fat and fry over a high heat until heated through and well browned. You don't have to fry a whole leg at a time, but make sure anything left behind is completely coated in fat.

A QUICK ALTERNATIVE METHOD

This pressure cooker method isn't quite a confit, but the result is similar – the flesh has a wonderful texture: very soft, spreadable and without a hint of dryness, a bit like hot smoked mackerel when you've mashed it into a pâté. The skin disintegrates to parchment and the meat takes on an almost marbled effect as the fat pushes into it.

To make, salt the chicken if you prefer, then put in a pressure cooker, cover with water and add any aromatics you like. Cook on high pressure for 45 minutes, then let the pressure drop naturally. Save the liquid for stock, then shred the chicken, discarding any bones or tendons.

To use, you can mix it with spices, pastes or other condiments such as mustard and use in sandwiches or as a dip. You can also fry it. It will not keep in the same way as confit, but you can freeze it.

Smoked chicken

Smoking – and here I mean hot smoking – is a remarkably easy process if you have a barbecue or just a wok.

Firstly, it is best to salt and air-dry your chicken (see pages 22–23). This should be done overnight in the case of a whole chicken; 2–3 hours is long enough for chicken breasts.

Next, you can either hot-smoke your chicken for as long as it takes to cook, or you can steam it first then smoke it afterwards. For a *Chinese-style whole smoked chicken*, I always steam it first (for instructions, see page 54). This is because it can take a couple of hours to hot-smoke a chicken and the flavour will be quite intense; smoking for 15–20 minutes will give you a subtler effect.

It isn't worth steaming small pieces of chicken prior to smoking as they don't take so long to cook. Just line a wok with foil and

put any smoking ingredients on top. Then you can either use a mere 1 tbsp of unsoaked hardwood chips or sawdust – such as apple, cherry or hickory, and add in some other aromatics if you like, such as juniper, rosemary sprigs or allspice berries. You can also tea-smoke chicken (see page 54) which is endlessly variable, as long as you still use the rice and sugar.

Once you have put your chosen smoking ingredients on the foil, place a rack on top for the chicken, making sure they can all fit in one even layer. Put a tight-fitting lid over the wok if possible, otherwise cover the whole thing with foil. Heat the wok over a medium heat to start with. You will smell the smoke after a couple of minutes or so if using wood chips or sawdust, anything else will take several minutes to start working. At this point, reduce the heat to low and leave the chicken to smoke. A chicken breast will take 20–30 minutes, depending how thick it is. To check for doneness, either use a probe thermometer to make sure it has reached 75°C (167°F), or pierce with a skewer: the tip should be too hot to hold comfortably against bare skin.

Chicken is best smoked with the skin on, as it's a layer of protection and will help keep the meat moist; if you want to eat the skin, you can brown it after smoking under a hot grill or in a frying pan. Or you can remove the skin before serving and save it up to add a smoky note to schmaltz and gribenes (see pages 20–22). You can also smoke chicken skin on its own, for later use. When doing this, I tend to parcel up the smoking ingredients in foil and punch holes in it, as I worry about the fat dripping on to them. Smoke for around 20 minutes for a subtle flavour; I like using hickory for this.

Other ways to add a smoky flavour

If you don't want to hot smoke, but still want a smoky flavour, invest in some smoked salt. Smoked salt – especially a hickory smoked salt – will impart a good, if subtle, smoky flavour if you use it for overnight salting and add it judiciously to any dish in place of regular sea salt.

Since I discovered smoked salt, I have stopped using liquid smoke as it is too strong and there are some quite unpleasant additive-filled varieties on the market.

The other thing you can do is marinate chicken in something naturally smoky, such as a smoked ham stock. I tried several different stock and water ratios before I was happy, as I wanted to ensure the chicken had a smokiness to it but retained a good, dominant chicken flavour. I most often do this with wings, but it will work with a whole bird, too. Make a smoked ham stock with a bone, a ham hock or a piece of smoked gammon. Take 500ml of it and dilute with one litre of very cold water (use the rest of the stock for something else, a soup perhaps). Prick the chicken all over with a sharp skewer and put into a plastic container you can fit into the fridge. Cover with the stock mixture. Leave a whole chicken overnight or for at least five hours; for chicken breasts or wings an hour or two is ample.

You can add other flavours to this, too. You can also dissolve 100g soft light brown sugar into the stock for a sweeter result, cooling the liquid completely before covering the chicken.

2. CHICKEN LIQUOR

Broths, Soups & Stews

"To feel safe and warm on a cold wet night,
all you really need is soup."
Laurie Colwin

There is an image I have in my head of a duffle coated boy, leaving the house on a cold and drear winter's morning, insulated by the bright orange glow that surrounds him. This comes straight from a popular TV advert from the 1980s, but it is still a good visualisation of the effects of chicken soup.

In all its myriad forms, chicken soup is seen as so good for mind and body, so warming and nourishing, that the mere thought of it is comforting. It will make most people feel better, whether they need their spirits lifting or a flu-ridden body soothed. It isn't just Jewish penicillin, it's a universal panacea.

These days all kinds of claims are made about its medicinal efficacy and it seems there may be some truth in them (see page 28). Of course, whether or not it can cure a cold is immaterial, the important thing about chicken soup is that regardless of whether you are eating a minimalist but well-flavoured broth, a creamy chowder, or a spicy, aromatic stew is that it tastes good *and* tastes as though it's good for you.

People have felt the effects of this for centuries, so it isn't really surprising that just about every omnivorous food culture in existence has some variant of chicken soup at its heart. It also makes sense in the context of economy. In a world which always had old chickens (often past-their-prime egg-laying birds), the best thing to do with them was to boil them up to make broth. The version most embraced by Western cultures is based upon the classic Jewish chicken noodle soup, but this type of soup is not unique to the Jewish tradition. Broths feature everywhere, it's just the aromatics and bulking ingredients that vary; the common ground seems to be onion and garlic and a type of starch, though that could be rice, noodles, pasta, potatoes, even barley or millet.

A COUPLE OF PRACTICAL NOTES

Traditionally all these soups would have started with a boiling fowl which would give up all its flavour after a very long, slow simmer. These days it is practically impossible to get hold of an ethically reared boiling fowl. I have no idea why – something must be done with all those organic, free-range layers – but there it is. For that reason I don't use them. Instead, I use my regular free-range chicken, simmer it for a shorter period of time (thus ensuring the chicken itself retains a good flavour and texture) and supplement the flavour by using a light chicken stock in place of water, or wrapping up a couple of chicken backs in muslin and adding those to the pot, too. All the broth-based soups in this chapter can be made in this way if you like but, for ease, I've instead given quantities for the amount of stock and cooked chicken needed for the finished dish.

One of the problems of making a soup from scratch the old-fashioned way is the amount of fat it will add to your finished soup. While some fat is desirable, you don't want the top of your broth to be covered in a thick layer of it, you just want a few droplets scattered about. There are a couple of ways to deal with this: you can make the stock for the broth in advance and skim it when chilled, as the fat will be easier to remove. Or, instead of cooking the chicken with the skin on, you can half-skin it. What I often do is take off the skin around the breast and legs – in one piece if possible – and leave the skin on the wings and back. This will provide enough fat and skin to make schmaltz and gribenes, or simply roast chicken skin, which you can use as a garnish for the soup.

All the soups in this chapter will serve four to six people, unless otherwise stated.

Chicken noodle soup (Jewish soup with matzo balls)

This is the soup that could be quite intimidating to approach unless you have been making it on a weekly basis for your entire adult life. This isn't because of anything to do with the preparation; it is not a hard soup to make. It is simply that it is endowed with so many qualities and steeped in so much historical and cultural allusion that you could almost feel as though you are doing more than making soup. This is all very silly of course. What is important about this soup is that it can and will make you feel better when you have a cold. There is apparently now a scientific basis for this and it's all to do with those golden spheres of fat which collect on top. Chicken fat contains large amounts of a monounsaturated palmitoleic acid, which boosts the immune system. And of course the combination of heat, fat and collagen soothe the throat.

Serves 6–8

1 chicken
2 litres chicken stock, or 2 chicken carcasses tied up in muslin
1 large onion, cut into 8 wedges
2 large carrots, cut into chunks
3 celery sticks, cut into chunks
1 head of garlic, halved horizontally
large sprig of parsley, plus very finely chopped parsley leaves to serve
large sprig of thyme
sea salt and freshly ground white pepper
handful of spaghetti or vermicelli (lokshen)

Remove some of the skin of the chicken (see above). Check inside the chicken, especially around the neck end, and pull out any large pieces of fat you can see. Save the skin and fat in the freezer for rendering into schmaltz (see pages 19–20). Put the chicken in a large saucepan. Pour over the chicken stock, or add the chicken carcasses and pour in two litres of water, making sure the chicken is well covered.

Bring to the boil and start skimming off any mushroom-coloured foam that collects on the surface. When the foam turns white, stop skimming. Reduce the heat and simmer for 30 minutes.

Add all the vegetables, garlic and herbs and simmer for a further 30 minutes, or until the vegetables are tender. Season well with salt and white pepper.

Strain the soup. Pull the chicken meat from the bones and return around half of it to the soup. (Keep the rest for something else.) Return the vegetables to the soup as well, then add the spaghetti or vermicelli. Simmer for a further 10 minutes, until the vermicelli is cooked. Serve sprinkled with very finely chopped parsley.

ADDITIONS: There are all kinds of things that can be added to this soup. Often a pinch of saffron strands is added toward the end.

You can add any kind of starch: simmer barley, rice or other types of pasta in it, or add them ready-cooked if you want to preserve the clarity of the broth.

You do not have to limit yourself to onion, carrot and celery; any root vegetables are good, especially parsnips and turnips. You can also add a chopped tomato.

MATZO BALLS are very traditional; here is a recipe for the light and fluffy sort.

I also like chicken meatballs in the soup (see pages 164–165).

125g medium matzo meal
2 tsp baking powder
sea salt and freshly ground white pepper
150ml chicken stock or water
50g unsalted butter, melted
1 large egg, lightly beaten
1 tbsp finely chopped parsley or dill leaves

Put the matzo meal and baking powder in a bowl. Whisk together so the baking powder is evenly distributed and season with salt and white pepper. Pour in the stock or water and mix thoroughly. Whisk the butter into the egg and whisk this into the matzo meal, then mix in the parsley. Leave to stand for around 30 minutes, to allow the matzo meal to absorb the liquid and swell. Form the mixture into walnut-sized balls.

At this point you can open-freeze the matzo balls on a tray, then decant into a freezer bag; that way you have a store of them to hand every time you want to add them to some broth. When you want to cook them, simmer them in water or broth, but not the soup you are serving them in, as they can give out a little starch and make it cloudy. They will be done when they float, in 10–12 minutes.

A QUICK VARIATION: This is rich, garlicky and also quite fatty unless you skim it well. I don't normally bother. Take some chicken pieces. Brown them in a little olive oil. Add around 1 litre of well-flavoured chicken stock and a pinch of turmeric. Add quartered onions, large chunks of celery and carrot and any other vegetables you fancy. Break up a head of garlic, add half the cloves whole and reserve the rest. Season with salt and pepper. Simmer for 10 minutes. Add a thickly sliced leek or two and the rest of the garlic, finely chopped. Simmer for a further

15–20 minutes until the meat is tender. Add noodles, if you like, or a cup of cooked rice. Serve with either the meat pulled from the bones and left in chunks, or just serve the chicken pieces still intact (they should be breaking up anyway). Add a sprinkling of parsley, a grating of nutmeg and a squeeze of lemon juice.

Other broth-based soups

You can of course make the above soup just by using a very well-flavoured stock and simmering vegetables and noodles before adding cooked chicken. Here are some other broths which I make in this way for speed, but remember you can make it the other way, too, if you have a whole chicken to hand.

An oriental chicken and mushroom soup

I started using dried seaweed in all kinds of broths when experimenting with a pressure cooker recipe for Fiona Bird's book on seaweed. It isn't essential here, but it does add another dimension to the flavour and is also very nutritious, so worth adding. I use Irish or Scottish wakame or kombu (see page 52).

1 litre well-flavoured chicken stock
15g dried seaweed, soaked for 20 minutes
15g dried Chinese mushrooms
15g root ginger, thickly sliced
1–2 star anise
5cm piece of cinnamon stick
1 tsp Szechuan peppercorns (optional)
5 garlic cloves, peeled and sliced
1 bunch of spring onions, half sliced into rounds, half shredded
250g mushrooms, preferably shiitake, sliced
½ head of Chinese leaf, or any other type of greens, thickly shredded
2 nests of egg noodles
200g cooked chicken
2 tbsp soy sauce
2 tbsp Shaoxing rice wine (or sherry or mirin)
sea salt
coriander leaves, to serve (optional)

Heat the chicken stock in a large saucepan or casserole. Drain the seaweed and shred it quite finely. Drain the dried mushrooms and do the same, this time reserving the soaking liquor. Pour this liquor into the chicken stock, making sure you leave any gritty bits behind. Add the seaweed and dried mushrooms to the stock with the ginger, star anise, cinnamon, Szechuan peppercorns if using, garlic and rounds of spring onion. Simmer very gently for 30 minutes. You can strain the stock at this point if you like, discarding all the aromatics, but it isn't strictly necessary.

Add the fresh mushrooms and cabbage and simmer for a further five minutes. Separately cook the noodles until al dente, according to their packet instructions, and add these with the cooked chicken. Pour the soy sauce and rice wine into the soup, then check for seasoning, adding salt if necessary. Serve with the shredded spring onions and some coriander leaves, if you like.

VARIATION: QUICK AND EASY PHO
This is a Vietnamese noodle soup. It can be made with a whole chicken as a full meal, but this is the lighter version. Good additions to the stock for this soup are a split pig's trotter and a roasted onion.

Take 1 litre of rich, well-flavoured chicken stock. Add 2 star anise, a 5cm piece of cinnamon stick, 2 black cardamom pods, 1 tbsp coriander seeds and 1 tbsp fennel seeds. Simmer for 30 minutes, then strain. Add 100g beansprouts, greens such as bok choi, any other shredded vegetables you fancy (carrot and white cabbage are good), large handfuls of mint and coriander leaves, rice noodles and as much cooked chicken as you like. Stir in a couple of tbsp of fish sauce. Simmer until both vegetables and noodles are cooked through. Serve with various condiments, including lime wedges, chilli sauce and hoisin sauce.

Ramen

Like pho, this soup is very much about the quality of the stock and the condiments. Proper tonkotsu ramen will be a milky white colour, as it is cooked for so long and so slowly that all the collagen and fat breaks down into the liquid and emulsifies. This doesn't sound appealing, but the result isn't remotely greasy, it's smooth, rich and savoury.

As the method for achieving this is quite involved, I have also given a couple of quicker, easier methods. It's entirely up to you which you follow: the flavours will be very good with all, it is the colour (and to a lesser extent texture), which is affected.

Regardless, this recipe calls for a large vat of stock simmering slowly away for most of the day, so it's definitely one for a day when you are quite happy staying close to the kitchen. You could even make schmaltz at the same time.

For the broth
2 pig's trotters, split lengthways
1kg pork bones from your butcher
2kg chicken carcasses (with as much fat and skin removed as possible)
1 onion, roughly chopped (unpeeled)
1 large carrot, roughly chopped
2 leeks, roughly chopped
cloves from 1 head of garlic, unpeeled
5cm piece of root ginger, sliced
200g white mushrooms, sliced
1 tsp black peppercorns

For the eggs
4 eggs
125ml soy sauce
125ml mirin or rice wine
75g caster sugar

For the chicken
2 chicken breasts, skinned (around 400g)
50ml soy sauce
2 garlic cloves, crushed

250g ramen noodles

And the extras
shredded Chinese leaf, or any other greens
carrot, cut into matchsticks
beansprouts

For the garnishes
shredded spring onions
coriander leaves
kimchi (see page 161 for a cucumber variety, but a Chinese leaf version would be better here)
sesame oil
chilli oil
soy sauce or tamari

To make the stock in a pressure cooker, put the trotters, bones and carcasses in your cooker and cover with water. Bring to the boil and skim until the foam turns white. Add the remaining ingredients, put on the lid and bring to high pressure. Cook for one hour.

To make the stock conventionally, use a stockpot instead of a pressure cooker. When you have added the aromatics, reduce the heat to the barest of simmers. Cook for several hours – at least six and up to 12 – topping up the water as necessary.

Strain and chill the stock until needed. Skim off the fat that will harden on the top of the stock and either whisk some of it back in or reserve for a different use. This will give you a very well-flavoured brown ramen.

For a milky white stock, there is an extra step. When the water first comes to the boil, boil hard for a couple of minutes, then drain and thoroughly wash the bones and carcasses. The aim is to get rid of anything remotely brown looking, you should be left with white bones and flesh. Wash out the stockpot too, cover with fresh water, bring to the boil again, then proceed as before. I promise, whichever method you follow, the stock will taste wonderful.

When the stock is ready and you want to eat, prepare the additions: Boil the eggs for six minutes or steam them in a pressure cooker at medium pressure for four minutes (the pressure-cooked eggs will be much easier to peel). Mix together the egg marinade ingredients and pour over the peeled eggs. Leave to marinate for at least four hours, preferably longer.

To prepare the chicken, slice it as thinly as you can. Mix the soy and garlic together and pour over the chicken. Leave to marinate for one hour. Cook the noodles according to the packet instructions.

To assemble, skim the chilled stock, which will have set to a jelly in the fridge. Simmer and check for seasoning. Add any of the extra vegetables you like and simmer until tender, then add the chicken; it should cook almost instantaneously. Pile noodles and a couple of egg halves into individual deep bowls, then ladle over the stock, chicken and vegetables. Garnish with anything you like. When I eat this I start by eating it plain, to enjoy the flavour of the stock, then when I get to around two-thirds of the way through I add some kimchi or chilli oil.

A trio of Italian broths

All of these serve 4.
There are three exceptional Italian soups that rely on a well-flavoured, preferably clarified, chicken broth. I include a generous amount of herbs, usually parsley, thyme, a single sprig of tarragon and some basil stalks. I will also add a couple of strips of lemon zest, but never lemon juice as it will make it go cloudy.

For ***Pasta in brodo*** use the finest angel hair-type pasta you can find, or very fine shapes, such as little stars or small *alfabeto*, which really appeal to children. Cook a few handfuls in boiling water until almost al dente, then add them to one litre of simmering broth to finish off. This keeps the broth pure and fairly starch-free (so it won't go cloudy or thicken). Add as much grated parmesan as you like, perhaps some parsley as long as it is very finely chopped as you don't want any real texture here. You can also use tortellini instead of pasta and, if you are making it yourself, try filling it with finely ground minced chicken with a hint of parsley, lemon zest and nutmeg. It works beautifully.

Passatelli in brodo has been a favourite of mine since some friends made it as a starter for our Christmas dinner one year. It's a bit more involved than *pasta in brodo*, but is fun to make with children as they will love the whole process. Bring one litre of broth to the boil. Mix 75g of very fine breadcrumbs with 75g finely grated parmesan. Season with salt and a little grated nutmeg. Put this mixture in a bowl or on a work surface and make a well in the middle. Break in 2 eggs, then gradually work them all in together until you have a well bound but soft dough. If you feel it is too wet, add more breadcrumbs and parmesan. Put a sharp knife in the broth, so it heats up and will be perfect for cutting the dough. Push the dough through either a potato ricer, the coarse plate of a vegetable mill, colander or a passatelli press if you are lucky enough to have one. As you push the dough through, cut it off at intervals directly into the broth. When it's all in the broth, simmer for another minute, then leave to stand for another five. Serve with more grated parmesan.

Stracciatella (Egg-drop soup) is a deconstructed version of *passatelli*. Again, bring one litre of broth to the boil. Beat together 2 large eggs with 50g finely grated parmesan and a scant grating of nutmeg. Start stirring the broth and, at the same time, pour in the egg and cheese mixture. Keep stirring for a few more moments, then remove from the heat and allow to stand for a few minutes. You can also add pasta to this if you like. Either way, serve with more grated parmesan and finely chopped parsley.

A chicken broth with rice, mint and lemon juice

This is based on *canja*, a Portuguese broth/pasta combination. The pasta is rice-shaped, like orzo, but it is often substituted with long-grain rice. Traditionally, a chicken was cooked in water, then the whole lot was smashed up and pressed through a sieve to extract as much goodness as possible. I don't recommend that here.

Season one litre of well-flavoured stock. Add a couple of large parings of lemon zest and some sprigs of parsley. Bring to a simmer and add either 100g cooked basmati rice or 75g al dente pasta. Add around 150g cooked chicken. Fish out the lemon zest and sprigs of parsley and stir in lots of finely chopped mint leaves. Serve at the table with lemon wedges for squeezing over the soup (I don't add this earlier as it can make the broth cloudy). For a meatier soup you can also add some sliced Portuguese sausage and chicken liver.

A herb-scented, summery chicken and vegetable broth

If you ever make the *Freekeh-stuffed chicken with a herb butter* (see pages 69–70), this is the soup you need to make with the leftovers. The herb-scented chicken will bring all the flavours in the soup and vegetables together, it's summer in a bowl. You can use any vegetables you like here, I just wander round the garden or market for inspiration. (*Photo overleaf.*)

Serves 4
For the soup
1 litre well-flavoured chicken stock
sea salt and freshly ground black pepper

1 lime
1 fennel bulb, finely sliced lengthways
1 small bunch of chard, stems and leaves separated
4 baby leeks or spring onions
2 courgettes, sliced thinly on the diagonal
handful of fresh peas
handful of baby broad beans
handful of runner beans, cut into thin strips
200g leftover chicken, finely sliced

To serve
handfuls of herbs: basil, tarragon, lemon thyme, parsley
olive oil
a few borage flowers, courgette flowers, or any other herb flowers you may have in the garden; lemon thyme flowers are especially lovely to eat

Pour the chicken stock into a large saucepan and season with salt, pepper and a thin paring of lime zest. Add the fennel, chard stems and baby leeks or spring onions and simmer for a few minutes until they are approaching al dente. Add the courgettes and simmer for another couple of minutes, then add the peas, broad beans, chard leaves and runner beans. After a further minute of simmering, add the chicken and give the whole thing a very gentle stir, you don't want the chicken to shred. Taste for seasoning and add a very little lime juice, if you like.

Put the herbs and olive oil in a blender or food processor and blend until combined.

Serve the soup in shallow bowls, with the herb oil drizzled over and topped with a few more herb sprigs, borage flowers and shredded courgette flowers.

Chicken, lentil and chard soup

This is a favourite soup that I always make with chicken stock, adding the lemon washed chicken in this recipe as it does wonderful things to the flavour.

2 tbsp olive oil
1 onion, sliced
1 large bunch of chard, stems and leaves separated, both shredded
2 garlic cloves, finely chopped
5cm piece of root ginger, grated
1 tsp ground cumin
1 tsp ground coriander
¼ tsp ground cinnamon
¼ tsp ground ginger
½ tsp turmeric
½ tsp dried mint
1 small bunch of coriander, stems and leaves separated
200g red lentils, well rinsed
sea salt and freshly ground black pepper
1.5 litres chicken stock
4 chicken thighs, skinned and boned, or 200g cooked chicken
juice of 1 lemon (if using chicken thighs), plus more to serve
chopped mint and parsley leaves, to serve
Greek-style natural yogurt, to serve

Heat the olive oil in a large casserole or saucepan.

Add the onion and the chard stems and sauté for a few minutes until starting to soften. Add the garlic, ginger, all the spices and mint and the finely chopped coriander stems. Add the lentils and stir to combine. Season with salt and pepper, then pour in the stock. Bring to the boil, cover and simmer for around 20 minutes, until the lentils have broken down.

If using the chicken thighs, rub them with the lemon juice and salt. Slice them finely. Add them to the soup, along with the shredded chard leaves and coriander leaves. Simmer until the chicken has cooked through and the chard leaves are tender. If you are using cooked chicken, add it at this point, to warm through. Serve with lemon juice, freshly chopped herbs and dollops of yogurt.

Winter sunshine soup

Around the end of January, my food cravings go through a schizophrenic period. I want rich, creamy comfort food to see off the final throes of gloom and cold, but my taste buds start rebelling and demand brighter flavours. This soup attempts to combine the two. It's filling enough, but will also inject a welcome amount of warmth and colour to your table. It's a good soup to make just as all the sour and blood oranges come into season, but you could use a combination of limes and oranges instead. As for the chillies, the choice is yours, but both scotch bonnets or the smoky flavour of chipotle will work well here. You can use chilli pastes or powders if you prefer. (*Photo opposite.*)

1 tbsp olive oil
100g smoked bacon, cut into lardons (optional, I don't always want it)
1 onion, sliced into wedges
1 large piece of pumpkin or other squash, cut into chunks
1–2 red peppers, finely chopped
3 garlic cloves, finely chopped
1 scotch bonnet or 1 dried chipotle soaked until soft, both left whole
1 bunch of coriander, stems separated from leaves
large sprig of thyme
½ tsp turmeric
½ tsp ground allspice
¼ tsp ground ginger
200g frozen sweetcorn kernels
50g basmati rice, well rinsed
1.5 litres well-flavoured chicken stock
sea salt and freshly ground black pepper
about 200g cooked chicken
juice of 2 sour or blood oranges OR juice of 1 orange and 1 lime
1 tbsp sherry
hot sauce (optional)
lime wedges, to serve

Heat the olive oil in a large saucepan. Add the bacon, if using, and all the vegetables. Sauté for a few minutes until they have started to soften. Then add the garlic and chilli. Finely cut the coriander stems and add those, too. Sauté for a further couple of minutes.

Add the thyme and spices, sweetcorn and rice. Stir everything to combine, then pour in the stock. Season with salt and pepper. Simmer for 20 minutes until the rice has cooked. Add the chicken, orange juice and sherry, allow to simmer for a couple of minutes. Fish out the chilli. If you want something spicier, add some hot sauce. Serve with coriander leaves and lime wedges.

Smoky chicken chowder

This soup uses cooked chicken and smoky bacon but, if you have any to hand, smoked chicken works beautifully, too. I make this as a very mellow, creamy soup; those who want more spice can sprinkle some in. What usually happens is that the children add a handful of cheese, while the adults swirl through a tomato and chipotle paste.

1 tbsp olive oil
100g smoked bacon lardons
1 small onion, finely chopped
1 celery stick, finely chopped
1 small carrot, finely chopped
500ml chicken stock
sea salt and freshly ground black pepper
1 leek, finely sliced
2 potatoes, peeled and finely chopped
150g piece of pumpkin or squash, peeled and finely chopped
500ml whole milk
150g sweetcorn kernels (I use frozen)
200g cooked chicken, chopped
1 tbsp finely chopped parsley leaves

To serve
large handfuls of grated cheddar
handful of coriander leaves
1–2 very ripe tomatoes, finely chopped
1 tsp chipotle paste
pinch of ground cumin

Heat the oil in a large saucepan or casserole. Add the bacon and fry until crisp and brown. Add the onion, celery and carrot and stir for a minute or two, then pour in the chicken stock. Season with salt and pepper. Add the leek and potatoes. Bring to the boil, then reduce the heat and simmer for eight minutes, then add the pumpkin. Simmer for a further five minutes. Add the milk and sweetcorn.

Continue to simmer very gently for a few minutes until the soup has thickened slightly from the starch in the potatoes. Add the chicken and parsley. Heat through, then serve with your choice of garnish if, indeed, you want any at all.

Classic cream of chicken soup

I think this one could almost pip the traditional chicken noodle soup to the post in terms of pure comfort (*Photo opposite*). It's old-fashioned, reminiscent of, but fortunately far removed from, the canned stuff and unashamedly calorific. This means that as lovely as it is, it is not quite as life-affirming as the broths, but is useful to have when only the full fat kind of comfort eating will do.

This can be garnished with very finely chopped parsley or tarragon.

Serves 4
30g unsalted butter
4 leeks, white part only, finely chopped
1 celery stick, finely chopped
1 garlic clove, finely chopped
500ml chicken stock
250ml whole milk
large sprig of tarragon
sea salt and freshly ground white pepper
1 chicken breast, cooked
grating of nutmeg
50–75ml double cream, depending how rich you want it
1 egg yolk

Heat the butter in a saucepan. Add the leeks, celery and garlic. Sauté very gently for several minutes, making sure nothing takes on any colour, until the leeks are translucent and soft. Pour in the chicken stock and the milk. Add the sprig of tarragon and season with salt only. Simmer very gently for around 15 minutes. Remove from the heat and allow to cool slightly. Fish out the tarragon sprig and transfer the soup to a blender.

Cut up the chicken and add it to the blender. Blitz until very smooth. (You can also put this through a sieve if you like, to

make it even smoother.) Return the soup to the saucepan and heat gently. Grate in a little nutmeg and some very finely ground white pepper. Whisk the cream with the egg yolk until smooth. When the soup is heated through (piping hot to serve), remove it from the heat and, in a slow, steady stream, add the cream and egg yolk mixture, stirring or whisking until it has completely combined with the soup. Serve immediately.

Variations: the flavours above are quite delicate. You can make it much more robust by adding woodier, more pungent herbs such as thyme to the broth, or spicier by making up a bouquet garni with a few cloves, a piece of mace and some crumbled pieces of bay leaf. There is also a German version of this, flavoured with caraway. Add bay, sprigs of parsley and thyme to the soup with 1 tsp caraway seeds and just make sure you sieve it well after you have blended it. Finally, another favourite combination of mine involves chopped tarragon and basil leaves and 1 tsp of finely grated unwaxed lemon or lime zest mixed in at the end. It injects a little bit of freshness without becoming overpoweringly citrusy.

Avgolemono

This is an excellent standby, storecupboard soup that's very popular in my family. It's simple, fresh and nourishing; very good pick-me-up food.

I have been told that this soup does not reheat. This isn't strictly true, but you must not allow it to reboil as the texture will be ruined. As it is, I never think the texture is quite as velvety after reheating, so I will often just make a half quantity for a quick lunch for two.

For the soup
50g orzo or basmati rice
1 litre well-flavoured chicken stock
2 bay leaves
2 eggs, separated
juice of 1 large lemon
100g cooked, shredded chicken (optional)

For the meatballs (optional)
1 tbsp olive oil
1 small onion, finely chopped
250g minced chicken (you can also use lamb)
1 egg yolk
½ tsp dried mint
2 tbsp finely chopped parsley leaves
25g breadcrumbs
grating of nutmeg
sea salt and freshly ground black pepper

To serve
handful of very finely chopped dill, mint or parsley (or all three)
grating of nutmeg (optional)

If serving with the meatballs, make these first. Preheat the oven to 220°C/fan 200°C/425°F/gas mark 7. Heat the olive oil in a frying pan and add the onion. Cook over a medium heat until softened. Put the chicken in a bowl with all the remaining ingredients including the onion. Season with salt and pepper and mix thoroughly. Form into small meatballs of around 15g each, you should have enough mixture to make 18–20. Place on a baking tray and bake for around 10 minutes until browned and cooked through. Keep warm while you make the soup.

To make the soup, cook the orzo or rice in plenty of water. Drain. Heat the chicken stock with the bay leaves and add the cooked orzo or rice. Whisk the egg whites until stiff, then whisk in the egg yolks. Finally, add the lemon juice and whisk for another minute. Take a ladleful of the simmering stock and hold it at a height above the whisked eggs. Pour it into the eggs very gradually, whisking all the while, until it is all combined. Remove the soup from the heat and pour the egg and lemon sauce into it, again, gradually and whisking all the time. Season to taste. Serve immediately, it should not need reheating. If you do want to reheat, be very careful.

To serve, divide either the shredded chicken or the meatballs between your bowls and ladle the soup over them. Sprinkle with the herbs and a very fine grating of nutmeg.

Thai chicken and galangal soup

You don't have to make this with coconut milk if you don't want to. Make it hotter and sourer, by adding more chilli and increasing the amount of stock to 1 litre.

For the broth
750ml light chicken stock
4 bone-in skinless chicken thighs
2 lemon grass stalks, bruised
2 kaffir lime leaves, shredded
½ head of garlic, cloves lightly bruised
3cm piece of galangal, cut into slices
1 green bird's eye chilli, lightly bruised
stems from 1 bunch of coriander

For the soup
400g can of coconut milk
1 lemon grass stalk, tender part only, finely sliced
2 kaffir lime leaves, very finely shredded
2cm piece of galangal, peeled and very finely chopped
2 green chillies, sliced
juice of 1 lime, plus more if needed
1 tbsp fish sauce
1 tsp palm sugar or soft light brown sugar, plus more if needed
¼ tsp shrimp paste (optional)
leaves from 1 bunch of coriander, roughly chopped
handful of mint or Thai basil leaves, roughly chopped
3 spring onions, shredded

Put the chicken stock in a large casserole or saucepan. Add the chicken thighs and all the other aromatics. Bring to the boil, then reduce to a low simmer and cook gently for 20 minutes. Remove the chicken, take out the bones and roughly shred the meat. Leave the broth to stand for 30 minutes, then strain into a clean saucepan.

Add all the remaining ingredients to the broth. Check for seasoning, then simmer for a few minutes. Taste and adjust the seasoning and amounts of lime juice and sugar if necessary. Add the chicken thigh meat and warm through. Serve piping hot.

Chicken, barley and yogurt soup

This is an Armenian soup and is another Jewish classic. In fact, it's so integral to the cuisine it gave its name to an Arnold Wesker play about a Jewish East End family, *Chicken Soup with Barley*.

It's a simple soup. You don't have to add chicken, the broth is really enough, but you can do so if you want to make it a bit more substantial. Some recipes add up to ½ tsp of sugar at the end. I don't think it needs it; taste yours and add it if you think it does.

200g pearl barley, soaked overnight
1.2 litres chicken stock
3 skinless bone-in chicken thighs
large sprig of parsley
1 shallot, left whole
sea salt and freshly ground black pepper
500ml thick natural yogurt
1 egg, lightly beaten
25g unsalted butter
2 tsp dried mint
mint, dill and/or parsley leaves, finely chopped, to serve

Drain the barley and put it in a saucepan with the chicken stock and the chicken thighs. Bring to the boil and skim off any starchy foam. Add the sprig of parsley and the shallot. Season with salt and pepper. Reduce the heat, cover, and simmer for 35–40 minutes until the barley is very tender. Remove the parsley and shallot, then also the chicken. When the chicken is cool enough to handle, remove the bones. Pull the meat into chunks and return it to the broth.

Meanwhile, strain the yogurt, by standing it in a colander or sieve lined with cheesecloth or muslin. Stir regularly. The point to this is that the soup will not be diluted by the water content of the yogurt and will consequently be creamier. Remove the yogurt from the strainer. Whisk it with the egg. Take a small ladleful of the soup and pour it into the yogurt and egg mixture from a height, whisking constantly. Then pour this mixture into the barley broth, whisking all the time.

Melt the butter and whisk in the dried mint. Pour this into the soup. Serve with finely chopped herbs.

Traditional chicken stew

This is the stew I have been making since I was a child. It is never the same twice, and is often the receptacle of all kinds of other types of meat, too. In that respect it's a bit like the Caribbean 'Saturday soup' which uses up the week's leftovers in one amorphous dish.

There's a routine about this soup. I always make it after a roast chicken dinner, rather than any other meal which is likely to give me chicken leftovers, purely because I like to add roast dinner leftovers to the pot too. This means any roast potatoes or parsnips, carrots, greens, stuffing and – if a Christmas dinner – bacon and chipolatas, too. This might sound too much, but it really isn't. If you have enough stuffing leftover, you don't need to make dumplings (although they're always good). Smoked pork of any sort will always taste good with chicken and, as for the vegetables, if they've been roasted they'll just add depth of flavour to the final stew and, if they're not, just add them at the end and heat through to supplement the other vegetables; the twice-cooking will make them soft and sweet. The other thing which makes this really quite special is leftover gravy. It will improve the flavour no end.

So what I will do is strip as much meat off the chicken carcass as possible and make a quick stock with the remains, enriched with the chicken neck if I have it, plus a couple of wings and/or chicken backs if they are to hand. When I'm ready to make the stew I scrape the fat off the top of the gravy and melt it in a large saucepan or casserole or, failing that, add a mixture of olive oil and butter or schmaltz. I use this to sauté onion, chunks of carrot and celery, then any other root vegetables I have – often swede or celeriac – and if I'm not using up roast potatoes, a floury potato or two which will eventually break up into the stock. Garlic can be added here, finely chopped, and very occasionally some bacon if I have some that must be used up (but this is rare, this is not a stew that really needs bacon). I will let everything take on a bit of colour, then add any aromatics I fancy: parsley, a woody stem of thyme, some tarragon. I will then pour over the stock – about one and a half litres – and season, then simmer until the vegetables are tender. At this point any vegetable leftovers can be added along with essential leeks, which are cut into rounds and simmered until tender. Cabbage too, but usually nothing darker than a Savoy or spring green. If I have a meat- or bread-based stuffing which holds its shape this will go in, too (although I will hold some back for roast chicken and stuffing sandwiches).

Then there's the dumplings. In winter these have to be suet. Take 200g self-raising flour and season it. Mix in 100g suet, then add milk or water, just enough to make a fairly sticky dough. Drop heaped tablespoons of this into the stew and cover. They will need to simmer for 15 minutes. If you want the top of them to have a brown crust, put in an oven or under a hot grill for a few minutes.

Gumbo

Like any dish of murky and hotly contended origins, there isn't one definitive or authentic way to make gumbo. It can be quite runny, or thick like a slightly soupier version of risotto. It can be thickened with roux – as brown as you can bear to get it – or okra, or filé powder or, as in the version below, can contain all three. Filé powder is ground sassafras leaf, first used by Native Americans; it has a subtle flavour which I can only describe as both peppery and creamy at the same time. It will contain the holy trinity of Louisianan food – onion, celery and green pepper – but can also include garlic in powder form as part of a Cajun seasoning. It is rare to find gumbo without andouille sausage; the nearest we can get here is a garlicky French sausage or a fairly soft, fat Polish kielbasa.

Usually when I cook I taste constantly throughout. Not so with gumbo. Taste it early on and you will be almost tempted to throw it out and start again. But something quite magical happens when the dark roux, chicken and stock start melding with the bay and other aromatics: the result is a soup that is richly, intensely savoury and with that glossy, oleaginous texture you would normally only get from a proper oxtail soup or a bone marrow-enriched gravy. And when I say magical, I mean it. My family could not get enough of it. My children even turned down a treat lunch out because we had leftovers and that's what they wanted to eat.

The Cajun seasoning included will make more than you need for this dish, but it will store well and can be used in either *Jambalaya* (see page 105) or *Cajun spiced wings* (see page 222).

Serves 6–8

For the Cajun seasoning

1 tbsp sea salt
2 tsp sweet smoked paprika
2 tsp garlic powder
1 tsp freshly ground white pepper
1 tsp onion powder
1 tsp dried oregano
1 tsp dried thyme
½ tsp ground cumin
½ tsp cayenne pepper

For the gumbo
8 chicken thighs or 1 chicken jointed into 8
2 tbsp Cajun seasoning, plus 1–2 tsp
up to 75ml groundnut oil, or a combination of oil and unsalted butter (half and half is good)
75g plain flour
1 large onion, very finely chopped
2 celery sticks, very finely chopped
1 large green pepper, very finely chopped
2 garlic cloves, finely chopped
1 litre chicken stock
3 bay leaves, scrunched up
250g okra, sliced into rounds
200g smoked sausage, sliced
a few dashes of red Tabasco or other hot sauce

To serve
6–8 servings of steamed rice
1–2 tbsp filé powder (optional)

Mix together all the ingredients for the Cajun seasoning.

Pat dry your chicken pieces, then sprinkle them with the 2 tbsp of Cajun seasoning on both cut and skin sides. Put on a rack in the fridge to dry out for an hour or so. (You can leave them overnight if you prefer.)

Heat around 3 tbsp of the oil in a large casserole, then fry the chicken pieces until well browned on all sides, up to five minutes for each side. You may need to do this in two batches, as you don't want to crowd the pan. Remove the chicken from the casserole. Pour any rendered chicken fat and oil in the casserole into a jug and make up the amount to 75ml with more oil, or mixed oil and butter. Return this to the casserole. If using butter, wait for it to melt. Add the flour, and cook, using either a very long-handled spoon or whisk. The colour of the roux here is important: the lighter the roux, the more it will thicken the gumbo, but the darker, the more complex and interesting the flavour. I aim for a rich brown, just very slightly lighter and redder than oxtail soup or HP sauce. It is harder to go much darker than this without burning. I find this usually takes 10–15 minutes. Be careful: you have to keep stirring and there is a risk that the mixture will spit at you.

When you are satisfied with the colour, add the onion, celery, pepper and garlic. Cook in the roux for several minutes until starting to soften. Sprinkle in a little more of the Cajun seasoning, just 1–2 tsp. Gradually add the stock, stirring just as you would for a béchamel or veloute, until it is all incorporated.

Return the chicken to the casserole, along with the bay leaves. Cover and simmer gently for at least one hour, until the chicken is close to tender, then add the okra and sausage. Cook for a further hour, until the sausage has softened and the okra has all but melted into the stew.

Remove the chicken from the casserole. Remove it from the bone and cut into small pieces. It's up to you whether you keep the skin or not, I like to. Add a few dashes of Tabasco and taste for seasoning.

Serve in bowls, ladled over a mound of steamed rice and sprinkled with filé powder if you have some.

3. POACHED & STEAMED CHICKEN

This is all about slow, gentle cooking, mellow flavours developing in the pot and enlivened – or not, as you wish – with a variety of sauces. It's also about creating food for more than one meal, as poaching will provide you with a whole cooked chicken and its cooking liquor which you can drink as a broth or use as a stock later.

The broth is also used to make sauces for the chicken. I poach chicken in just water, flavoured with different aromatics for a light, summer dish; other times I use a light chicken stock to intensify the flavour of robust dishes, such as *Poule au pot* (see page 47). It's up to you what you do.

In terms of end result, I don't see a huge amount of difference between poaching and steaming. Steaming gives a slightly drier, firmer finish to the skin, which is useful, as it will keep its shape better so can be browned afterwards if necessary. It's also useful if you want to smoke the meat afterwards because, again, it will be drier. You can use the cooking liquor left over from either.

How to poach a whole bird

First of all, you need to decide whether or not you want to include the skin. Leaving it on will result in softer, more tender meat, as you are not removing all the fat. But it does mean that your broth will have a layer of fat on the top. This can be skimmed off with a spoon or ladle and some patience or, if you are not using the poaching liquor immediately, you can strain, chill and skim off the hardened fat later to be used as schmaltz.

I sometimes part-remove the skin, leaving the trickier bits such as the skin around the wings. Then the removed skin will be reserved for making schmaltz and gribenes, or fried up immediately for a garnish.

There are more methods for poaching chicken than I care to list here. To poach a whole bird, timings vary wildly – from 10 minutes, then leaving it to stand in the cooling liquor for another hour which, frankly, I don't trust – to simmering for a couple of hours, which is far too long.

I choose a happy medium. For an average-sized bird, weighing around 1.5kg, I will cook as follows:

Put the chicken in a large casserole or saucepan. Pour in water until the thickest part of the legs are immersed: around one-third of the top of the breasts and the tips of the legs will be left sticking out of the water. This is fine, the breasts will steam more gently during the cooking time. Add 1 tsp of salt, then bring to the boil and skim until any foam that appears turns from mushroom grey to white. Then add any aromatics you want and perhaps some wine. Reduce the heat to the lowest possible simmer and cover. Leave to cook for around 45 minutes, then turn off the heat and leave to stand for a further 15 minutes. This will have the dual effect of continuing to cook and rest the bird at the same time.

At this point the chicken is ready to use. To keep it warm, just let it sit in the poaching liquor until you need it. When I store poached chicken in the fridge, I will break it up into large chunks, discarding bone and sinew where necessary, then put into a fairly shallow container and ladle over some of the broth, which I will not have skimmed of fat. This collagen-rich broth will help keep the chicken moist and tender.

A whole poached chicken – because it tends to come with bits and pieces that have cooked around it – will serves six people.

How to poach a chicken breast

I don't often poach anything other than a whole bird, as I don't buy breasts. However, some recipes do call for breast meat, or cooked meat, so there may be times when this is what you prefer to do. To poach chicken breasts, put them in a single layer in a shallow, lidded pan. Completely cover with stock or water and any other aromatics you choose. Bring to a simmer, then cook over the lowest possible heat for seven to 10 minutes, depending on the size of the chicken breast. Start checking for doneness after seven minutes. The easiest way to do this is by inserting a skewer: if it comes out too hot to touch for more than a second, the chicken is done. Alternatively, if you have a probe thermometer, it should be cooked to 75°C/167°F. Poached chicken breasts are useful added to soups, salads and slightly more elegant dishes. You could use them in any of the dishes below, with any of the sauces. I serve them sliced on the diagonal and slightly fanned out across the plate, with plenty of sauce spooned over.

Poaching in a pressure cooker

A whole chicken poaches brilliantly in a pressure cooker. I don't add quite so much liquid as for conventional cooking; I will make sure the stock just comes halfway up the bird, then bring it to high pressure and cook for 20 minutes, then allow it to drop pressure naturally. It will be perfectly cooked in that time. A chicken breast will take just three to four minutes, with natural release; an on-the-bone thigh or leg just 10 minutes.

Sauces for plain poached chicken

I say a plain poached chicken, but I will still include in the cooking liquor a glass of wine or vermouth, bay leaves, tarragon, parsley, garlic and peppercorns. And probably a piece of pared unwaxed lemon zest, too.

CAPER SAUCE

Old fashioned, but a winner. It's especially good with poached chicken when you need some kind of sauce, but it would also work with a roast chicken, with or without gravy.

You can add herbs if you like, but remember, this sauce will also hint at any of the aromatics you have poached the chicken with, as it is cooked with the poaching liquor. It's non-traditional, but I love this with *Poule au pot* (see right).

Serves 4
25g unsalted butter
25g plain flour
300ml chicken stock, from poaching
3 tbsp salted capers, rinsed, drained and roughly chopped
sea salt and freshly ground black pepper
1 tbsp double cream (optional)

Heat the butter in a saucepan. When it has melted, add the flour and stir to make a smooth roux. Cook for a further couple of minutes to cook the raw flavour of the flour out, then start gradually incorporating the stock, stirring constantly between additions until you have a smooth sauce.

Stir in the capers; taste for seasoning (you may not need salt) and add the double cream, if using.

PARSLEY SAUCE
Follow the recipe for caper sauce but, instead of capers, add lots of finely chopped parsley leaves. This is lovely – very mellow – but it's also very good with a heap of Dijon mustard added to it.

LEMON AND SAFFRON SAUCE
Follow the recipe for caper sauce but add a large pinch of saffron strands to the liquor and a squeeze of lemon juice at the end.

Poule au pot

This is a French institution. The thought behind this dish was originally well meant, with Henri IV proclaiming that he wanted every peasant or farming family in the land to be able to afford a chicken for the pot each Sunday. I'm not sure how many families still cook this on a Sunday, as I think these days a lot of people just buy a rotisserie chicken, which has also become an institution.

There is a certain economy about poule au pot. The stuffing and all the vegetables mean that the chicken goes further, while the stuffing itself – made with stale breadcrumbs and chicken livers – is quite parsimonious. You can use any of the stuffings in the Roast Chicken chapter if you prefer; the Toulouse sausage and green olive version (see page 66) is very good for this dish. Adding prunes to the stock isn't traditional, despite them being a product of south west France. I quite like to add a few, it conflates this dish with Cock a Leekie (a Scottish broth with poached chicken, leeks and prunes). The sauce is traditional, but you could use any of the above in its place. I am in favour of caper sauce myself. Another conflation, this time English and French but, really, as long as it tastes good, who cares?

Serves 6–8
For the stuffing
25g unsalted butter, melted
1 onion, finely chopped
2 garlic cloves, finely chopped
50g smoked ham, finely chopped
100g breadcrumbs
½ tsp ground allspice
2 tbsp finely chopped parsley leaves
1 egg yolk
sea salt and freshly ground black pepper

For the poule au pot

1 large chicken (make sure you get one that will fit into your largest pot)
200ml white wine
up to 1.5 litres light chicken stock or water
2 onions, peeled and quartered
4 carrots, peeled and cut into chunks
3 celery sticks, cut into chunks (plus leaves from the centre)
1 tsp peppercorns
1 tsp allspice berries
bouquet garni of bay, thyme, parsley and chervil if you can find it
100g plump prunes (optional)
500g small new potatoes
2–3 leeks, cut into chunks
½ small Savoy cabbage (optional)

For the green sauce

3 egg yolks, hard-boiled
1 tbsp white wine vinegar
100ml olive oil
1 shallot, finely chopped
small bunch of parsley, finely chopped

First make the stuffing. Mix all the ingredients together (no need to sauté first) and season well with salt and pepper. Use it to stuff the cavity of the bird. Pull the skin tightly up over the cavity entrance and either tie up with string or secure with a couple of cocktail sticks.

Put the chicken in a large casserole or pot. Add the wine and enough stock or water to almost cover the bird, as described (see pages 45–46). Follow the instructions for poaching on those pages, adding the vegetables, spices and bouquet garni and increasing the cooking time to 1–1¼ hours to take the stuffing into account. Add the prunes (if using), potatoes, leeks and cabbage (if using) 15 minutes before the end of the cooking time. Turn the heat off and leave everything to rest or finish its cooking for 15 minutes.

To make the sauce, mash the egg yolks up, then mix with the vinegar. Season with salt and pepper. Start dripping in the olive oil as you would to make mayonnaise. When the mixture starts to emulsify, add it in a steadier stream. When it is all added, stir in the shallot and parsley.

Poached chicken with lentils

This is a really good way of immediately using up some of the chicken poaching liquor. You could use pieces here but as I like to have poached chicken leftovers I poach a whole bird; it takes longer, but gives you more scope for further dishes so, in reality, you're saving time. Add any other vegetables you fancy to the lentils; I like root vegetables, especially celeriac.

1 chicken
enough water or light chicken stock to cover
350ml red wine
large bunch of thyme
4 garlic cloves
1 strip of pared unwaxed lemon zest
100g bacon lardons
1 onion, finely chopped
2 garlic cloves, finely chopped
200g Puy or other brown or green lentils, well rinsed
1–2 heads of spring greens or Brussels sprout tops
Dijon mustard, to serve

Poach the chicken as described (see pages 45–46), including in the stock or water 250ml of the red wine, the thyme, garlic and lemon zest. Add the greens for the last five to 10 minutes, allowing them to sit on top to steam.

Meanwhile, when the chicken is nearly cooked, start the lentils. Fry the bacon lardons in a large casserole until plenty of fat has rendered out, then add the onion and garlic. Stir in the lentils, then pour over the remaining 100ml of red wine. Bring to the boil and reduce down to almost nothing, then add 600ml of the chicken poaching liquor. Return to the boil, then reduce the heat to a simmer and cook until the lentils are tender, around 45 minutes. (The poached chicken should be resting during this time.)

Serve the lentils with large chunks of the chicken and plenty of Dijon mustard.

Chicken, summer veg and a tomato and basil scented sauce

This is a dish to make when you have very ripe, sweet tomatoes, as they will make or break it. If you prefer, you can simply add some cherry tomatoes at the end and wait for them to burst, before serving with lots of freshly torn basil leaves. (*Photo overleaf.*)

1 chicken
enough light chicken stock or water to cover
1 large sprig of tarragon
4 garlic cloves, finely sliced
zest of 1 unwaxed lemon, in pared strips
12 small new or salad potatoes
small bunch of baby carrots
4 baby fennel bulbs, or 1 large fennel bulb cut into wedges
2 leeks, finely sliced
1 courgette, sliced on the diagonal
handful of peas or broad beans
handful of runner beans, shredded

For the tomato and basil sauce
100g sweet cherry tomatoes, chopped
handful of basil leaves

Follow the instructions for poaching a chicken (see pages 45–46), using the light chicken stock or water and adding the tarragon, garlic and lemon zest at the beginning. After 30 minutes, add the potatoes, carrots and fennel. After 40 minutes, add the leeks, courgette, peas or broad beans and runner beans. When the chicken is cooked, leave to rest for 15 minutes, then remove the chicken and vegetables and strain, reserving the broth.

Cut up the chicken and arrange on one serving plate, or individual plates, surrounded by the vegetables. Skim the broth. Take a ladleful and put in a frying pan. Add the cherry tomatoes and boil fiercely for a couple of minutes. Taste for seasoning, then stir in the basil. Spoon over the chicken and serve.

GOAT'S CHEESE DUMPLINGS

I'm not a fan of chicken stuffed with cream cheese or goat's cheese. I don't like how it almost always curdles and, as it's usually to keep the inside of a chicken breast moist, I'd rather just eat thighs instead. But I do love chicken with these little dumplings, which are light, billowy and absolutely perfect with chicken, broth and especially with the cherry tomato sauce above.

200g plain flour
2 tsp baking powder
sea salt and freshly ground black pepper
1 egg, lightly beaten
75ml whole milk
75g soft goat's cheese
finely grated zest of 1 unwaxed lemon
finely chopped herbs: basil, tarragon, mint, parsley

Whisk the flour and baking powder together and add salt and pepper. Make a well in the middle, then start whisking in the egg. When it is all incorporated, gradually whisk in the milk. Crumble the cheese in and combine thoroughly, then stir through the lemon zest and the herbs. You should end up with a fairly smooth dough.

Drop dessertspoons of the dough into the broth. They will only take two or three minutes to cook and will float when done.

Steamed chicken

I don't steam chicken very often. When I do, it's usually because I want it to stay firm and in one piece, such as in the smoked recipe on page 54. If you really want to steam chicken pieces, as opposed to a whole chicken, the most economical way is to do it over something else. So, for example, it takes 15–20 minutes to cook rice by the absorption method. If you sat chicken breasts or flattened-out thigh fillets in a steamer basket above this, it would steam perfectly in the same amount of time, with the added bonus that you will add flavour from the chicken juices dripping into the rice.

Here's one simple recipe, not using rice, which is a good one when you want something supremely virtuous. Of course, I would probably ruin it all by adding copious amounts of soy, chilli sauce and sesame oil at the end, but the intention is there.

2 chicken breasts or flattened thigh fillets, skinned
sea salt
200ml water or chicken stock
1 lemon grass stalk, bruised
a few slices of root ginger
a few slices of garlic
a few florets of broccoli or sprouting broccoli

Sprinkle the chicken with a couple of teaspoons of sea salt and leave to stand for around 30 minutes. Place in a steamer basket.

Put the water or chicken stock in the base of the steamer. Add the lemon grass, ginger and garlic. Place the steamer basket on top. Bring up to a gentle simmer, then steam for 15–20 minutes until the chicken is done. Add the broccoli after 10 minutes.

Remove the basket from the steamer. Leave the chicken to rest for a few minutes. Slice the chicken up, fan out over a plate and serve with the strained broth and broccoli.

TWO VARIATIONS

With lemon and thyme butter sauce. Steam chicken on a bed of bay leaves or other herbs, and scent the cooking broth with strips of lemon zest. A lemon- and thyme-scented broth with a well-seasoned chicken breast is lovely, especially if you add some slices of courgette after 10 minutes and a few cherry tomatoes for the last two. To make it richer, take some of the broth and whisk in some cold butter for a very quick lemon and thyme sauce.

With lime, allspice and coriander. Another version has lime zest and leaves in the base with a couple of lightly crushed allspice berries, some coriander stalks and sliced garlic cloves. Finish the liquor off with butter and lots of chopped coriander leaves, then stir in a very ripe, finely chopped tomato.

THE OVEN METHOD

If you don't want to use a steamer on the hob, you can make parcels with foil or baking parchment for the chicken. This is good if you are making a lot, as you can simply cover the chicken with aromatics, ladle over a little stock, water or alcohol, then seal up, put in a preheated oven (200°C/fan 180°C/400°F/gas mark 6) and steam for 25–30 minutes. These can look and smell amazing when they are opened at the table and all the aromas spill out. Try cooking them with thyme, slices of orange and a glug of sherry or vermouth for something really fragrant. The other thing I like to do here is sauté lots of slices of leek first, then pile them into the parcels, add the chicken breasts, pour over some vermouth and top with a slice of lemon. That way you have an instant sauce as well.

Mizutaki: a Japanese hot pot

This is what you get when you combine Japanese precision and elegance with economy: a hot pot that is prepared and served in a very specific way, but which is infinitely variable in terms of the ingredients used. Discrete little groups of vegetables and meat are arranged in a shallow casserole, then gently cooked in broth. This is often done at the table, with more and more ingredients being added as others are removed. The trick is to keep the different kinds of vegetables apart.

The dipping sauce is very sour, but is a perfect foil for the mellow hot pot. You can find yuzu (a citrus fruit which is very popular in Japan), or bottled yuzu juice, easily now, thanks to larger supermarkets stocking them. (*Photo opposite.*)

For the hot pot
1 large piece kombu
½ head of Chinese leaf cabbage, cut into thin wedges
6 boneless chicken thighs, skinned and cut into slices
2 leeks, sliced into 5cm pieces on the diagonal
1 large carrot, peeled and cut into very thin batons
100g shiitake mushrooms, sliced
handful of sprouting broccoli or any kind of oriental green vegetable
glass noodles, preferably made from sweet potatoes (optional)
up to 1 litre of light chicken stock
sea salt

For the ponzu dipping sauce
100ml dark soy sauce
50ml brown rice vinegar
50ml yuzu or lemon juice
finely grated zest of 1 yuzu or unwaxed lemon

Lie the kombu in the base of a casserole. Cover it with the Chinese cabbage; this will serve as a base for the other ingredients and make them easier to arrange. Mentally divide your pot into six wedges and arrange the chicken, four types of vegetables and noodles over the cabbage, making sure they remain apart from one another.

Gradually pour over the stock until it reaches the top of the vegetables, chicken and noodles; they should not be completely immersed. Season with salt, then cover and bring to a simmer. Simmer for eight to 10 minutes, until everything is cooked through. To make the dipping sauce, simply combine the ingredients together.

Serve, passing round small bowls and chopsticks for everyone to help themselves, providing plenty of ponzu dipping sauce.

Whole smoked chicken, Chinese style

The main cooking in this recipe is done via steaming; that cuts the smoking time down so the flavour is very mildly aromatic. You can use the steaming liquor afterwards as the basis of any Chinese-style noodle soup or rice dish. The smoked chicken can be eaten immediately with some of the stock poured over and just some plain rice and greens, it can be eaten cold, or can be used in a stir-fry.

For the chicken and marinade
1 whole chicken
2 tbsp sea salt
2 tsp Chinese 5-spice powder
1 tbsp ground Szechuan peppercorns (optional)
5cm piece of root ginger, sliced (no need to peel)
3 garlic cloves, sliced

For the broth
1 litre light chicken stock or water
5cm piece of root ginger, sliced
4 garlic cloves, sliced
2 star anise
1 cinnamon stick
1 tsp black peppercorns
1 tbsp mirin

For the smoke
50g black Chinese tea
50g long-grain rice (jasmine or basmati)
50g demerara sugar
2 star anise, broken up
1 cinnamon stick, broken up
1 tsp fennel seeds

Put the chicken on a rack over a plate that will fit comfortably in your fridge. Mix the salt with the Chinese 5-spice and the Szechuan peppercorns, if using, and use this to sprinkle the chicken, inside and out. Stuff with the ginger and garlic. Put into the fridge and leave overnight.

When you are ready to cook the chicken, put the water or stock and all the ingredients for the broth, except the mirin, in a pan and set the chicken over it, either on a rack or in a separate steaming basket, just make sure the chicken isn't touching the water. Pour the mirin over the chicken. Cover, bring to the boil, then reduce the heat to a steady simmer. Steam for 1–1¼ hours until cooked through.

To smoke the chicken, line a wok with foil and put all the smoke ingredients on top. Put a rack over this and place the chicken on it. Heat the wok until the smoke ingredients begin to burn. Reduce the heat, then cover the wok and the chicken with foil and leave to smoke for 15 minutes. Turn off the heat and leave to stand, still covered, for another 10–15 minutes.

GLAZED SMOKED CHICKEN
You can also glaze this before you smoke it (*photo opposite*). Mix together 2 tbsp hoisin sauce, 1 tbsp soy sauce, 1 tbsp honey or maple syrup, 1 tsp sesame oil and 1 tsp ground ginger or Chinese 5-spice powder. Brush this over the chicken once before smoking it, then once or twice during the process as well. You should end up with a richly burnished skin, similar to Peking duck.

Ginger-scented chicken

This is my version of a Hainanese chicken, a classic hawker stall dish I've eaten in Singapore. It's a very refreshing summer dish and the leftovers are superb in the salad on pages 203–205.

For the chicken and rice
1 chicken
sea salt and freshly ground black pepper
enough water or light chicken stock to cover
4 garlic cloves, peeled and sliced
5cm piece of root ginger, peeled and thinly sliced
1 bunch of spring onions
large knob of unsalted butter, or vegetable oil
300g jasmine rice, rinsed thoroughly until the water runs clear
1 pandan leaf (optional)
300g choi sum or sprouting broccoli
1 tbsp tamari or soy sauce
a few drops of sesame oil

For the chilli sauce
8 mild red chillies, deseeded and roughly chopped
20g root ginger, peeled and roughly chopped
6 garlic cloves, peeled and roughly chopped
2 tsp palm sugar or soft light brown sugar
2 tbsp groundnut oil
juice of ½ lime
1 tsp white wine vinegar
1 tsp fish sauce
freshly ground white pepper

To serve
½ a cucumber, peeled, deseeded and cut into thin crescents
handful of coriander leaves

Look inside the cavity of the chicken and pull out any fat you can see. Reserve for cooking the rice. Season the chicken with salt and pepper. Put in a saucepan or casserole and cover with water, or a combination of water and stock if you have any to hand. Add the garlic and ginger. Take half the spring onions and finely slice. Add these as well. Poach according to the instructions on pages 45–46.

Remove the chicken from the pot, skin it and break into fairly large pieces. Spoon some of the cooking liquor over the chicken and keep it warm. Return the discarded pieces of chicken carcass to the broth and simmer until it has reduced to around one litre in volume. Strain.

To cook the rice, heat the butter or oil and the reserved chicken fat in a saucepan until the chicken fat has melted (you could instead use some ready-made schmaltz here, see page 21, and just add the reserved fat to the next batch you make). Add the rice and stir until coated with the fats. If you have one, fold up the pandan leaf and add to the saucepan, then pour over 550ml of the poaching liquor. Season with salt, then bring to the boil and cover. Simmer for 10 minutes, then remove from the heat and add the choi sum. Leave to steam in its own heat for a further 10 minutes.

To make the chilli sauce, blitz all the ingredients together.

To serve, pile a mound of rice in a bowl and top with the greens and cooked chicken. You can either moisten the whole with some of the remaining broth – but only a little, it's not supposed to be a soup – or serve it separately in bowls.

Drizzle with soy or tamari and a few drops of sesame oil. Serve with slices of cucumber, the reserved shredded spring onions and the coriander, with the chilli sauce on the side.

4. ROAST CHICKEN

If I had to choose just one way to eat chicken, a roast would be it. It has everything that is good about chicken, from the crisp, burnished, buttery skin, to the juicy thighs and sticky wings. There are also hidden delights: the oysters on the chicken backs are particularly good on a roast and so bitterly fought over at the table that I now regret telling the children of their existence.

But, if I must give up my (once) chef's perks of the oysters, there is some small consolation in that there is plenty of skin to go round. My favourite bit is the skin that covers the small hollow at the base of the breast, just below the wishbone; it will be particularly sticky underneath from the hot fat which will pool there during roasting time and can catch you unawares when it spills out. It has the best flavour and texture.

There are also the leftovers. Some cooked chicken is one of the most useful things to have in the fridge and I do often roast a chicken particularly for this reason. I say this though the truth is that sometimes I roast the chicken purely because I want to eat all the skin, then put the meat in the fridge for later use. There are other bonuses: the jelly that collects around the carcass which is concentrated stock and useful for adding to any sauce. Or the pot of roasting juices, or gravy, which sits in the fridge with a lovely layer of schmaltz on top, to be used in anything, but never better than when spread on hot toast with a sprinkling of salt.

A roast chicken is also the meal which, more than any other, says 'home' to me. Growing up, chicken was a treat, only ever eaten roasted or pot-roasted, or very occasionally put in a pie, apart from leftovers of course. It was always served on Sunday and I loved the routine of it, especially in winter. Roast lunch was followed by my mum's weekly bread-making session. Then the evening meal would be a vegetable stew bolstered by the freshly made chicken stock from the carcass (the leftover meat was reserved for later in the week), served with warm-from-the-oven bread rolls. Add a good novel, a comfy Chesterfield and the smell of our slightly smoking log fire and you have my idea (and memory) of Sunday bliss.

Roasting a chicken is really one of the easiest of things to do – high returns for little effort. But as there are so many methods out there – usually all trying to solve the dry breast conundrum – it has become very complicated. So the first part of this chapter is as much about how not to roast your chicken.

How to roast a chicken

I have strict criteria when it comes to a perfectly roasted chicken. The skin is vitally important and must be very crisp and brown, no pale flabbiness allowed. The wings must be crisp, sticky and slightly chewy, the legs must pull away from the carcass easily and give up soft juicy meat and the breast meat must still be tender, not dry. Regardless of what I do with flavourings, stuffings, gravies and sides, these are all non-negotiable. I am talking about texture here I know, but the beauty of a perfectly cooked roast is that you will get this huge variety of texture from just one bird. The flavour should be good if you have bought a decent chicken.

For years, my default method was the one that my mother taught me, which always seemed to come out right, even on her temperamental solid fuel Rayburn. It was 20 minutes per pound – which I now translate roughly to 500g – plus a further 20 minutes and it remains pretty much a failsafe, if roasting at around 200°C/fan 180°C/400°F/ gas mark 6. We would slather the chicken in butter and sit it on a bed of herbs to flavour the gravy. We did not agree on stuffing more on this below.

Then I discovered the method Simon Hopkinson made famous in *Roast Chicken and Other Stories*. This introduced the idea of the sizzle at the beginning of the cooking time. So I started roasting a chicken with the oven on full whack, reducing the temperature after 20 minutes to 200°C/fan 180°C/400°F/ gas mark 6, and roasting for another 30–45 minutes, depending on size. This method only works if you follow Simon's instructions to the letter and leave the chicken in the switched-off oven for a further 15 minutes, as it will continue to cook/rest during that time. This isn't so useful if you have other things in the oven you still need to cook – roast potatoes, for example – so instead I have incorporated the sizzle into my 20 minutes per 500g method.

Over the years I have toyed with other methods. I have roasted birds breast-side down, which means that the breast meat is constantly fed by the rest of the meat juices and consequently stays moist. This is fine but, even if you turn it upright at the end for a sizzle, the skin will never be quite as crisp, and it often tears.

A variation on the upside down chicken is the method in the impossibly nerdy *Cook's Illustrated*, a publication from America's Test Kitchen, which involves propping up your chicken on a V rack, or scrunched-up foil, so it cooks one wing-side up for 15 minutes, then is turned around so the other wing is facing up, then for the final 15 minutes it is cooked breast-side up. All at 190°C/fan 170°C/375°F/gas mark 5. I am impressed with the results of this, but it is not a method I would regularly employ as it's too fussy for me. The beauty of a roast chicken is you can usually go away and leave it for at least 45 minutes, you really don't want to have to be shifting it around every 15 minutes.

The problem for me with both this method and the breast-side down method is what happens to the back of the chicken. The best bits of meat on the whole bird are the oysters, as they are so soft, tender and have so much flavour, and these qualities can be lost if the back is exposed to too much direct heat. The final method I mention here is very purist and has been pointed out to me by several food writers and chefs. This is the Thomas Keller (chef patron of The French Laundry in Northern California) method. The chicken is trussed, put on a rack and dried out in the fridge. Then it is brought to room temperature, seasoned inside and out (on the outside from a height with sea salt), then roasted at 230°C/fan 210°C/450°F/gas mark 8 for 50–60 minutes. Then it is rested for 15 minutes and basted with any pan juices.

This is an excellent method and results in a good, crisp skin and succulent meat. But it's not my method of choice for a couple of reasons: firstly you need to use quite a small bird, as the breasts will dry out on anything larger than around 1.2kg. Also, you can't add anything else to the pan, as the crisp skin is dependent on dry heat and anything you add will create steam. This means no butter, no liquid in the roasting dish and, worst of all, no onions or garlic under the chicken. This latter point is a deal breaker for me. The onion is my cook's perk and I will usually eat it before serving up the rest of the meal. Half the garlic is mashed into the gravy, the rest is given to my husband, as it's his absolute favourite thing. Every chicken roasted without these is a wasted opportunity. With hope, I tried Keller's method with the onions: the chicken was excellent, but the onions weren't nearly soft enough. So, his is not the method for me.

The other method I discarded was the slow roast. Heston Blumenthal has a recipe which involves brining a chicken, roasting at 90°C/fan 70°C/194°F/gas mark ¼ for three to four hours, then removing from the oven, resting for 30–45 minutes, then browning at a temperature of 230–240°C/fan 210–220°C/450–475°F/gas mark 8–9 for five to 10 minutes. I did try this and found that the texture was close to that of confit and, really, I would rather use one of the methods specifically for that (see pages 23–24). You can slow-roast in the oven at a slightly higher temperature: 130–140°C/fan 110–120°C/266–275°F/gas mark ½–1 for three hours is about right. I can happily do this with the 40 cloves of garlic recipe (see pages 71–73), but I cover the dish for the first hour and watch the garlic like a hawk.

A complete roast chicken meal should serve four people and perhaps even six, depending on your side dishes and the size of your chicken. You should also manage to keep some back for leftovers.

My best roast chicken

This is the method and flavourings I use when I want a simple roast chicken – no adornments – when I hope to have leftovers, as I love the flavours of tarragon and garlic together. You can use other herbs, such as thyme, bay or parsley if you prefer.

For the chicken
1 chicken, 1.2–1.8kg, air-dried and salted (see pages 22–23)
sea salt and freshly ground black pepper
1 bunch of tarragon
1 onion, sliced into rounds
1 bulb of garlic, cloves separated
lots of unsalted butter
juice from ½ a lemon
125ml wine or vermouth, diluted with 125ml water

For the optional gravy
2 tsp plain flour (also optional, I waver)
100ml white wine
200ml chicken stock

An hour before you want to cook your chicken, remove it from the fridge and allow it to come to room temperature. Make sure it is dry, inside and out. Stuff with the tarragon.

Preheat the oven to 230°C/fan 210°C/450°F/ gas mark 8. If the chicken isn't already trussed, do so (see page 14).

Put the sliced onion in the centre of your roasting pan. Lightly bash the garlic cloves, leaving the skin on, and tuck into any gaps around the onion. Put the chicken on top, trying to make sure that the onion and garlic are completely covered. Rub the chicken breasts and the tops of the legs liberally with butter, then squeeze over the lemon juice. Season the outside of the chicken with salt; to get a very even spread, do this from a height. Pour the liquids around the chicken.

Roast the chicken for 15 minutes, then turn the heat down to 200°C/fan 180°C/ 400°F/gas mark 6. Roast for a further 45 minutes to one hour; this will depend on the size of your chicken, work it out using the 20 minutes per 500g method (see page 58). To ensure it is cooked, insert a skewer into the thickest part of the thigh. Any juices should run clear and the skewer should feel slightly too hot to be comfortable when pressed against bare skin. The leg should also feel loose, as though it will pull away very quickly. Otherwise insert a probe thermometer, you need the internal temperature of the chicken to reach 75°C/167°F. It is important to note here that, if you are cooking a free-range or organic bird, there will likely still be some pinkness about the legs; do not mistake this for undercooking, instead rely on one of the other tests for doneness above.

You can serve this bird as is, with the roasting juices poured over, but I usually prefer to make a gravy as well. Remove the chicken to a hot serving dish and cover loosely with foil. Leave to rest for 15 minutes. Drain off all the liquid into a bowl, spooning off some of the fat that will collect on top, if you wish. Remove the onion and put to one side (chef's perk! Or be generous and serve with the chicken). Squish the garlic into the roasting dish and remove the garlic skins, then put the roasting pan over a low heat and sprinkle over the flour (if using). Stir vigorously, scraping up any brown bits which will stick to the pan, then pour over the wine. Allow to bubble furiously, then continue stirring, making sure that all the goodness in the pan is becoming part of the gravy. Add the stock and simmer until slightly thickened. Drain off any juices from the resting chicken and add those too. Check for seasoning, then pour into a serving jug. If you have been thorough, the roasting pan should look clean.

Other ways to roast chicken

FLAT ROASTED CHICKEN

This is a very fast method. Spatchcock a chicken (see page 11) and press firmly down on the breast bone to flatten the whole thing out. Preheat the oven to 230°C/fan 210°C/ 450°F/gas mark 8. Lie the chicken flat in a roasting dish. Roast for 30–45 minutes, depending on size (15 minutes per 500g is ample), then rest for 15 minutes.
The meat cooks very evenly with this method. The first time we ate it, I had rubbed it with butter, sprinkled over hickory smoked salt and dried herbs and squeezed over some lime juice. There wasn't a sliver of meat left.

THE BRICK-FLATTENED ROAST

This is very similar to flat roasting. It's apparently an Italian institution, and an import the Americans have embraced. I think it works better on a barbecue, but if you want to cook it in an oven, do as follows: salt and air-dry a spatchcocked chicken overnight

(see pages 22–23 and 11). Rub with olive oil and dried herbs. Preheat the oven to 230°C/fan 210°C/450°F/gas mark 8. Heat a large non-stick frying pan or griddle (a cast-iron skillet is best, you need one that is ovenproof) and drizzle with a very little olive oil. Put the chicken skin-side down on the skillet and weigh down with either a brick wrapped in aluminium foil, or another frying pan weighted down with something heavy (such as cans or bags of rice). Cook for 15 minutes until the skin is brown. Turn the chicken over and transfer the whole thing to the oven. Cook for another 20–25 minutes until the chicken is completely cooked through. Remove and allow to rest for 15 minutes.

THE VERTICAL ROAST

I imagine this is the closest you can get to a home-made rotisserie chicken, without investing in a rotisserie. Your other option is to skewer the chicken, or employ a small child to turn a spit for you (I can only manage this for around 30 seconds).

You can buy vertical roasters in supermarkets, they usually consist of a reinforced wire frame which interlocks into a drip tray. There are also more solid, ceramic versions available which would have the same effect as *Beer-can chicken* (see page 211).

The main benefit to roasting this way is that you will prevent fights breaking out over the skin, as the whole bird will be burnished and crisp. The gravy is also incredible. You can even stuff the neck cavity if you wanted. The downside, for me, is that, as the back of the chicken is so much thinner than the rest of the bird, the meat will cook very quickly and the oysters will therefore be overcooked. I save the cooked oysters for warm salads and poach them lightly first, to soften them up.

For the (optional) salting
2 tbsp sea salt
2 tbsp fennel seeds, crushed
1 tsp sweet smoked paprika

For the chicken
1 tbsp fennel seeds
1 tsp black peppercorns
50g unsalted butter
1 tsp sweet smoked paprika
1 tsp sea salt
finely grated zest of 1 unwaxed lemon and juice of ½
200ml vermouth or white wine

If salting your chicken, do so following the instructions on pages 22–23, adding the fennel seeds and paprika to the salt. Regardless of whether you are salting or not, try to air-dry the bird on a rack in the fridge overnight.

Preheat your oven to its highest setting. Grind the fennel seeds and peppercorns. Mash into the butter with the paprika, salt and lemon zest. Smear this over the entire chicken, then squeeze over the lemon juice. Stuff the neck end if you like (see pages 64–67 for stuffing suggestions).

Put the chicken on the metal rack and make sure that the top point is poking out of the neck of the chicken. Fill the drip tray to two-thirds full with a choice of liquid: it could be water, or beer or cider, but I personally prefer a vermouth or white wine.

Place in a roasting dish and put in the oven. Roast for 15 minutes, then reduce the heat to 200°C/fan 180°C/400°F/gas mark 6 and roast using the 20 minutes per 500g method (see page 58). By this time, the skin should be very well browned and the flesh completely cooked through.

The drip tray should be filled with what

will be an absolutely wonderful gravy that I don't believe needs any embellishment. If you want it thicker, make it so in the usual way (by using flour, see page 60).

How to enhance your roast chicken

While I love the flavour of my best roast chicken (page 59), it is possible to enhance it in all kinds of ways, still maintaining its integrity. There are three main methods: through the stuffing; through adding flavour to or under the skin; and by whatever else you decide to put in the roasting dish with the bird. There are plenty of examples of all, below, but first here are three things I avoid:

MILK AND CHEESE: Unless in very small amounts in stuffing, I don't want these anywhere near a roast chicken. I have tried chicken with variously flavoured cream or goat's cheeses stuffed under the skin. They always curdle slightly and, although everyone always likes the flavour of whatever has been mixed with the cheese, the appearance and texture is never great. If you want to stuff under the skin, use butter as a flavour carrier instead, or potatoes (see page 67 for a good use of potatoes under the chicken skin).

ROOT VEGETABLES IN THE ROASTING TIN: There is one main reason I avoid this. Gravy. Or, rather, lack of gravy. If you roast potatoes and other root vegetables with the chicken, they will soak up all the cooking juices and you will end up with a dry tin. This isn't something I can live with. I also like keeping the flavours of my side dishes distinct from the chicken, with the exception of stuffing, which I think is integral.

GLAZED SKIN: I do this very occasionally and always wish I hadn't, because I want the crisp skin and I don't really like the way a glaze interferes with this and the flavour of the chicken. I do love maple syrup, honey, pomegranate molasses, tamarind – and even love those flavours with chicken – but not when the bird is roast. I find that they're all too sweet, unless tempered with heat, and I don't really want a chilli-hot roast chicken. I'll save these flavours for the barbecue; the combination of savoury chicken, sweet glaze, heat, smoke and the slightly bitter note from charring is sublime.

TO STUFF OR NOT TO STUFF?

I don't always make roast chicken with stuffing, but I always regret it when I don't, it's such a wasted opportunity not to bother. Use the right ingredients and a stuffing really enhances the whole meal and, when you consider that many stuffings are based on storecupboard ingredients or leftovers, it's quite obvious that they can eke out the other components of the meal at very little cost. It might even mean you end up with more chicken leftovers, which I think can only be a good thing.

Not everyone agrees with me on this. I own a book on roast chicken which roasts chicken in 20 different ways but doesn't have one version with stuffing. My mother is suspicious of stuffing the bird. If you remember the annual Christmas day argument over gravy in *Bridget Jones* (to strain or not to strain), you will understand the degree of our disagreement and how frequently it re-emerges. My mother doesn't stuff the cavity as she's worried about whether it will cook properly. I do. Yes, it takes slightly longer to roast, as you have to include the stuffing in the weight of the chicken to work out what the cooking time will be. I know people worry that this will result in a dried-out chicken breast. Well it doesn't, not if you are careful with your cooking method.

I am quite happy stuffing both the neck end and the inside cavity. The reason is that, either way, the flavour of the chicken permeates the stuffing, so they marry together much better than if they are cooked separately. I also like soft stuffing as opposed to the crunchy stuff. Also, if the stuffing isn't stuffed in the cavity, then – really – what is it? It's just another extra dish with little real relevance to the chicken, creating, I might add, more washing up in the process.

If you aren't convinced, by all means make stuffing and bake it separately. But if you are doing this, I would moisten the whole thing with some well-reduced chicken stock or gravy and spread liberal amounts of schmaltz on top, then cover with foil for most of the cooking time. At least then you are imbuing it with essence of chicken, which really, to me, is the whole point. The other option is to make a kind of chicken/stuffing tray bake. If, when roasting chicken pieces, you decide to put pieces of stuffing underneath, you can end up with the best of both worlds, as you will get the flavour of chicken throughout and it will be soft/crunchy as you are unlikely to completely cover it all. Win-win.

Types of stuffing

Traditional stuffings are generally made from things you want to use up. What kitchen is often without a bit of stale bread, an onion, some dried herbs, a lemon? Breadcrumbs and ground meat, both separate and combined, are always my default. However, these days, most of us use a wider variety of grain-based foods. These can be divided in two for me: those I will use in stuffing and those I won't. And I will rarely bother cooking any of them just for the purpose of stuffing; leftovers only, please. I do like: long-grain varieties of rice, if still al dente; as well as couscous; bulgar wheat; quinoa; and freekeh. These all give quite a light, crumbly stuffing. What I am not keen on is those which are stodgier; any leftover risottos, whether made with short-grain rice, barley or spelt just aren't pleasant as they tend towards claggy. Also worth considering are potatoes and pulses. Chickpeas make an excellent base for chorizo, with a thyme-scented sherry gravy, while nutty Puy lentils are wonderful with bacon and a gravy sweetened with apple or redcurrant jelly.

Roast chicken with stuffing

If you want to stuff the cavity of a chicken, you will need to cook the bird for slightly longer. This is fine, as long as you take steps to protect the breast. Trussing will help. The other answer is butter or schmaltz. I often put butter on and under the skin: on helps the skin crisp up, under helps the breast stay moist. To stuff the butter under the skin, you need to work from the neck of the chicken: pull out the flap of skin that is usually tucked under when trussed and, very gently, work the skin away from the flesh. The easiest way to do this is with your fingers, but use the handle of a wooden spoon if you prefer. When you have loosened the skin right the way up to the top and round the legs, take a large piece of butter and soften it in your hands a little. Smear it liberally over the breast, then smooth the skin back over again, massaging the butter so it spreads evenly over the bird. Season the skin.

If you want to use schmaltz, I think it works better on top of the skin, it will certainly help crisp it up. Smear a layer over the breast. Truss the bird (see page 14).

To roast a stuffed bird, weigh it after stuffing, so you can work out the time it will take to cook. Preheat the oven to 230°C/fan 210°C/450°F/gas mark 8. Roast it for 20 minutes at this temperature, then reduce to 190°C/fan 170°C/375°F/gas mark 5. Cook for 20 minutes per 500g. Check that the chicken is cooked in the same way as before, but make sure the stuffing has reached 75°C/167°F as well as the meat. Follow the recipe for *My best roast chicken* (see page 59), or one of the variations below.

Other ways to flavour chicken

There are all kinds of flavours that can be added to the chicken skin before it is roasted. I will usually just use butter, salt, pepper and lemon juice, however spices can be fantastic. Paprika and fennel work brilliantly together, as in *The vertical roast* (see page 62). The River Café gives chickens a light dusting of nutmeg which is really comforting, especially with a lemony, creamy gravy. Bizarrely, both Scandinavian and Caribbean countries use allspice. Any rubs are a good idea, as they are essentially flavoured salts, so you can add them while you salt the chicken. As for the rest? I am a big advocate of butter and citrus juice, under and over the skin. I also like using flavoured butters.

Christmas roast stuffings

This is really an extension of *My best roast chicken*, the recipe I make most frequently (see page 59). With a regular-sized chicken, I will assemble either one of these stuffings below. If I'm feeding more than just the four of us, I will either roast two chickens, or a capon (so much better than turkey). And even with a regular-sized chicken, it's not unusual for me to stuff the cavity with one and the neck end with the other.

The sausagemeat stuffing was the first recipe I ever had published (in an adapted form from the one published here, which is my favourite), in a video for *The Guardian*.

For the sage and onion stuffing
25g unsalted butter
1 onion, finely chopped
100g breadcrumbs
2 tsp dried sage, crumbled, or a handful of fresh sage, finely chopped
finely grated zest of 1 unwaxed lemon
sea salt and freshly ground black pepper
a little chicken stock (optional)
1 egg, lightly beaten (optional)

For the sausagemeat, chestnut and quince stuffing
25g unsalted butter
1 onion, finely chopped
200g sausagemeat
50g cooked chestnuts, crumbled
2 tsp thyme leaves
½ tsp ground allspice
½ tsp ground mace
1 quince, grated (you can replace this with eating apples or fresh apricots)

For the sage and onion stuffing, melt the butter in a frying pan and add the onion.

Sauté until the onion is soft and translucent. Put the breadcrumbs in a bowl with the sage and lemon zest. Add the onion and its buttery juices, then season with salt and pepper. Mix thoroughly. Check to see if it needs extra liquid: if, when you squish it, it clumps together, it's fine. If it's too crumby, add a little chicken stock or water. You can also add an egg, which is very binding but can make it a bit on the chewy side.

For the sausagemeat stuffing, melt the butter in a frying pan and add the onion. Sauté until the onion is soft and translucent. Put the sausagemeat in a bowl with all the other ingredients. Add the onion and its buttery juices, then season with salt and pepper. Mix thoroughly.

It is up to you what you stuff where. I usually put the sage and onion stuffing in the cavity and the sausagemeat stuffing in the neck end. Truss the bird (see page 14).

To roast a stuffed bird, weigh it after stuffing, so you can work out the time it will take to cook. Preheat the oven to 230°C/fan 210°C/450°F/gas mark 8. Roast it for 20 minutes at this temperature, then reduce to 190°C/fan 170°C/375°F/gas mark 5. Cook for 20 minutes per 500g. Check that the chicken is cooked in the same way as before, but make sure the stuffing has reached 75°C/167°F as well as the meat.

Roast the chicken on a bed of onion and thyme, with garlic if you like and make the gravy according to the instructions for *My best roast chicken* (see page 59). I will serve this with all the trimmings: bread sauce; roast potatoes and parsnips; chipolatas wrapped in bacon; Brussels sprouts cooked with marsala, chestnuts and bacon; and glazed carrots. A friend who always spends Christmas with us also contributes home-made cranberry sauce.

A THANKSGIVING-INSPIRED STUFFING

Finely chop 200g pumpkin (or squash) and boil it until just tender. Finely chop some streaky bacon, a small onion and a celery stick and sauté in butter. Add the pumpkin and fry until starting to brown. Mix in 75g finely chopped pecans. Season with salt, freshly ground black pepper and some dried herbs (sage or thyme are best). Stuff the chicken and proceed as above. I prefer to add vermouth to the gravy here in place of wine and may sprinkle the skin with a mixture of dried herbs and smoked paprika.

PORK SAUSAGE WITH FENNEL

This is a traditional recipe from south west France. Use the same quantities as for the sausagemeat stuffing (see page 65); remove the casings from Toulouse sausages and mix with around 20 green olives, sliced, the finely grated zest of 1 unwaxed lemon and 1 finely chopped onion, sautéed in butter. I like to roast this chicken sitting on thin slices of fennel, with lemon zest and some garlic cloves as before (see page 60).

POTATO, BACON AND PRUNE STUFFING

This was a huge surprise, as my first thought about a potato stuffing was that it couldn't possibly be nice. I have no idea why I had that preconception. You don't have to crush potatoes in the way described here; instead, a fairly firm, buttery mash (read, no milk) will work just as well. Peel, chop and boil 500g potatoes until just tender. Sauté a finely chopped leek, a few leaves of thyme and around 75g finely chopped streaky bacon in some unsalted butter, then add the potato. You could also add a pinch of allspice and/or nutmeg. Keep frying gently until the potato starts to break down a little and crisps up a bit round the edges. Mix in around 50g finely chopped prunes and season well with salt and freshly ground black pepper. Stuff into the cavity and roast according to the instructions for roasting a stuffed bird (see pages 64–65), adding allspice and/or nutmeg to salt before sprinkling it over the well-buttered chicken skin.

The success of potato stuffing inspired me to try other root vegetables. I found that most were good in small quantities, with either sausagemeat, minced pork or grated into a breadcrumb-based stuffing. Carrots and celeriac are particularly good this way. The one vegetable which worked well in place of the potatoes above was – surprisingly – Jerusalem artichokes.

POTATOES WITH MUSHROOMS
This idea comes from Edward Lee's *Smoke and Pickles*, which is brilliantly and unusually about his own brand of Korean and Southern US fusion. He grates a large potato, dries it out as much as possible (wringing out in a tea towel works for me), fries it in butter for two minutes, seasons, allows it to cools down and stuffs it under the skin over the breast and top of the legs. I love this. I loved it even more when I added some dried mushrooms I'd soaked and fried with the potatoes, along with very finely chopped rosemary. The gravy for this is good with a glug of marsala added at the end. I have some porcini powder which I like to mix with butter and smear on top of this chicken (you can blitz dried porcini for the same effect).

Roast chicken with spiced lamb stuffing

This is another one I wasn't sure would work; we often put chicken and pork together, but chicken and lamb? But it's lovely, especially with these spices. As it's based loosely on North African flavours you could use ras el hanout or harissa paste here in place of the spices and rose petals. I tend not to, as I don't want heat with my roast chicken, just gentle warmth and fragrance. Serve with a herby couscous or some boiled new potatoes. (*Photo overleaf.*)

For the stuffing
200g minced lamb
50g soft dried apricots, finely chopped
50g breadcrumbs
leaves and stalks from a small bunch of parsley, finely chopped
1 tsp dried mint
finely grated zest of 1 unwaxed lemon
¼ tsp ground cinnamon
¼ tsp ground cloves
¼ tsp ground allspice
¼ tsp ground cardamom
¼ tsp ground ginger
1 tbsp dried rose petals, crumbled
juice of ½ orange

For the chicken
1 chicken, salted and air-dried overnight (see pages 22–23)
1 onion, sliced into rounds
lots of unsalted butter or olive oil
200ml chicken stock or water
juice of ½ orange
1 tsp rose water (optional)
the same spices as used in the stuffing, including the rose petals

For the gravy
1 tbsp pomegranate molasses
100ml chicken stock
handfuls of finely chopped parsley, mint and if you fancy it, coriander leaves

Mix all the stuffing ingredients together and use to stuff a chicken. Put the chicken on top of the slices of onion. Rub the chicken with butter or olive oil then mix the juice and rose water (if using) with the spices. Pour this over the chicken and add the stock to the roasting tin. Truss the bird (see page 14).

Roast according to the instructions for roasting a stuffed bird (see pages 64–65).

When the chicken is resting, make the gravy in the usual way, but whisk in the pomegranate molasses with the stock. Add the herbs at the last minute.

Freekeh-stuffed chicken with a herb butter

I love this way of cooking freekeh. There is probably slightly more than you need for the stuffing, but it's very good left over. There's also definitely more herbed butter than you need, but it's useful to make this much as it is so good with so many other things: stirred into rice or couscous, used to crisp up cooked potatoes, melted on toast (see page 239). Chill leftovers and keep in the fridge for a few days, or slice and wrap up portions individually for the freezer.

For the stuffing
150g freekeh
25g unsalted butter
1 onion, finely chopped
2 garlic cloves, finely chopped
½ tsp ground allspice
2 tbsp finely chopped parsley stems
300ml chicken stock
sea salt and freshly ground black pepper

For the chicken
1 chicken, salted and air-dried overnight (see pages 22–23)
1 onion, sliced into rounds
finely grated zest and juice of 1 lime
200ml chicken stock or water

For the herb butter
250g unsalted butter
1 tbsp sea salt
very large handfuls of finely chopped parsley, coriander and mint leaves
2 garlic cloves, very finely crushed

First, cook the freekeh. Put it in a bowl and cover generously with water. Leave for five minutes, then drain it well. Heat the butter in a heavy-based saucepan. Add the onion and garlic and sauté over a low heat for around five minutes until softened. Add the allspice and the parsley stems. Now tip in the drained freekeh and stir for a couple of minutes until well coated with the buttery onions. Pour in the stock and season with salt and pepper. Bring to the boil, then reduce the heat and cover. Simmer very gently until all the liquid is absorbed. Remove from the heat and leave to steam with the lid on for a few minutes. Allow to cool, then use to stuff a chicken.

Mash or beat together all the ingredients for the herb butter. Loosen the skin from the chicken flesh around the breast and the top of the legs (see page 64). Slather as much of the butter inside the skin as you can. Put the onion in the roasting tin and sit the chicken on top. Sprinkle the chicken with salt and squeeze over the lime juice. Sprinkle the zest over the chicken and the tin and add the stock. Truss the bird (see page 14). Roast according to the instructions for roasting a stuffed bird (see pages 64–65).

VARIATION: ROAST CHICKEN WITH QUINOA STUFFING

I like using the same herb butter with this stuffing. Sauté 1 finely chopped onion in unsalted butter. Mix it with 150g cooked quinoa (if making from scratch, rinse 50g quinoa well, then cover with 100ml water. Bring to the boil, cover, then simmer gently until all the liquid is absorbed and the grain is still al dente.) Add the finely grated zest of 1 lime, the juice of ½ lime (use the rest on the chicken skin), the juice of ½ orange, 2 tbsp finely chopped coriander stems and leaves, ½ tsp ground allspice and ½ tsp ground cumin. Stuff this into the chicken and proceed as before, using the herb butter if you like and adding a bit more orange juice to the gravy.

A stuffing that dispenses with chicken breast

This is a dish to make when you are only serving a couple of people and would rather save the uncooked chicken breast for a future dish. It comes from my mother, to whom that very often applies. Peel back the skin from the breast as carefully as you can (see pages 64–65), you want to avoid tearing it. Cut out one or both chicken breasts by working down either side of the breastbone, following the contour of the ribs. Replace the breast with any stuffing – the firmer, bread- or meat-based versions work best – and mould the skin back over to an approximation of what the bird would normally look like, breasts intact. Roast as for *My best roast chicken* (see page 59).

Roast chicken with ginger and pasta gratin

I've included this recipe as it reminds me of one of the best meals I ever ate in France. I was in a ramshackle bed-and-breakfast chateau somewhere between Grenoble and Valance and they cooked us roast chicken which was then cut into pieces, plated in its own roasting juices and served with a gratin of coquillettes, a French-style pasta a bit like elbow macaroni, but much smaller and thinner. The pasta was just cooked in chicken stock, with some fresh tomato stirred through, then gratinéed with cheese on top. The combination of the two was superb.

It sounds very extravagant to use chicken stock to boil pasta. However, you can reuse the stock elsewhere, it will just help thicken anything in which you use it, because of the starch from the pasta.

1 roast chicken, cooked as for My best roast chicken *(see page 59)*
1 tbsp grated root ginger (see method)

For the pasta
chicken stock if you have it, or water
sea salt
350g coquillettes, or other short pasta
1 tbsp olive oil
2 garlic cloves, finely chopped
2 very ripe tomatoes, finely chopped
1 sprig of thyme
some hard cheese to grate over, such as Gruyère or Comte; cheddar at a pinch

Prepare the chicken as for *My best roast chicken*. Grate very fresh root ginger into a bowl. Squeeze it out over the chicken, then put the remaining flesh inside the cavity. Bring a large saucepan of stock or water to the boil. Add lots of salt, then add the pasta and cook until al dente, according to the packet instructions (usually 10–12 minutes).

Meanwhile, heat the olive oil in a frying pan, give the garlic a quick sauté, then add the tomatoes and swirl them round the pan for a minute or two. Ladle some of the pasta stock into the tomatoes, just to moisten, then drain the pasta and pile it into a gratin dish. Stir in the tomato mixture and sprinkle in the leaves from the sprig of thyme. Grate over the cheese and brown under a preheated hot grill for around 15 minutes. You can do this while the chicken is resting; as it is already cooked, you just need the cheese to melt and brown a little. Serve the chicken with its pan juices spooned over, with the pasta and – perhaps – a floppy green salad.

ANOTHER ROAST CHICKEN WITH PASTA (*Photo overleaf.*)
This is *tagliatelle 'frisinal'*, or tagliatelle from the Venetian ghetto, which I first had to try when I read about it years ago in Nigella Lawson's *How to Eat*. It also appears in Claudia Roden's *The Book of Jewish Food*. The original dish contains raisins, which I replace with chopped apricots as I'm not keen on raisins in savoury dishes, but use whatever you like, just make sure you soak either in warm water for 30 minutes before using. I also add a pinch of saffron strands to the soaking water. Not authentic, but I like it.

Roast a chicken as for *My best roast chicken* (see page 59). Soak 50g raisins or chopped dried apricots and a large pinch of saffron strands in enough warm water to cover for 30 minutes. Cook 500g tagliatelle in plenty of salted water. Let the chicken rest for 15 minutes, then drain off any juices it gives out into a saucepan, along with anything left in the roasting tin. Add the dried fruit and its soaking liquor with some finely chopped rosemary, and also some sage if you like it. I will chop up the onion from roasting the chicken, too, and add that. Simmer just to let everything meld together a bit. Tear the chicken apart into chunks and discard all the bones. Mix this with the gravy and the pasta in one glorious mess, and garnish with around 100g toasted pine nuts.

Chicken with 40 cloves of garlic (version 1)

I do a very mellow pot-roast version of this, too (see page 79), but this recipe is useful as it serves as the basis for so many good things. The garlicky infused oil in particular can be used in all kinds of ways, not just for making mayonnaise (see page 229) but also for salad dressings and for drizzling over poached and braised dishes, while the garlic will have confited to an intensely sweet creaminess.

250ml olive oil (not the good extra virgin stuff)
1 chicken, salted and air-dried overnight, trussed (see pages 22–23 and 14)
several branches of thyme
2 sprigs of tarragon
40 garlic cloves (around 4 large bulbs), separated but unpeeled
unsalted butter, for the chicken breasts
juice of 1 lemon
sea salt and freshly ground black pepper

Preheat the oven to 190°C/fan 170°C/375°F/gas mark 5. Heat 1 tbsp of the olive oil in a frying pan. Brown the chicken all over. Put half the thyme and tarragon in a roasting tin and the rest in the chicken cavity. Place the chicken on top of the herbs.

Pierce all the garlic cloves very lightly with the tip of a sharp knife. Scatter these around the chicken, then pour over the remaining olive oil. Smear the chicken breasts with butter, then pour over the lemon juice. Put one of the squeezed lemon halves in the cavity of the chicken. Season generously with salt and pepper.

Cover the chicken with foil, then put in the oven for a minimum of 1½ hours, basting regularly with the olive oil. Remove from the oven as soon as it is cooked (test with a skewer or probe thermometer, see page 60).

Allow the chicken to rest for 15 minutes before serving with some of the garlic cloves to squish at the table. You can, if you wish, use some of these to add to a gravy.

Sauces for roast chicken

While I will usually serve roast chicken with a pan juice gravy, sometimes I want a more elaborate sauce. These two sauces in particular are wonderful with roast chicken. The first is time-consuming, but still easy and can be made far in advance, just finished by the addition of roasting juices. The second is very simple and doesn't need the pan juices, but add them if you like (if you intend to do so, reduce the amount of liquid you add to the roasting tin by half).

A LEMON AND GARLIC SAUCE

I have tried to simplify this from a recipe in Paula Wolfert's *The Cooking of South West France*, but realised that it's not really possible. There is no denying this is quite a labour-intensive sauce but, I promise, it is worth it.

1 chicken, roasted as for My best roast chicken *(see page 59), with ½ lemon and some sprigs of thyme in the cavity)*

For the sauce
2 bulbs of fresh (green) garlic, cloves separated
1 large or 2 small unwaxed lemons, plus a little lemon juice, if necesssary
½ tsp caster sugar
sea salt
300ml single cream
200ml strong-flavoured chicken stock

Blanch the cloves of garlic in boiling water for two minutes, then drain and peel. Pare off the zest from the lemon: strips are preferable here, so best not to use a zester. Slice off and discard as much of the white pith from the lemon as you can, then slice the fruit across, flicking out any pips as you go.

Put the garlic, lemon zest and lemon slices and the sugar in a saucepan with 1 tsp of salt. Cover with 1 litre of water, bring to the boil, then reduce the heat and simmer, uncovered, very, very slowly, until almost all the liquid has evaporated. Towards the end of this process, stir regularly just to make sure nothing is catching on the base of the pan. The garlic should be light golden brown and tender. Add the cream and simmer until it has reduced by half. Strain through a sieve, pushing as much of the garlic and lemon through with the back of a spoon as possible. Set aside until the chicken has roasted.

Pour all the roasting juices into a pan with the stock and the reserved lemon and garlic sauce. While the chicken is resting, simmer until reduced and creamy; you should end up with around 300ml. Taste for seasoning and add a squeeze of lemon juice if necessary. Serve poured over the chicken.

A SOUR CHERRY SAUCE

I was convinced that chicken and fresh cherries, as opposed to the dry, sour sort, should be a good match, but early experiments were disappointing. Then I realised that I should actually be using sour cherries, as sweet cherries lose their flavour when cooked. Sour (or cooking) cherries are slightly misnamed, as when perfectly ripe they are sweet enough to eat raw, but really come into their own when cooked.

If you want to get cherry flavour into the chicken too, you can add sour cherries to any meat- or bread-based stuffing, or simply stuff them into the cavity of the chicken (which I've done; it was really quite good). You could serve this sauce with a plain roast chicken, or perhaps with the *Freekeh-stuffed chicken with a herb butter* (see page 69).

25g unsalted butter
500g morello or other cooking cherries, pitted
1–2 tbsp caster sugar or mild-flavoured honey, to taste
pinch of ground cinnamon
pinch of ground allspice (optional)
squeeze of lemon juice

Melt the butter in a saucepan. As soon as it is foaming, add the cherries. Cook briskly for a minute, then pour over 100ml of water. Cook for a few minutes over a medium heat until the liquid in the saucepan is deep purple and the cherries have softened slightly. Add the sugar and spices.

Stir over a gentle heat until the sugar has dissolved and the liquid has reduced and thickened. Add a squeeze of lemon juice and serve with the chicken.

ELABORATE WAYS WITH ROAST CHICKEN

There are all kinds of ways chefs make more of a roast chicken. In some ways I think this is a pointless exercise: no matter how many times I cook and eat a roast chicken, it still seems an extravagance, a feast of a meal. If I want to be really extravagant – and if I'm feeding a large crowd – I will just roast two or even three chickens. Possibly with different stuffings.

So I don't want to mess around with turduckens (a turkey, stuffed with a duck, stuffed with a chicken) or any different permutations of. I also don't want to bone a chicken. I honestly don't see the point: the bones help with flavour and structure and, however nice the stuffing within is, I can never get away from the thought it would work just as well with an intact bird. However, there were one or two other things I wanted to try, which in the end did give a good result.

Chicken in a Mountain

I'd heard a lot about this, ever since seeing a recipe by Fanny Cradock called 'Chicken in a Mountain'. Her description, as usual, was breezy and made the whole thing sound so simple. Cover a chicken in salt, bake in a hot oven, crack it open at the table, et voila! A perfectly roasted, moist, crisp-skinned chicken, right? Wrong. Unfortunately, my first attempt was disastrous. Here's why:

First of all – mea culpa – I misread the recipe. In the preamble Fanny Cradock does mention that you must use coarse rock salt. I missed this completely and bought several kilos of table salt.

Next, it was quite an operation. She advises getting someone to help. I ignored this at my cost. You cover a roasting tray with two sheets of foil, crossed, pour over about an inch of salt, put the chicken on top, then bring up the sides of foil and pour in the rest of the salt until the chicken is completely covered. This turned out to be nigh on impossible on my own. I ended up hugging the foil walls to my chest in an attempt to halt the waves of salt which seeped out relentlessly, forcing my walls to collapse. After a couple of failed attempts, I finally managed to parcel it all up, using much more salt than is probably necessary. I roasted it as per the instructions. When I opened it at the table, the top cracked pleasingly, the skin was crisp, if a little salty – but the bottom was a different story. The salt was a quagmire, seeping round the chicken wings and making them unbelievably salty. A complete failure. So as I hadn't at this point realised my error with the salt, I tried a different tack. This recipe was French and involved making a pastry with flour, salt and wine, spreading it with slices of garlic, placing the chicken breast-side down on top of it, then moulding the pastry over the rest. I was promised that when this was broken open at the table, my guests would be overwhelmed by the wonderful aromas of chicken and garlic. Wrong again. The chicken looked a bit anaemic and, worse still, the garlic flavour had not really reached the chicken at all and the skin was too salty to eat. What a waste of flour, wine and garlic.

I decided the whole idea was too gimmicky and really for those who believed the scaremongering about dried-out breast meat and wanted a novel solution. The other thing that annoyed me was that there was no gravy or edible (rather than too salty) juices. I would have left it at that. But my kids kept pestering as they liked the spectacle, so I revisited it and eventually came up with one that works. Here it is. And, yes, there isn't any gravy. I suggest you make this when you have some left over in the freezer, or are happy to make a gravy without tin scrapings.

1 bulb of garlic, cloves separated
1 chicken, trussed (see page 14) and air-dried perfectly (see pages 22–23)
large bunch of thyme
finely grated zest and juice of 2 limes (reserve the squeezed halves of 1)
1kg coarse rock salt (definitely not fine table salt)

Preheat the oven to 200°C/fan 180°C/400°F/gas mark 6.

Pierce each clove of garlic with a knife tip or skewer. Put them in the cavity of the chicken, with a large sprig of thyme and the reserved lime halves.

Put the salt in a large bowl, then add the lime zest and juice. Bruise the remaining thyme a little in a mortar and pestle, then chop the sprigs fairly finely. Add them to the salt. Add some water very gradually, mixing thoroughly as you go, until you have a very crumbly paste – like damp sand – that will just clump together.

Put a layer of foil on the base of a roasting tin, just enough to go up the sides. Cover the foil with a layer of the salt, to a depth of 1 generous cm. Put the chicken in the centre of the roasting dish, then pack with the salt paste. Do this by the handful, imagining the way you might pack handfuls of damp sand round someone you are burying on the beach. Make sure the chicken is entirely covered, then encase the whole thing with another sheet of foil.

Bake in the oven for 1½ hours, then remove from the oven and take off the foil. Serve the chicken in the tin at the table. The salt should have dried to a hard crust which you can crack open, revealing a lovely browned chicken within. Brush off any salt that is clinging to the skin and serve up.

An extravagance

There are lots of things paired with roast chicken which are ostentatious, but I find don't really improve or add anything of value to the dish. They include most kinds of seafood. I have seen chicken – mainly breasts – stuffed with lobster, crab and shrimp and smothered in a bisque-type sauce. It's a variant on surf 'n' turf, I know, but not one for me; it's one of those occasions when I find the flavours fight and subsume one another rather than complement.

I also found a recipe which stuffed the cavity with oysters. This piqued my curiosity: would the oysters absorb the chicken flavour and plump up? Would they disintegrate into nothing and just add a whiff of ozone to the cooking aromas? I did go so far as to buy a large pile of unshucked oysters but, when faced with them, I just couldn't bring myself to stuff them in a chicken as I wanted to eat them raw. So the oysters became a starter that day instead of part of the main event. There is also a bread stuffing or 'dressing' in the US which contains oysters, though often canned. Again, when I thought about trying it, I came to realise that actually I just don't want to cook oysters, unless they're deep-fried for something like a po' boy.

What I did like was the chicken and truffle combination, particularly with mushrooms. This is the kind of thing I would cook for my husband's birthday, as they are exactly the flavours he loves. That heady, earthy truffle flavour enhances all the savoury qualities of chicken, without overpowering it:

Chicken in half mourning

The poetic title comes to me courtesy of Jane Grigson's *The Mushroom Feast* and refers to the fact that the slices of truffles show up black when slipped under the skin. In her version, this is more dramatic, as she poaches her chicken in stock. You could do this too if you like, following the instructions for poaching a chicken (see pages 45–46). I love this version though. There are few things better than the combination of chicken, truffle, garlic and lots of butter.

It's not necessary, but a couple of handfuls of wild mushrooms, lightly sautéed and added to the gravy at the end, would be no bad thing. Neither would a drop of cream.

1 chicken
1 fresh or preserved truffle, thinly sliced
1 bulb of garlic, halved horizontally
a few large sprigs of thyme
2 bay leaves
1 glass of white wine
unsalted butter, to coat
sea salt

Prepare the chicken the day before you want to roast it. Carefully separate the skin from the flesh, around the breasts and tops of the legs (see pages 64–65). Push the slices of truffle under the skin and spread them as evenly as you can across the breast and the top part of the legs. Put on a rack in the fridge overnight. Remove from the fridge at least 30 minutes before you want to roast it.

Preheat the oven to its highest setting. Put the garlic, cut-side up, in a roasting dish. Cover with some of the thyme and put the rest in the cavity of the chicken with the bay leaves. Put the chicken on top of its garlic-thyme bed, then pour the wine around. Smear butter all over the chicken and sprinkle liberally with salt. Roast as for *My best roast chicken* (see page 59).

When you are satisfied the chicken is done, allow it to rest for 15 minutes. Mash the garlic cloves into the pan juices.

If you like, you could add cream and a pile of sautéed wild mushrooms to this.

One lone leftover dish: chicken hash with fried eggs

This is pretty much the contents of your roast dinner, fried. It works better with the remnants of a traditional version with potatoes rather than anything healthily whole grain. You will also need some leftover gravy, or at least make sure that, when you strip the chicken meat from the carcass, you scrape off and reserve any jellied bits of stock.

Strip the chicken carcass of all of its meat and tear or cut it into bite-sized pieces. If there are any bits of skin left, shred those, too; it doesn't matter if the skin isn't crisp, it will be by the time you've finished. Chop up any potatoes, parsnips or carrots you may have left over. If there are bacon and chipolatas, chop those up as well. Greens? They won't hurt; you will have something between a hash and a bubble and squeak.

Heat 1 tbsp of either schmaltz, dripping or unsalted butter in a large frying pan. Sauté 1 chopped onion over quite a high heat until starting to brown. Add all the chicken, the chicken skin and everything else, stirring regularly until crisp and brown. Pour over any gravy and mix. Leave to cook for a few minutes over a medium-low heat, then, if you like (this isn't essential), put under a grill for a few minutes more. You will end up with a mixture that is crisp in places, soft in others, but it should all stick together quite well. Top with a fried egg and serve.

Eat with any condiments you fancy. I like HP sauce.

5. POT ROASTS & BAKED CHICKEN DISHES

Pot-roasting is a technique that combines poaching (or braising), steaming and roasting, with the result that you will get different textures on the same bird: the back of the chicken will be tender and sticky, the rest will be moist from the steaming but with a crisp, burnished skin. The best of all worlds?

I pot roast either in a large cast-iron casserole or a fairly deep tray, depending on a few things. I think whole chickens work better in a large casserole and you can fit everything else snugly round them. If you are using chicken pieces, you are better off using a roasting tin or baking tray, because you can put them in one layer; that means you will get a crisp skin and a soft underside, not just of the chicken, but of the vegetables, too.

Incidentally, a pot-roast chicken, made in the pressure cooker, is probably the most useful recipe in the world when you want something that looks as impressive as a roast chicken but takes a fraction of the time. Simply brown the chicken all over, then use all the ingredients in the recipe opposite, but cook at high pressure for 20 minutes, then leave the pressure to drop naturally. I usually stuff this chicken, too. Of all the recipes in this book, I think this is the one I have cooked most frequently over the past few years. It remains my fallback, even now.

A pot-roast chicken, with the other bits from its pot, should serve six people.

Pot roasting a whole bird

This is the halfway house between a roast and a poached chicken. It's useful when you want an instant gravy as opposed to a stock. If you want the skin really crisp, you can uncover the bird for the last few minutes of cooking time.

2 tbsp olive oil
large knob of unsalted butter
1 onion, chopped
1 chicken
1 bulb of garlic, separated into cloves, unpeeled
sprigs of fresh herbs (oregano, parsley and tarragon are all good)
250ml chicken stock or water
250ml white wine
sea salt and freshly ground black pepper
a little unsalted butter (optional)
50ml single cream (optional)

Preheat the oven to 200°C/fan 180°C/400°F/ gas mark 6.

Heat the olive oil and butter in a large casserole. Add the onion and fry until it has browned. Push to one side and add the chicken. Brown on all sides.

Add the garlic and herbs to the pot, then pour over the stock or water and the wine. Season with salt and pepper. Bring to the boil, then cover and put in the oven.

Cook for around one hour, removing the lid for the last 15 minutes so the skin of the chicken can brown. You might want to baste it with a little butter at this point.

Remove the chicken from the oven. Take it out of the casserole and keep warm by covering it with foil. Put the casserole on the hob and boil the remaining liquor until it has reduced by about one-third. Strain. Return the onion to the sauce. Take the garlic out of the skins and mash the cloves back into the sauce. Add the cream, if using, and cook for another minute.

Serve the chicken with the sauce for pouring over. This is particularly good with mashed potato.

VARIATIONS

With 40 cloves of garlic For an ultra-garlicky sauce, break up 4 bulbs of garlic (roughly 40 cloves). All the tiny cloves – those that sit around the stem of the garlic in the centre – are pierced with a knife point and put in the cavity, along with some sprigs of thyme. The rest will end up outside the bird, as before. (*Photo on page 2.*)

With bacon and mushrooms Add 100g bacon lardons at the beginning with the onion, then, halfway through the cooking time, add around 250g whole chestnut mushrooms you've sautéed first in oil and unsalted butter. Serve with lots of chopped parsley.

With assorted vegetables Put vegetables such as fennel or leeks, which are best when meltingly tender, underneath the chicken. Put root vegetables such as new potatoes, small carrots or chunks of celeriac around the outside.

With stuffing You can add any stuffing to pot-roast chicken, but you will need to increase the cooking time a little. (Though not if using a pressure cooker.) Cook for one hour, then uncover and cook for a further 15 minutes. For a very buttery pot roast, you could also rub some *Herb butter* (see page 69) under the skin.

A sharper-tasting pot roast This uses red wine in place of white, along with 1 tbsp red wine vinegar and a couple of chopped tomatoes. Omit the cream. Add some pitted black olives towards the end. Serve it with sautéed potatoes and lots of parsley.

POT ROAST CHICKEN, USING PIECES

These are useful meals as they tend to be more one pot than those using a whole bird (i.e. no need for sides). They also take less time to cook.

One-pot chicken with leeks and new potatoes

Once you've browned the chicken a bit, this is one of those throw-it-all-in-and-forget-it dishes. As it is, it's very mellow. For an extra savoury note you could add some bacon lardons as a good contrast to the tender sweetness of the chicken.

1 tbsp olive oil
large knob of unsalted butter
8 bone-in skin-on chicken thighs
500g new potatoes, sliced
2 leeks, sliced into rounds
150ml white wine
150ml chicken stock
sea salt and freshly ground black pepper
1 small bunch of tarragon
100g seedless grapes

Preheat the oven to 200°C/fan 180°C/400°F/ gas mark 6.

Heat the oil and butter in a large casserole which can comfortably take the chicken in a single layer. Fry the chicken thighs, skin-side down, until crisp and brown. Remove and set aside. Add the potatoes and leeks to the casserole. Stir for a few minutes just to start the softening process, then pour over the wine and stock. Season with salt and black pepper, then lay the tarragon sprigs on top.

Top with the chicken, skin-side up. Put in the oven, uncovered, and bake for around 30 minutes. Add the grapes for the last five minutes. Check that the vegetables are tender and the chicken is cooked through.

Remove from the oven. Serve with the cooking liquor spooned over.

Chicken with caramelised chicory

I cannot recommend this dish highly enough; if you like chicory (or Belgian endive, as it's also known) I am sure you will love this as much as I do. It will work equally well with fennel, just use two fat bulbs and quarter them, making sure the layers are attached at the base. Oh, and as this is based loosely on a Belgian dish, beer is appropriate, but really, use anything you like. (*Photo opposite.*)

1 tbsp olive oil
8 bone-in skin-on chicken thighs
large knob of unsalted butter
2 tsp caster sugar
4 heads of chicory, trimmed and halved lengthways
2 garlic cloves, finely sliced
a few sprigs of thyme
100ml beer, white wine or cider
50ml double cream
squeeze of lemon juice (optional)

Preheat the oven to 180°C/fan 160°C/350°F/ gas mark 4.

Heat the olive oil in a large casserole and fry the chicken thighs, skin-side down, until crisp and light brown. Remove. Add the butter to the casserole. When the butter starts to foam, add 1 tsp of the sugar, stirring to help it dissolve, then add half the chicory, cut-sides down. Reduce the heat and leave to cook for a few minutes, until the chicory is starting to soften and caramelise on the cut side, then turn over and cook for a couple of minutes more. Remove, then add the remaining sugar and cook the rest of the chicory in the same way. Return all the chicory to the casserole and add the garlic and thyme. Put the chicken pieces on top, then pour over the beer, wine or cider.

Put in the oven, uncovered, for 40–45 minutes, until the chicken is cooked through. Remove from the oven, pour in the cream and simmer for a couple of minutes. Taste for seasoning and add a squeeze of lemon juice, if you like.

BAKED CHICKEN

The next couple of recipes are more bakes than pot roasts, as the process is roasting more than roast/poach/steam. This doesn't mean the dishes don't have a sauce – they do – they are just much more reduced and therefore more intense.

Chicken cooked with bay, saffron and oregano

This is a dish cooked for me every time I visit my mother in Greece. She has an abundant supply of dried oregano flowers, as the mountains surrounding her home are filled with wild herbs, but dried oregano leaves can be used instead. Don't worry if the basting sauce separates very slightly; this is perfectly normal.

1 chicken, jointed into 10, or equivalent
sea salt and freshly ground black pepper
1 onion, sliced
1 red pepper, sliced
slice of unsalted butter
a few bay leaves
2 tsp dried oregano or oregano flower buds, crumbled
200ml fruity dry white wine
250ml double cream
2 tbsp Dijon mustard
¼ tsp cayenne pepper
pinch of saffron strands, soaked in a little warm water for 30 minutes
juice of 1 lemon
6–8 artichoke hearts, halved

Preheat the oven to 200°C/fan 180°C/400°F/ gas mark 6. Season the chicken with salt and leave to stand for one hour.

Take a large, shallow casserole or ovenproof dish. Strew the base with the onion and red pepper, then dot with the butter and put the bay leaves on top. Arrange the chicken over, then sprinkle with the dried herbs and a grinding of black pepper. Pour in 100ml of the white wine.

Whisk together the cream, mustard, cayenne and saffron with its soaking water, the remaining 100ml wine and the lemon juice. Spoon most of this over the chicken pieces and reserve the rest for basting. Bake in the oven for 20 minutes, then remove and baste with a little more of the cream mixture.

Reduce the oven temperature to 180°C/ fan 160°C/350°F/gas mark 4 and cook for a further 15 minutes, basting once more. Tuck in the artichokes, then bake for a further 15 minutes. By this time the chicken should be cooked through with a brown, slightly curdled crust.

Maple-glazed chicken

Calling this dish 'maple-glazed' doesn't really do it justice; the sweetness is there, yes, but the red wine and aromatics give it a rich and savoury flavour.

This uses a very small amount of chicken stock. It's one of those times when freezing well-reduced stock into ice-cube trays comes in very handy. (*Photo overleaf.*)

For the chicken
1 chicken, jointed into 8, or the equivalent in pieces
juice of 1 lime
1 tbsp olive oil
1 large red onion, sliced into wedges
sea salt and freshly ground black pepper
50ml red wine
finely chopped parsley

For the sauce
75ml red wine
50ml chicken stock
4 tbsp dark soy sauce
2 tbsp red wine vinegar
1 tbsp tomato purée
2 tbsp maple syrup
1 tsp hot sauce
1 tsp ground ginger
1 tsp mustard powder
1 tsp finely chopped rosemary
3 garlic cloves, crushed

Preheat the oven to 200°C/fan 180°C/400°F/gas mark 6.

Put the chicken pieces in a bowl and pour over the lime juice. Rub it over the entire chicken and leave for a few minutes. Heat the olive oil in a casserole. Fry the chicken for several minutes on each side until the skin is crisp and well browned. Remove the chicken and fry the onion for another few minutes in the rendered chicken fat. Return the chicken to the pot and season with salt and pepper.

Combine all the sauce ingredients together. Pour this over the chicken and put in the oven for 20–25 minutes, basting a couple of times with the sauce.

Remove the roasting dish from the oven and place over a medium heat. Remove the chicken and keep warm. Pour in the 50ml of red wine and let it bubble for a couple of minutes.

Serve the chicken with the sauce and onions, with a generous sprinkling of parsley. This is very good with mashed potatoes.

CHICKEN TRAY BAKES

Tray bakes are one-pot roast dishes, made with chicken pieces instead of the whole bird, without a sauce or gravy. So the vegetables and other additions tend towards crispness and caramelised edges. It's also a useful way of making chicken go further, as you can adapt the chicken-to-vegetable ratio to suit.

They're also good for meals for one. When I was testing a lot of different stuffings, I realised that if I put some stuffing in the middle of a small oven dish, put a chicken leg on top and vegetables around the side, I had a good one-person roast dinner. Sometimes I did these with some liquid in the dish – so it was halfway between a roast and a pot roast

– and sometimes I would add vegetables, often Mediterranean-type vegetables, and make it fairly dry. Both work. Here are a few suggestions for other tray bakes:

Chicken and sausage tray bake

In this recipe, you can either add the sausages to the tin as they are, or you can break them up and mould under the chicken pieces.

4 large bone-in skin-on chicken pieces (legs or breasts)
about 6 merguez sausages, or Toulouse if you prefer
2 red peppers, thickly sliced
2 red onions, cut into wedges
500g new or waxy potatoes
olive oil
1 tsp dried oregano
½ preserved lemon, flesh scraped out and discarded, skin finely chopped
½ tsp ground cinnamon
pinch of saffron strands, soaked in 100ml warm water for 30 minutes (optional)
sea salt and freshly ground black pepper

Preheat the oven to 220°C/fan 200°C/425°F/ gas mark 7.

Arrange the chicken pieces, sausages and vegetables in a large roasting tin, preferably in a single layer, and drizzle with olive oil. Sprinkle over the oregano, preserved lemon and cinnamon, turning everything over to make sure it is coated in the flavourings. If using, pour over the saffron in its liquid, otherwise add 100ml water to the pan. Season with salt and pepper.

Bake in the oven for 50 minutes to one hour, until everything is tender, cooked through and well browned.

Chicken and Mediterranean vegetable tray bake

This is one of the few times I dried herbs as their pungency, along with the citrus juices and olives, helps to balance out some of the sweeter ingredients in this dish.

4 bone-in skin-on chicken pieces
200g new or waxy potatoes, sliced
1 large aubergine, cut into thick rounds
1 red pepper, thickly sliced
1 red onion, cut into wedges
2 tbsp olive oil
juice of ½ lemon
juice of ½ orange
1 tsp herbes de Provençe
sea salt and freshly ground black pepper
12 cherry tomatoes, left whole
handful of black olives, pitted and roughly chopped
large handful of basil leaves

Preheat the oven to 220°C/fan 200°C/425°F/ gas mark 7.

Put all the chicken pieces and vegetables (not the tomatoes or olives) in a large roasting tin, preferably in a single layer. Whisk together the olive oil and citrus juice then drizzle this over the contents of the tin. Sprinkle over the herbs and season with salt and pepper.

Cover with foil and put in the oven for 30 minutes. The vegetables should feel tender when pierced with a knife. Remove the foil and add the cherry tomatoes. Return uncovered to the oven for a further 15–20 minutes, until the chicken is well browned and cooked through. Serve with the olives and basil sprinkled over.

Autumnal chicken tray bake

If possible, avoid the orange skinned, 'carving' type of pumpkin here, as the flesh tends to collapse. I use a denser fleshed Crown Prince, or firm-fleshed squash instead. (*Photo opposite.*)

4 bone-in skin-on chicken pieces
100g smoked bacon lardons
600g pumpkin or squash, peeled and cut into 1.5cm-thick wedges
2 parsnips, peeled and cut into thick batons
2 carrots, cut into thick batons
2 leeks, thickly sliced
1 celery stick, finely chopped
½ tsp sweet smoked paprika
1 tsp dried thyme
1 tsp dried sage
sea salt and freshly ground black pepper
olive oil
50ml vermouth
1 tbsp maple syrup (optional)

Preheat the oven to 220°C/fan 200°C/425°F/gas mark 7. Put the chicken, bacon and vegetables in a roasting tin, preferably in a single layer, but if that's not possible, put the chicken on top. Sprinkle over the smoked paprika, the thyme and sage. Season with salt and pepper. Drizzle over some olive oil, turn everything over to make sure it is coated. Pour in the vermouth and 50ml of water.

Roast for 45 minutes, then drizzle over the maple syrup, if you like. Finish cooking with another 10 minutes or so in the oven, until everything is well browned and caramelising around the edges.

VARIATION: JERUSALEM ARTICHOKES
Drop peeled Jerusalem artichokes into a bowl of water acidulated with a good squeeze of lemon juice before adding to the tin in place of the pumpkin. Omit the smoked paprika and replace with the finely grated zest of 1 unwaxed lemon and some olive oil-tossed chestnut mushrooms for the last 10 minutes. Leave out the maple syrup.

THE 'FAKE FRY'

These days I bake an awful lot of things that were traditionally shallow- or deep-fried. This isn't just because it's supposed to be healthier (it's certainly less calorific), it's also because it's much easier. Lining everything up on a baking tray and putting it in the oven is so much easier than watching them on the hob, and it's much less messy, too.

Chicken goujons

These are good drizzled with any of the dips or dressings in this book. The quantities below will serve a family of four with sides, or work as an appetiser for up to eight. You could probably add another breast without increasing the other ingredients.

For the chicken and marinade
300g pot of buttermilk
juice of 1 lemon
1 tsp garlic powder
sea salt and freshly ground black pepper
3 large chicken breasts, butterflied out (see page 11), but not flattened

For the coating
150g fine breadcrumbs
50g finely grated parmesan
handful of basil leaves, finely chopped
finely grated zest of 1 lime

Put the buttermilk in a bowl and add the lemon juice and garlic powder. Season with salt and pepper. Thinly slice the chicken and add to the bowl. Make sure everything is coated with the marinade, then cover and leave in the fridge for an hour or two. Remove from the fridge for 30 minutes before cooking, to allow to come to room temperature.

Preheat the oven to 220°C/fan 200°C/425°F/gas mark 7. Line a couple of baking trays with baking parchment.

Mix together the coating ingredients and season with salt and pepper. Spread half of them out on a shallow tray (the rest is for the second batch; if you use all the crumbs at once they're likely to get wet with buttermilk and start clumping together).

To avoid getting too messy, follow this technique: remove a piece of the chicken from the marinade and allow the marinade to drip off. Give it a shake. Lie the chicken on the breadcrumbs. Do not touch the breadcrumbs. Repeat until the whole tray is covered with strips of chicken. Rinse your fingers, dry them thoroughly, then flip each strip of chicken over so it becomes completely coated. Place on the lined baking trays. Repeat until you have used up all of the breadcrumbs and chicken.

Bake in the oven for around 10 minutes until cooked through and the coating has nicely crisped up and browned.

WITH A SUMAC COATING AND A FENNEL AND POMEGRANATE MOLASSES DIP: Omit the parmesan (if you like, you don't have to), basil and lime zest from the coating and add instead 1 tbsp sumac, 1 tsp dried mint and, optionally, ½ tsp ground chilli powder. Proceed as before. For the dip, pound 1 tbsp of fennel seeds in a mortar and pestle (or blitz in a grinder) and add to 100ml Greek-style natural yogurt. Drizzle in 1–2 tbsp pomegranate molasses to taste.

KATSU-STYLE, WITH A PONZU OR A YUZU DIPPING SAUCE: Find a fresh, non-wrinkly piece of root ginger, around 5cm in length, and grate it into a small bowl. Squeeze out the flesh and add the ginger juice to the buttermilk marinade. Use panko breadcrumbs for the coating; I like to still use the cheese and basil, but it's not essential. The lime zest is, however. Serve with either Ponzu (see page 52) or add 1 tbsp yuzu juice and ½ tsp hot sauce to 100ml Greek-style natural yogurt (or mayonnaise if you prefer), with lots of seasoning.

Buffalo wings

These gave me a bit of trouble. I blame America. They go ga-ga over buffalo wings and devote a huge amount of time and energy to trying to perfect their recipes. And everyone disagrees with one another, just as much as they do over fried chicken. I spent hours – days – messing around with egg whites and bicarbonate of soda and even different brines, to try and make wings with the most tender insides and crisp skin, before realising they were all pretty much of a muchness and just giving me a headache.

I have two ways of cooking wings. One is on the grill, the other is baked. I use the two methods interchangeably, but I do this one most frequently as it's so easy. This is my version of buffalo wings.

These are traditionally deep-fried but, as the coating makes the wings literally drip in butter anyway, I prefer to bake them.

I think the smoked ham stock (see page 26) complements the other flavours here; so if you want to marinate the wings first, do so, (see pages 215–223), then air-dry them, without added salt, overnight, as in this recipe. (*Photo on previous page.*)

For the wings
as many wings as you want to eat; I would say 3–4 per person
1 tbsp fine sea salt
1 tsp garlic powder (optional)
celery sticks, to serve

For the sauce
50g unsalted butter
100g hot sauce (traditionally Frank's, which can be found in the UK)
1 tbsp cider vinegar
sea salt and freshly ground black pepper

For the blue cheese dip
150ml buttermilk
150ml crème fraîche or sour cream
75g stilton or other blue cheese, crumbled
½ onion, very finely chopped
a few drops of cider vinegar

For the wings, cut off the tips and separate into what the Americans call 'drumettes' (as they look like miniature drumsticks) and 'flats'. You should be able to get a butcher to do this for you.

Put a metal rack on a baking tray. Put the wings in a bowl and sprinkle with the salt and garlic powder, if using. Make sure they are completely coated and use a little more if necessary. Arrange on the rack and leave in the fridge overnight to air-dry.

Preheat the oven to 220°C/fan 200°C/425°F/gas mark 7. Bring the wings to room temperature by taking them out of the fridge for 30 minutes and pat them dry if necessary. Bake the wings in the oven for 25 minutes, then turn them all over and cook for a further 20–25 minutes. The wings should be just the right combination of crisp, brown, sticky and tender.

Meanwhile, make the sauce and dip. Melt the butter, hot sauce and cider vinegar together and whisk thoroughly to combine. To make the dip, put everything in a food processor or blender and blitz, then thin out with a little water if necessary. Season both sauce and dip with salt and pepper.

To serve, the traditional thing is to smother the wings in the sauce: to do this the traditional way, put them in a bowl, pour over the sauce and toss. I keep a handful of wings back, as I like them as is. Serve with the blue cheese dip and celery sticks.

6. BRAISED CHICKEN

Most of the recipes in this section rely on fairly slow, gentle cooking. They are, for the most part, one-pot dishes that can be bunged in a low oven if you like, but I prefer to do them on the hob. They are best made in wide, shallow casseroles or lidded frying pans, so the meat can all be cooked in one layer, and so that any liquid in the sauce won't cover the skin (so it won't lose any crispness). Most also work well in a pressure cooker.

The trick with these braises is to take your time over searing the chicken skin. The aim is to end up with tender, falling-off-the-bone meat and skin that is alternately crisp and sticky, with plenty of the fat rendered out. To achieve this, you will need to spend at least 10 minutes frying it at the start of any recipe. If you don't have time to do this, or don't care about the chicken skin, you can skip that stage and simply use skinless thighs instead. (Though still give the chicken a quick sear before proceeding with the rest of the recipe.) In addition to the initial searing, which is important for rendering out some of the fat to ensure a very crisp skin, you can also put it under a hot grill for five minutes at the end of the cooking time. This will make a huge difference to the skin, but have little or no impact on the rest of the dish.

I will normally use bone-in thighs for these braises as I think they give the best flavour and have a texture to suit this kind of fairly slow cooking, but I do occasionally use a whole jointed bird instead. To make sure the thighs cook through in the times given, I open them out slightly and cut round the bone, leaving the thigh attached to the flesh, but making room for more of the heat and sauce to penetrate. You can use boneless thighs if you prefer, though reduce the covered cooking time by 10–15 minutes if doing so and remember that you may need to reduce the sauce for slightly longer. (The same applies if you are using chicken breast in place of thighs.)

I reckon that braised dishes with six chicken thighs will feed four, as there's always at least one person who only wants one and one who wants two.

Chicken with bacon, lettuce and peas

This is a variation on one of the gentlest of French dishes, the classic poulet à la Clamart.

I once made this with a jar of artichoke hearts in place of the lettuce, which was quite wonderful. Keeping a jar or can of these to hand makes this dish a good standby, as it means almost all the ingredients can be gleaned from the storecupboard or freezer.

1 tbsp olive oil
100g bacon lardons
6 bone-in skin-on chicken thighs
5mm-thick slice of unsalted butter
2 leeks, cut into rounds
2 garlic cloves, finely sliced
1 sprig of tarragon
3 Little Gems, halved (try to make sure the leaves are still attached to the stem)
100ml white wine
200ml chicken stock
200g petits pois
sea salt and freshly ground black pepper
50ml single cream

Heat the oil in a large, shallow casserole or lidded frying pan. Add the bacon and fry briskly until browned. Remove with a slotted spoon, then add the chicken. Fry until crisp and golden brown; this will take up to 10 minutes. Set aside with the bacon.

Drain off any excess fat from the pan and add the butter. When the butter starts to foam, add the leeks, garlic, tarragon and the Little Gems, cut-sides down. Leave for a couple of minutes without stirring, then pour over the wine. The wine will bubble up; when it does so, cover and leave the leeks and lettuce to braise in the buttery juices for five minutes.

Add the stock and peas to the pan, then season with salt and pepper. Return the bacon and chicken, making sure the chicken pieces are skin-side up. Half-cover and simmer over a low heat until the vegetables and chicken are tender and cooked through (about 30 minutes). Stir in the cream and simmer for a few more minutes until the sauce has reduced and thickened. This is good served with mashed or sautéed potatoes.

Chicken with coriander, garlic and sour orange

This is another dish with peas at the heart of it, but it couldn't be more different from the last. Orange, normally associated with duck, is just as good with chicken if not better; they're cooked together frequently in Mexico and Latin America. The contrast here between the sweet, tender peas, savoury chicken and zingy orange and coriander makes it one of my favourite flavour combinations in the whole book.

50g bunch of coriander, plus a few sprigs to serve
1 red chilli, deseeded
½ bulb of garlic, cloves separated and peeled
2 tbsp olive oil
large knob of unsalted butter
6–8 bone-in skin-on chicken thighs
1 onion, finely chopped
sea salt and freshly ground black pepper
1kg new or waxy potatoes
250ml sour orange juice (or 200ml orange juice plus 50ml lime juice)
250ml chicken stock
250g fresh or frozen peas

Preheat the oven to 200°C/fan 180°C/400°F/ gas mark 6.

Blitz the coriander, chilli and garlic together with 1 tbsp of the olive oil and just enough water to help it along.

Put the remaining oil and butter in a large casserole. Melt over a medium heat, then fry the chicken, skin-side down, until the skin is well-browned and crisp. Remove from the casserole, then add the onion. Sauté until soft, then add the coriander paste. Cook for a minute or two. Return the chicken to the pan. Season with salt and pepper. Add the potatoes and pour over the orange juice and the stock.

Bake in the oven for around 30 minutes, adding the peas for the final 10 minutes and topping up with water if necessary.

Serve in shallow bowls with the slightly syrupy cooking liquor spooned over and a sprinkling of coriander leaf.

Flambéed chicken with cider, chestnuts and Brussels sprouts

Proper winter food this, best served with buttery mashed potatoes or perhaps a large pile of crushed and buttery carrots and swede. Despite their difference in flavour, I often alternate juniper, allspice and paprika, as they seem to work so well individually with the other ingredients. So it is up to you whether you want this to have fruity, spiced or smoky aromatics perfuming it. (*Photo opposite.*)

1 tbsp olive oil
8 skin-on boneless chicken thighs
25ml Calvados or apple brandy
5mm-thick slice of unsalted butter, plus another for the apples
1 onion, thickly sliced
200g Brussels sprouts, trimmed and halved
100g cooked chestnuts (the vacuum-packed sort are fine, though roasted are best)
large sprig of thyme
2 lightly crushed allspice berries, or 1 tsp crushed juniper berries, or 1 tsp sweet smoked paprika
sea salt and freshly ground black pepper
200ml sweetish cider
50ml single cream
2 firm eating apples, cored and cut into wedges
1 tsp demerara sugar

Heat the olive oil in a casserole or ovenproof frying pan. Fry the chicken thighs until well browned on both sides. Drain off any excess fat. Heat the Calvados or apple brandy in a small saucepan or ladle and ignite. Pour this over the chicken. When the brandy has stopped bubbling and has completely boiled off, remove the chicken from the casserole.

Add the butter and, when it is foaming, add the onion and Brussels sprouts. Cook over quite a high heat for several minutes as you want some colour here: the cut edges of the sprouts should have patches of brown.

Add the chestnuts, thyme and your choice of aromatics, then season with salt and pepper. Pour over the cider and stir until you have completely deglazed the base of the pan. Return the chicken to the casserole, skin-side up and cook on the hob until the sauce has reduced and the chicken is cooked through; probably just another 10 minutes. Add the cream and simmer for a few more minutes until reduced and slightly thickened.

Meanwhile, heat the 1 tbsp of butter in a separate frying pan. As soon as it is foaming, add the apple wedges. Sprinkle over the sugar and fry until slightly caramelised on all sides. Serve with the chicken.

VARIATION: WITH BOURBON, PUMPKIN AND PECANS. Replace the Calvados with bourbon and the cider with a light and fruity beer. Increase the onions to two and take out the Brussels sprouts and chestnuts. Instead, add 200g chopped pumpkin and ¼ small red or savoy cabbage, shredded, and crumble in a few pecans. You will need to cook this dish for slightly longer: make sure the pumpkin and cabbage have taken on some good colour then, when braising, check the liquid levels regularly and top up with a little water if necessary. Replace the apples with peaches if you like (either are good), fried in butter and maple syrup. You can flavour this with allspice or paprika, but not juniper.

Chicken with sausages, fennel and orzo

Use gutsy sausages for this. I like the Italian varieties with garlic and fennel, or a classic, sage-rich Lincolnshire banger. The chicken is skinned and chopped here for a change, because it works better with the pasta. However, if you have the chicken skin, you could crisp it up in the oven or frying pan and sprinkle it on the dish, if you like. My family also like this with butternut squash and a grating of nutmeg, which does suit its heartiness and makes it firmly autumnal.

1 tbsp olive oil
4 large sausages
5mm-thick slice of unsalted butter
1 fennel bulb, chopped
2 garlic cloves, finely chopped
4–6 boneless skinless chicken thighs, chopped
200g orzo (or other type of short pasta)
100ml vermouth or white wine
500ml chicken stock
sea salt and freshly ground black pepper
1 sprig of thyme
1 tsp finely grated unwaxed lemon zest, chopped
200g sprouting broccoli, chopped (any greens would work here)
finely grated parmesan, to serve

Heat the olive oil in a large casserole. Add the sausages and brown quickly on all sides. Remove from the casserole and cut into chunks. Drain off any excess fat and add the butter. Sauté the fennel for a few minutes over a medium heat, the idea is for it to take on some colour and start softening.

Add the garlic and chicken and stir briskly until the chicken has sealed on all sides. Stir in the orzo and keep stirring for another three or four minutes until it is turning a light golden brown and is completely coated with the oil and butter. At this point it should feel as though you are making a risotto.

Pour in the vermouth or wine and allow to bubble for a minute or two, then add the stock. Return the sausages to the casserole. Season with salt and pepper, then tuck in the sprig of thyme and add the lemon zest. Bring to the boil, then reduce the heat and leave to simmer, uncovered, until most of the liquid has absorbed, stirring every so often just to make sure the pasta isn't sticking on the base of the casserole. This should take around 15 minutes.

After 10 minutes, add the broccoli and let it just sit on top of the pasta. Cover, so the steam will cook the broccoli. When the broccoli is just tender and the pasta is al dente, give a final stir to combine. Serve with grated parmesan.

YOU CAN PRESSURE COOK THIS DISH TOO: make sure the orzo is just covered with liquid, bring up to high pressure and cook for five minutes. Fast release the pressure, then either add the greens and sit over a very gentle heat to allow them to cook in the steam, or return to high pressure and – as soon as it is reached – fast release.

PEARLED SPELT VARIATION
You will need to increase the amount of stock to 800ml and it will take a little longer to cook (around 20 minutes). I would also be tempted to replace the fennel with a finely chopped onion and some chestnut mushrooms and would definitely add butternut squash.

Chicken pepitoria

A Spanish classic; the chicken is braised in wine and saffron, then the sauce is thickened with egg yolks and ground almonds. I once read that the Spanish prefer not to use onion and garlic in the same recipe and, for once, I am taking heed, so the almost universal step of sautéing an onion is omitted here.

Serve with boiled or steamed potatoes.

1 tbsp olive oil
8 bone-in skin-on chicken thighs, or 1 chicken, jointed into 8
2 bay leaves
5 garlic cloves, crushed
pinch of saffron strands, soaked in warm water for about 30 minutes
200ml dry sherry or white wine
200ml chicken stock
sea salt and freshly ground black pepper
60g blanched almonds
40g pine nuts
25g flaked almonds
yolks from 2 hard-boiled eggs
freshly grated nutmeg
handful of finely chopped parsley leaves

Heat the olive oil in a large casserole and add the chicken pieces. Fry until well browned on all sides, then remove. Add the bay leaves and garlic. Sauté for a minute or two until the garlic starts to brown, then pour in the saffron and its liquid with the sherry or wine. Bring to the boil and simmer for five minutes, then add the chicken stock. Season well with salt and pepper, then return the chicken to the casserole.

Half-cover the casserole and leave to cook for 30 minutes, or until the chicken is tender.

Toast the almonds and pine nuts in a dry frying pan, shaking them and watching constantly as they can burn in a second of inattention. Remove and cool. Do the same to the flaked almonds (be even more watchful as these burn even more quickly). Grind the whole almonds and pine nuts, then crush in the egg yolks and mix in a few tbsp of the chicken cooking liquid until you have a fairly smooth paste.

Remove the chicken pieces from the casserole and keep warm. Stir the paste into the cooking liquid and simmer for a couple of minutes, until the sauce thickens. Serve poured over the chicken, with a grating of nutmeg and some of the flaked almonds and parsley sprinkled over.

Walnut chicken

Chicken and walnuts are a very popular combination. The Middle East has *fesenjan*, which is made with walnuts and pomegranates, and the Georgians have several, including this one which I have adapted from Silvena Rowe's book, *Feasts*, and which she called *chicken imereti*. Dried marigolds are quite easy to come by now, but look for them online if your local shops fail you. The quality of the walnuts is important here as anything too tannin or bitter can ruin the dish. (*Photo opposite.*)

1 tbsp olive oil
8 bone-in skin-on chicken thighs
2 large onions, finely sliced
200g shelled walnuts
1 bulb of garlic, cloves separated and peeled
½ tsp chilli powder, or 1 dried chilli
1 tbsp powdered marigold (blitz the petals in a blender or, if you can't find it, use 2 pinches of saffron)
1 pinch of saffron strands
1 tsp ground cumin
50ml white wine vinegar
300ml chicken stock

To serve
steamed rice, or A fragrant Middle Eastern pilaf *(see pages 110–112, omit the chicken)*
a few marigold petals
finely chopped coriander leaves (optional)

Heat the oil in a large shallow casserole and brown the chicken pieces thoroughly. Remove from the casserole and add the onions. Sauté until soft and translucent.

Put the walnuts, garlic, chilli powder, powdered marigold, saffron and cumin into a food processor and pulse to a paste. Gradually add the white wine vinegar and keep pulsing until the paste turns from coarse to smooth.

Stir the paste into the onions, then slowly add the chicken stock, stirring constantly.

Return the chicken to the casserole, part-cover, then cook for 45–50 minutes until the chicken is tender.

Serve with rice or pilaf and sprinkle over some marigold petals and coriander, if you wish.

Chicken tagine with preserved lemon and olives

It's really difficult to pin down just one tagine recipe; in the end I decided on this as it's a classic and the version I think works best with chicken. And I prefer the tart saltiness of olives and preserved lemons to those tagines containing sweeter fruits. The fennel here is not authentic, but I think its sweetness helps balance out the other flavours without being too cloying.

1 tbsp olive oil
8 bone-in skinless chicken thighs
2 large fennel bulbs, each cut into 8 wedges
3 garlic cloves, finely chopped
large pinch of saffron strands, soaked in cold water for 30 minutes
1 tsp ground ginger
¼ tsp ground cinnamon
300ml chicken stock or water
sea salt and freshly ground black pepper
skin from 1 preserved lemon, finely chopped
100g green olives, pitted and chopped
handful of parsley leaves
handful of coriander leaves

Heat the olive oil in a large casserole and brown the chicken on all sides. Remove from the casserole and discard any excess rendered fat. Add the fennel and sauté until starting to soften and caramelise around the edges. Add

the garlic and cook for a further minute, then add the saffron and its water, the ginger and cinnamon. Pour in the stock or water and return the chicken to the casserole. Season with salt and pepper.

Simmer half-covered for around 20 minutes, then add the preserved lemon and olives. Simmer for a further 20 minutes, by which time the chicken should be very tender and the liquid reduced.

Sprinkle with lots of fresh parsley and coriander and serve with new potatoes or couscous, if you like.

A QUICK HERBY COUSCOUS
You can use any kind of small grain couscous: white, whole grain or barley. Follow the packet instructions and leave to stand, covered, for as long as possible, as that will result in fluffier couscous. I usually add 1 tbsp olive oil and a slice of unsalted butter to couscous along with boiling water. However, if I have a batch of *Herb butter* in the fridge or freezer (see page 69) I will add this, then chop in lots more fresh herbs. A few toasted pine nuts or flaked almonds are also good here.

Chicken with chickpeas, morcilla and chorizo

Another Spanish dish, this one adopted by many British because of our ongoing love affair with chorizo (*photo opposite*). I use morcilla here, too, the Spanish version of black pudding. I particularly like the small variety sold by brindisa.com.

It is up to you whether you use *picante* or *dulce* chorizo here; I use the less spicy variety (*dulce*) most of the time, but that is purely to make this more child friendly.

1 tbsp olive oil
4–6 bone-in skin-on chicken thighs or other pieces
2 links of cooking chorizo, sliced into rounds
6 small morcilla, left whole
1 onion, sliced
2 garlic cloves, finely chopped
150ml red wine
250g cooked chickpeas (see note)
400g can of tomatoes
200ml chicken stock
1 large sprig of thyme
2 bay leaves
small bunch of kale, tough stalks removed and leaves thickly shredded
sea salt and freshly ground black pepper

Heat the oil in a large casserole. Add the chicken thighs and brown thoroughly on all sides. Remove from the casserole and pour off any excess fat which will have rendered out. Add the chorizo and morcilla and cook for a couple of minutes over a high heat, stirring so the morcilla is browned on all sides. Again, remove from the casserole and drain off any excess fat.

Add the onion and sauté until starting to soften and caramelise. Add the garlic and sauté for a further minute. Pour in the wine and allow it to bubble fiercely: it needs to reduce by about half. Add the chickpeas, tomatoes, stock, thyme and bay leaves, then stir in the kale and return the chorizo and morcilla. Arrange the chicken pieces on top, making sure they are half submerged in the cooking liquid. Season with salt and pepper. Simmer half-covered for around 35 minutes, until the chicken is tender.

Note To cook chickpeas conventionally, you need to soak them overnight, then change their water, bring to the boil and boil

hard for 10 minutes. Then reduce the heat and simmer for 1½ hours. Alternatively, you can cook from unsoaked in a pressure cooker for 28 minutes, allowing natural release of pressure, or from soaked for 18–22 minutes, depending on how soft you want them.

Chicken adobo

There are many kinds of adobo, most of which have been disseminated and adapted around the world from their original Spanish roots. This is a chilli-free Philippino version which, unlike the mellow braises in the rest of this chapter, still really packs a punch.

Coconut vinegar is quite easy to source in Asian supermarkets and online, but you can use other vinegars – I would use rice wine vinegar – instead.

This is an instant method (but you can marinate the chicken in all the other ingredients for a few hours first, if you prefer). Pat the chicken dry, fry it, and pour over the marinade ingredients at once instead of adding them separately. Incidentally, this is a very good marinade if you want to barbecue the chicken.

3 tbsp vegetable oil
8 bone-in skin-on chicken thighs, or 1 chicken jointed into 8
1 bulb of garlic, cloves peeled and roughly pounded with sea salt
4 bay leaves
1 tbsp ground black peppercorns
1 tsp annatto seeds, soaked in 2 tbsp water (optional, mainly for colour), or ½ tsp ground annatto
50ml dark soy sauce
25ml light soy sauce
250ml coconut vinegar

Heat the oil in a large, shallow frying pan or casserole. Fry the chicken pieces until well browned; at least five minutes on each side. Scrape in the garlic and cook for a minute, then tuck in the bay leaves, peppercorns and the annatto powder or the water drained off from the annatto seeds (discard the seeds).

Pour over the soy sauces and the vinegar, then cover and cook for 40–45 minutes until the chicken is tender. Remove the lid and continue to simmer until the sauce is well reduced. Serve with rice.

VARIATION: ESCABECHE. This has more complex spicing than the adobe (and most other escabeches, for that matter), but the process is very similar.

Mix together 1 tbsp each of salt, ground coriander, ground cumin, dried oregano and ground black pepper with 1 tsp ground Mexican chillies (chipotle or Anaheim are good), ½ tsp ground cinnamon and ½ tsp ground allspice. Mix half this with the juice of 2 oranges and 2 limes and 50ml of vinegar. Make cuts in 8 bone-in skin-on chicken thighs or pieces and pour over the marinade mixture. Leave for a few hours or overnight. Drain the chicken, reserving the marinade, then pat it dry and fry it as before. Remove. Sauté 2 sliced onions. Add 4 finely crushed garlic cloves and the rest of the spice mix. Return the chicken to the pan, then pour over 250ml chicken stock and part-cover. Simmer for 20 minutes, then add the reserved marinade. Cook for another 25 minutes, uncovered for the last 10 to reduce the sauce a little. Remove the thighs, shred the meat, then return it to the sauce. Serve on rice, or with warm tortillas.

7. CHICKEN & RICE

Maurice Sendak's story for children, *Chicken Soup with Rice*, is an absolute favourite of my children. It makes them laugh as the scenarios are so silly – but they also see nothing strange in the concept of eating warming bowls of chicken and rice all year long.

As a family we eat an inordinate amount of both, frequently together, and I'm sure both my children would describe it as the perfect comfort food. I can understand this – look at risotto. It's a joy to eat – rich, creamy and savoury, but also fairly homogenous, so quite soothing and unchallenging.

However, I was slightly surprised that some of the dishes I rarely cooked have now had to become part of the regular repertoire thanks to writing this book. I will never forget how the children turned down a treat lunch out, followed by a trip to the ice cream parlour, purely because we had leftover gumbo in the house (see the recipe on page 43) and as I write, it is the end of a particularly balmy August and we have just finished off a huge pile of garlicky jambalaya. This is good from my perspective, as really, few things lend themselves better to using up stock and leftover chicken than any form of rice.

A slight confession here: these recipes do focus on white rice rather than the healthier, more wholesome varieties. I do use white and brown rice interchangeably in my cooking and all the recipes using white basmati can be adapted to use brown basmati, simply follow the timings (a low simmer for 30 minutes, then leave to stand for a further 10 minutes) and ratios (by which I mean using double the volume of liquid to rice) as described for *A simple chicken and mushroom Chinese rice pilau* (see page 110).

The dishes in this chapter will serve four to six people, unless otherwise stated.

Risotto

This is probably one of the best things to make with some leftover chicken; as long as you have a well-flavoured stock you don't need to use much chicken and you can add all kinds of vegetables to it. Because of that, I do tend to use it as a dumping ground for vegetables I want to use up and it is never the same twice. Which is a good thing because I cook it virtually every week due to the fact that it's my step daughter's favourite meal. Here's my basic recipe, with a few suggestions for variations at the end.

This is one of the recipes I always make in a pressure cooker so I include instructions for this, too. I promise you'll be so amazed not only by the speed but by the perfect results that you won't ever want to go back to the longer method.

1 litre chicken stock
1 tbsp olive oil
25g unsalted butter, plus 25g
1 large onion or leek, finely chopped
2 garlic cloves, finely chopped
300g risotto rice
sea salt and freshly ground black pepper
75ml vermouth or white wine
25g grated parmesan, plus more to serve
100g leftover chicken, chopped
finely chopped parsley leaves

Put the chicken stock in a saucepan and heat it.

Put the oil and 25g of the butter in a large pan over a medium heat. When the butter is foaming, reduce the heat and add the onion or leek. Cook until the onion is softened and translucent. Add the garlic and stir for another minute. Add the risotto rice and stir until it is completely coated in the butter. Season with salt and pepper. Pour over the vermouth or wine and let it bubble away for a minute, then start adding the warm stock, just enough to cover the rice. Stir continuously, letting the stock simmer until it has been absorbed by the rice. Repeat until all the stock has been absorbed; the rice should be very creamy and roll in gentle waves when you run a spoon through it.

Beat in the remaining 25g of butter and the parmesan, then fold in the chopped chicken. Serve with more parmesan and finely chopped parsley.

To cook in a pressure cooker, you will only need 750ml stock. Proceed as above until you have added the vermouth, then add all the stock at once. Put the lid on, bring to high pressure and cook for five minutes. Fast-release the pressure, then proceed as in the previous paragraph.

SEASONAL VARIATIONS:

Our most frequent variation is to add mushrooms, butternut squash and sage, for a dish well suited to autumn. If cooking conventionally, I fry the mushrooms separately and use roasted butternut squash. When cooking in the pressure cooker, I put everything in at the same time as the onions.

A gutsier risotto for winter will contain other meats – I like good old Lincolnshire sausages with cavolo nero or kale. Cook the sausages, perhaps with some lardons of smoked bacon, then remove and cut up. Proceed as before. Blanch the greens and add at the end with the sausages and chicken. Here I might use red wine instead of vermouth or white wine. If cooking in a pressure cooker, you don't have to remove the sausages; they will become very tender, but keep their form.

I often have an abundance of chard in spring and summer, so use the chopped stems in the beginning with the onion, along with the finely grated zest of 1 unwaxed lemon. The leaves can be blanched separately and chopped, then added with the chicken at the end. I often add other greens, especially courgettes, broad beans and peas. Do not be afraid of adding the courgettes at the beginning: they will disintegrate, but that just adds to the creaminess of the finished risotto.

Another favourite summer risotto involves fennel and artichoke hearts. I will chop a fennel bulb quite finely and add it to the pan with leek instead of onion, the finely grated zest of 1 unwaxed lemon and 1 tsp fennel seeds. A 280g jar of artichoke hearts, drained, are added with the chicken at the end, when I will sometimes add 1 tsp of ouzo, too, along with lots of torn basil leaves.

Jambalaya

As jambalaya is often referred to as the US version of paella, people often make it with a Spanish sausage like chorizo. What really works better is a fat, Polish kielbasa or a French saucisse de Morteau; neither will leach out copious amounts of fat or paprika and both will plump up nicely, which is exactly what you want here.

6 skinless boneless chicken thighs, chopped
12 large prawns, peeled and deveined, heads intact
2 tbsp Cajun seasoning *(see page 43)*
2 tbsp olive oil (or, if you have it, rendered bacon fat)
1 large onion, roughly chopped
1 green pepper, roughly diced
2 celery sticks, chopped
4 garlic cloves, finely chopped
200g smoked sausage, thickly sliced
4 tomatoes, chopped (or 200g canned chopped tomatoes)
2 bay leaves
1 large sprig of thyme
1 sprig of tarragon (optional, I like the sweetness it adds)
400g long-grain rice, well rinsed
1 litre chicken stock
1 tsp hot sauce
sea salt and freshly ground black pepper
100g green beans, each cut into 4
handful of finely chopped parsley leaves

Put the chicken and prawns in separate bowls and divide the Cajun seasoning between them. Rub it in well so they are completely coated. Set aside.

Heat the oil or fat in a large casserole, then add the onion, pepper and celery. Cook over a medium heat until they start to soften and caramelise around the edges, then add the garlic and sausage and cook for another minute. Pour over the tomatoes, then add the bay leaves, thyme and tarragon (if using). Sprinkle over the rice, then pour over the stock, add the hot sauce and season with salt and pepper.

Cover and simmer over a gentle heat. After 15 minutes, add the chicken and beans to the casserole. Cook for a further five minutes, then add the prawns. By this point the rice should be cooked and most of the liquid absorbed. If it's starting to get dry, turn off the heat and leave the shrimp to stand for about five minutes, until most of the liquid has been absorbed. If it's getting dry, just take off the heat to steam for a few minutes until the shrimp are cooked through. Fork through and serve sprinkled with parsley.

A Spanish-flavoured rice dish

This isn't a paella, but is instead a wetter, soupier dish, more like an American 'bog', but made with short-grain rather than long-grain rice. I know it's yet another dish containing fennel and smoked paprika, but that is a wonderful combination much loved in my household. There is an argument for making this look much more impressive, by using whole chicken pieces and browning them well but this is supposed to be quite a quick dish and, really, I like the way the flavours manage to get right into the chicken. (*Photo opposite.*)

1 tbsp olive oil, plus more if needed
8 skinless boneless chicken thighs, chopped
2 leeks, finely chopped
1 red pepper, sliced
1 fennel bulb, sliced
4 garlic cloves, finely chopped
2 tsp fennel seeds, crushed
finely grated zest of 1 unwaxed lemon, plus lemon wedges to serve
1 bay leaf
1 tbsp tomato purée
300g short-grain or paella rice
pinch of saffron strands, soaked in a little warm water for 30 minutes
1 litre chicken stock
400g can of artichoke hearts, well rinsed (optional)
100g peas (frozen are fine)
100g podded broad beans
sea salt and freshly ground black pepper
handful of chopped parsley leaves

Put the olive oil in a large, heavy-based frying pan or casserole. Add the chicken and brown well on all sides. Remove from the casserole. Add the leeks, red pepper and fennel, with a little more olive oil if necessary, then fry quite briskly until they start to soften and take on some colour. Add the garlic along with the fennel seeds, lemon zest and bay leaf. Stir, for a minute, then add the tomato purée.

Tip in the rice, then stir to combine. When the rice is looking red and glossy, pour in the saffron and its liquid and the stock. Add the artichokes, if using, then sprinkle over the peas and broad beans and season with salt and pepper. Make sure the rice is evenly spread over the base of the pan, then bring to the boil.

Reduce the heat, partially cover, then simmer for around 20 minutes. By this point the rice should be al dente and the whole dish should have a slightly thicker-than-soup texture. Serve in bowls with lots of parsley and lemon wedges.

PILAUS, PILAFS, PLAVS AND PLOVS

There's a whole raft of rice dishes that clearly must have similar origins; here I've largely stuck to the ones I know well and love. All of these recipes using long-grain rice can be pressure cooked: it takes a mere three minutes, before a long, natural release of the pressure so it can keep steaming, so it's very economical on fuel.

Yogurt-marinated chicken and rice (*yakni pilau*)

This dish is often the centrepiece of a meal at my in-laws. It's very aromatic, very mildly spiced and the chicken is very tender, thanks to the yogurt marinade. I cook with whole spices here and have taught my children to

pick them out so they don't get an unpleasant mouthful of clove or cardamom, but if you prefer you could grind the spices and use them that way, or simply add a favourite mild curry powder. (*Photo opposite.*)

For the chicken and marinade
200ml natural yogurt
juice and finely grated zest of 1 unwaxed lemon
1 small onion, finely chopped or grated
2 garlic cloves, crushed
5g root ginger, finely grated
1 chicken, skinned, jointed into 10 (or equivalent)

For the rice
1 tbsp oil
1 large knob of unsalted butter
1 onion, finely chopped
1 tsp black peppercorns
4 cloves
2 black cardamom pods
1 tsp green cardamom pods
3cm piece of cinnamon stick
1 tsp coriander seeds
1 tsp cumin seeds
1 blade of mace
½ tsp turmeric
2 bay leaves
800ml chicken stock
400g basmati rice, well rinsed
sea salt and freshly ground black pepper

For the fried onion and other bits
1 tbsp vegetable oil
1 large onion, sliced into crescents
large handful of coriander leaves
a few green chillies, finely sliced

Mix together all the marinade ingredients. Cut shallow slashes in the chicken flesh, then put in a bowl and massage in the marinade, making sure it gets right into the cuts. Cover and leave to marinate in the fridge for several hours, or overnight.

When you are ready to cook the pilau, heat the oil and butter in a large casserole. Scrape off most of the marinade and fry the chicken over a medium–low heat until all sides are browned. Take your time with this, around 10 minutes. Remove the chicken from the pan and add the onion and all the spices and bay leaves. Fry for a few minutes, then pour in a little of the stock. Boil fiercely, stirring the entire time, just to make sure any brown bits stuck to the base of the pan are scraped up. Add the rice, turn it over a few times so it is well coated in the oil and spices, then pour in the remaining chicken stock. Season with salt and pepper then put the chicken on top.

Bring to the boil, then reduce the heat to a simmer and cover. Cook for 20–25 minutes until all the stock has absorbed into the rice and the chicken is cooked through. You can also cook this in an oven, if you prefer. Preheat the oven to 180°C/fan 160°C/350°F/gas mark 4. Cook for 30–35 minutes. Or, to cook in a pressure cooker, reduce the amount of stock to 600ml and cook on high pressure for three minutes, then allow to drop pressure naturally.

My mother-in-law always tops this with some fried onion. Heat the oil and fry the onion quite briskly until brown and blackening round the edges. Drain well and sprinkle over the pilau with the coriander leaves. Serve green chillies in a separate bowl at the table for those who want to add heat.

A simple chicken and mushroom Chinese rice pilau

This recipe uses brown rice; you can adapt any of the other rice recipes in this book for brown rice by using the cooking times and the 1:2 rice-to-liquid ratio used here.

300g brown basmati rice
1 tbsp groundnut oil
3–4 skin-on boneless chicken thighs, sliced
1 onion, finely chopped
200g shiitake mushrooms, sliced
3 garlic cloves, chopped
2cm piece of root ginger, finely chopped
600ml chicken stock
3cm piece of cinnamon stick
1 star anise
2 bay leaves
sea salt and freshly ground black pepper

Cover the rice in cold water and leave to soak for one hour. Drain thoroughly.

Heat the oil in a lidded saucepan or casserole. Add the chicken and stir-fry over a high heat until the skin is browned. Remove, then add the onion and mushrooms. Cook for a few minutes, again over a high heat, until they are all lightly browned, then add the garlic and ginger. Cook for another minute, then add the drained rice. Cook for a couple of minutes more to coat, until it looks glossy.

Return the chicken to the casserole, then pour over the stock. Add the cinnamon, star anise and bay, then season with salt and pepper. Bring to the boil, then reduce the heat and cook, covered, on a low simmer for 30 minutes until all the water is absorbed. Leave to stand for a further 10 minutes, covered, to steam and fluff up. This is wonderful on its own, but you could serve it with stir-fried or steamed greens and a dash of soy sauce.

A fragrant Middle Eastern pilaf

This can be as plain or as elaborate as you like (*photo opposite*). I tend to go all out with the garnishes as I love the flamboyance of nibbed pistachios and rose petals. Many pilafs have golden raisins or sultanas in, but I am not keen on those, so instead I add some finely chopped dried apricots to add a similar sweet note. The other important thing about a good pilaf is the *tah dig*, the golden crust of crisp rice which develops on the bottom.

It is up to you which cut of chicken you use here, but you will need 500–600g in total.

2 skinless chicken breasts, cut into bite-sized pieces
3 skinless boneless chicken thighs, trimmed of fat, cut into bite-sized pieces
sea salt
juice of ½ lime
juice of ½ orange
3 tbsp natural yogurt
1 tbsp olive oil
large slice of unsalted butter
½ tsp green cardamom pods
2–3cm piece of cinnamon stick
50g finely chopped dried apricots
800ml chicken stock
pinch of saffron strands, soaked in a little of the chicken stock for 30 minutes
400g basmati rice, well rinsed
1 tbsp orange blossom water, or rose water
25g flaked almonds
25g nibbed pistachios
handful of finely chopped parsley leaves
handful of dried rose petals

Put the chicken in a bowl and sprinkle with half a teaspoon of salt. Add the lime and orange juices and then spoon over the yogurt.

Stir to combine, cover and leave for one hour.

Heat the oil in a large casserole. Add the butter. When it starts to foam, shake off any excess marinade from the chicken and fry quickly. Add the cardamom pods and cinnamon stick, then stir in the apricots and rice. Stir for a minute or two until well coated. Use the chicken stock to 'rinse' out the marinade bowl and add this to the pan with the soaked saffron.

Bring to the boil, reduce the heat and cover. Simmer over a low heat for 15–20 minutes until all the liquid has been absorbed. Remove from the heat and drizzle over the orange blossom or rose water. Leave, covered, for around 10 minutes, so it continues to steam; this will result in a slightly drier, but fluffier rice.

Stir the almonds and pistachios through the rice and turn out on to a large serving platter, with the *tah dig* pulled off separately. The rice should be white-dappled-yellow from the saffron. Sprinkle with the parsley and rose petals and serve immediately.

AND A VERY GREEN ALTERNATIVE
Follow the recipe above, with the same spices. Take out the orange juice and orange blossom water or rose water. Use the juice of a whole lemon instead. Add 150g podded broad beans to the rice after it has been cooking for 10 minutes. Replace the pistachios and almonds with toasted pine nuts and stir in lots of dill, mint and parsley at the end.

COOKED RICE

There are often bowlfuls of leftover rice in my household, not least because, when you have Pakistani in-laws, it is *de rigeur* to provide mountainous platterfuls, even when you know most of it won't be eaten. The leftovers do get used up in all kinds of ways. I like adding cooked rice to any kind of chicken broth, with a dash of chilli sauce, some greens, and perhaps an egg broken into it, but mostly, I make egg-fried rice. It's important to store leftover rice properly: make sure that, as soon as it has cooled to room temperature, you put it in the fridge to chill. Even better, freeze it; it will defrost brilliantly as long as it has been cooked to the dry and fluffy stage.

I wonder how many households still regularly make a savoury rice with leftovers? It was quite common when I was growing up, but flavoured more often with Worcestershire sauce than soy. What I normally do is take leftover chicken and any lone vegetables from the fridge, along with a cupful of frozen peas. These will be stir-fried together, then I add garlic, ginger and pinches of curry or Chinese 5-spice before the rice goes in. The whole thing is finished with soy sauce, mirin and a few drops of sesame oil. I might also push it all to one side and fry a couple of beaten eggs, before they gets mixed in too. You can add any flavours to this: leftover curry paste or spice mixes, different meats (chorizo, with saffron and paprika perhaps). Then there are some dishes built around the concept of having cooked rice at hand:

Creole dirty rice

This would normally include making a stock with the chicken giblets (sans liver), so if you have any of these in the freezer, you could add them to your regular chicken stock for a gamier flavour.

Melt a generous amount of unsalted butter in a casserole and add around 200g trimmed chicken livers. Sauté for a minute or two on each side, then remove and slice them up, they should still be pink in the middle. Finely chop 1 onion, 1 green pepper and 2 celery sticks and sauté in the butter. After a few minutes, add a few finely chopped garlic cloves. Stir in some dried thyme. Return the livers to the pan, along with 300ml stock. Simmer until it is well reduced – you only want enough to moisten the rice – then stir in around 400g cooked rice. Serve with chopped herbs and spring onions.

Nasi goreng (Indonesian fried rice)

Variations of this are found all over Malaysia. I occasionally crave it for breakfast, with lots of extra sriracha sauce on the eggs. If you want to speed things up, the chicken doesn't have to be marinated and you don't have to grill it. Whether you've marinated it or not, you can just slice it up and add it to the wok once the shallots have had a chance to soften. I like to grill it because I like the smoky dimension it adds, but I must confess that I don't always bother.

For the chicken and marinade
1 tbsp groundnut oil
1 tbsp fish sauce
juice of ½ lime
1 tsp chilli powder
2 garlic cloves, crushed
1 tsp palm sugar or soft light brown sugar
2 skinless chicken breasts, butterflied and flattened (see page 11)

For the spice paste
4 garlic cloves, finely chopped
2 shallots, finely chopped
2 hot red chillies, finely chopped
½ tsp shrimp paste

For the rice
2 tbsp groundnut oil
4 shallots, sliced into crescents
2cm piece of root ginger, finely chopped
400g cooked basmati rice (preferably cooked in chicken stock)
1 tbsp light soy sauce, plus more to serve
2 tbsp kecap manis
4 eggs
handful of coriander leaves
chilli sauce, to serve

First prepare the chicken. Mix the marinade ingredients together, stirring to make sure the sugar dissolves. Coat the chicken with this mixture, cover and leave to marinate for a couple of hours, or overnight.

To make the spice paste, blitz the ingredients together, adding a little water if it is resistant, until you have a semi-smooth texture.

To cook the chicken, heat a griddle until smoking. Cook the chicken for no more than two minutes on each side (it should take less), then remove and leave to rest. After a few minutes, slice it.

Heat the groundnut oil in a frying pan or wok. Add the shallots and ginger and fry over quite a high heat until golden brown. Add the spice paste and continue to fry for another minute. Tip in all the rice and keep stir-frying until it is completely coated with all the paste and onions. Add the soy sauce and kecap manis and combine.

Now you have a choice with the eggs. You can either beat them together, lightly fry them and add them to the rice, or you can leave them whole, frying them individually. Either way, when the rice is cooked, decant into bowls. Top with the chicken, then a fried egg if that's the way you've taken it. Garnish with coriander leaves and serve with more soy sauce and chilli sauce.

Oyako-don (mother and child)

A Japanese rice dish of chicken and egg, hence the title. This is a quick lunch when you are on your own, hence the single serving. You can obviously scale up the ingredients to serve more people.

You can buy *dashi* stock in powdered form in many Oriental stores and some large supermarkets; to make *dashi* yourself, wash a piece of *kombu* (dried seaweed) then cover it in water, bring to a simmer and cook for 10 minutes. Add a handful of bonito flakes (*katsuobushi*), turn off the heat and let it steep for another five minutes. The flavour will be savoury, but very subtle possibly too subtle for the average Western palate, so, although it's very inauthentic, I like using a very light chicken stock in place of the water.

Serves 1
100ml dashi (see recipe introduction), or chicken stock
1 tbsp light soy sauce or tamari
1 tbsp mirin
pinch of caster sugar
1 leek, white part only, thinly sliced
1 skinless boneless chicken thigh, chopped
1 egg, lightly beaten
1 portion of leftover rice, warmed through with boiling water
2 spring onions, sliced into rounds

Put the dashi in a saucepan with the soy sauce, mirin and sugar. Bring to a simmer and, when the sugar has dissolved, add the leek. Simmer for a couple of minutes, then add the chicken.

Simmer until the chicken is done, then pour in the egg. Cook over a fairly high heat for at most two minutes, stirring constantly until the eggs have set, but are still pourable because of the stock. The texture will be a bit like runny scrambled eggs.

Put the rice in a soup bowl, then very quickly pour over the chicken and egg mixture. Sprinkle with the spring onion and, if you have some, eat with a few slices of kimchi on the side.

VARIATION
You can add other things to this; a hot-smoked chicken breast or thigh (see pages 24–26) adds a lovely dimension, or try frying some sweet-cured smoky bacon at the start. (The latter brings you about as close as I get in this book to bacon and eggs.)

Maqluba

I like making dishes which have a bit of risk about them; it adds to the theatre at the table if you have to turn something out. I have had disasters over the years with tarte Tatins that remained stuck to the pan, or steamed puddings which have become welded to their basin as though held tight by a suction only to fall out with a squelch, with the filling gushing everywhere. I find that, as long as the food still tastes good, people quite like these mishaps. This is a dish which I approach with trepidation, for the same reason. It's a layered dish of delicately spiced chicken, rice and vegetables, which is supposed to turn out, tarte Tatin-like, before serving. A pilaf with structure, if you will. (*Photo opposite.*)

Serves 8

1 large aubergine, sliced into rounds
olive oil
sea salt
1 small cauliflower, broken into small florets
1 tbsp vegetable oil
8 skin-on boneless chicken thighs
1 onion, roughly chopped
3 bay leaves
1 tsp black peppercorns
½ bulb of garlic, cloves separated but unpeeled, plus 4 garlic cloves, sliced
1 litre light chicken stock
4 tomatoes, thickly sliced
1 bunch of chard, leaves only, blanched for one minute
300g basmati rice, well rinsed
½ tsp turmeric
½ tsp ground cinnamon
1 tsp ground allspice
1 tsp ground cumin
pinch of ground cloves
grating of nutmeg
1 thick slice of unsalted butter
25g pine nuts

Preheat the oven to 200°C/fan 180°C/400°F/gas mark 6. Spread the aubergine slices over a baking tray. Drizzle over some olive oil and sprinkle with salt. Roast in the oven for around 30 minutes, turning once, until golden brown but still quite plump. Toss the cauliflower in olive oil and salt and put on a separate baking tray. Add this to the same oven when the aubergines have been cooking for 10 minutes. Remove at the same time.

Meanwhile, heat the vegetable oil in a large casserole. Add the chicken and fry until most of the fat has rendered out and the skin is crisp and brown. Drain off most of the fat, then add the onion, bay, peppercorns and garlic cloves. Pour over the stock, bring to the boil, then reduce the heat, cover and simmer for 30 minutes. Remove the chicken from the stock. Strain the stock.

To assemble the maqluba, take a large non-stick casserole or deep frying pan. (If you don't have a non-stick one, line the base with baking parchment and smear the whole thing with butter.)

Arrange the tomato and aubergine slices in the base, then drape slightly scrunched up chard leaves over them at intervals. Add the cauliflower and the chicken thighs. Make sure everything is evenly spaced. Sprinkle with some of the garlic slices, then spread the rice over in an even layer. Top with the remaining garlic.

Take 650ml of the reserved chicken stock and whisk in all the spices. Pour this over the rice, pressing the rice down to make sure it is completely covered. Put over a medium heat and bring to the boil. Reduce the heat to a low simmer, cover and cook for 20–25 minutes until all the liquid has been absorbed. Remove from the heat and leave to steam, covered, for a further 10–15 minutes.

Place a large serving dish over the casserole and turn it out. Leave it for a couple of minutes, then lift it off; the rice should have slowly but irrevocably peeled itself away from the casserole and dropped on to the serving dish.

Meanwhile, melt the butter in a frying pan and lightly toast the pine nuts. Pour them, butter and all, over the upturned maqluba. Serve with *Tzakziki* (see page 216).

8. RETRO CHICKEN

These are the dishes I think people do secretly still love, even though most of them are now deeply unfashionable. Some of them became so uncool that they have now become cool again.

Or something like that, anyway. I remember some of them from my parents' dinner parties and others from my own first forays into entertaining, well before they fell victim to ubiquity via the ready meal.

I haven't included any of the following dishes for purely nostalgic reasons. They're all dishes that my family enjoy eating, which makes them just as relevant now as they were several decades ago.

Chicken in aspic

Children can be very unprejudiced when it comes to food. I know lots of adults who have difficulty with the idea of savoury jelly but, to my kids, it didn't seem anything out of the ordinary and they love this. It's jelly, it wobbles, it tastes of chicken. What's not to like?

Actually this should appeal to everyone as it looks so pretty and delicate yet has such a savoury, chicken flavour.

Serves 4–6
For the poaching liquor
250ml white wine
250ml clear chicken stock
1 bay leaf
1 sprig of parsley
1 sprig of tarragon
1 piece of pared lime zest
1 celery stick, chopped
2 garlic cloves, sliced
1 tsp fennel seeds, lightly crushed
1 tsp peppercorns, lightly crushed
sea salt
3 leaves of gelatine
1 tsp cider vinegar

For the rest
2 skinless chicken breasts
1 large, very sweet tomato, deseeded and finely chopped (optional)
large handful of parsley leaves, finely chopped
1 sprig of tarragon, leaves finely chopped
4 spring onions, finely chopped
1 tbsp small capers, well rinsed
1 tbsp olives, finely sliced
squeeze of lime juice

Slice the chicken breasts in half lengthways so you have four fairly flat pieces. Put them in a saucepan and cover with all the ingredients for the poaching liquor except the gelatine and vinegar, seasoning with salt.

Bring to the boil, cover, then reduce the heat to the lowest possible and leave for 10 minutes. Remove the chicken from the liquor and leave to cool, then chill until ready to assemble the dish. Cover the liquor again and let it simmer for 30 minutes.

Taste the broth – you need to make sure the wine is cooked out and it has a good chicken flavour. Strain it thoroughly, preferably through muslin or cheesecloth, and leave in the fridge to chill. When it is cool, remove any fat from the top as well as any sediment that may have collected at the bottom.

Dice the chicken carefully – you don't want it to shred – then put it in a bowl with the tomato, parsley, tarragon, spring onions, capers and olives. Season again and squeeze over some lime juice. Transfer to whatever you intend setting the jelly into: a terrine dish, ramekins or glasses will all work.

Reheat the liquor gently. Soak the gelatine leaves in cold water. When they are soft, wring them out and add to the reheated liquor. Stir until completely dissolved, making sure you don't bring to the boil or you will inhibit the setting quality of the gelatine. Add the vinegar. Taste for seasoning once more. Let the liquor cool a little, then pour it over the chicken. Cover and, when cool enough, transfer to the fridge to chill, preferably overnight.

When you are ready to serve, dip the base of the terrine or other containers into hot water briefly, then turn the chicken out on to a platter or plates. Serve with thin slices of buttered toast and perhaps a few cornichons.

THE TOMATO JELLY VARIATION

This one is summer on a plate, made in the season's last throes, when tomatoes are at their best. Take 2kg very ripe, sweet tomatoes. Roughly chop them and put in a saucepan with sliced garlic, tarragon, lemon zest and 1 clove, then season. Bring to the boil, cover and simmer gently for 40 minutes, adding lots of basil – stems included – for the last 10. Strain through a coarse sieve without pushing through, then again through muslin or cheesecloth. (Don't throw away the tomato pulp, it can be used in a sauce.) Put the strained tomato liquor back in a saucepan and proceed as above, using 2 leaves of gelatine. Pour over 2 poached, chopped chicken breasts and any aromatics you like, but especially finely chopped basil leaves. A bruised lemon grass stalk is a good thing to add to the other aromatics if you have one.

THE BACON VODKA VARIATION

This should convert even the most rigid of jelly naysayers, as it involves making bacon vodka. Cut up and fry a few rashers of smoky bacon. Put it in a container and pour over 200ml vodka. Put this in the freezer for a few days, then strain, just as you would a stock you need to clarify (see pages 18–19). Decant this into a bottle and, if you want it spicy, add a chipotle chilli. Add a shot to either aspic version above. It will encase the chicken in a lovely sweet, smoky, spicy jelly which most people will find hard to dislike.

Chicken kiev

I imagine most people's experience of this is via the chiller cabinet – it was apparently Marks and Spencers' first ever ready meal – but a proper home-made chicken kiev can be sublime. My research tells me that the original recipe did not include garlic and some Russians still regard adding this to the herb butter as practically sacrilegious. Nowadays it's more likely the parsley will be left out. But this version has both in spades. You could also add *Herb butter* (see page 69) to this instead, with or without the garlic.

One of my least favourite kitchen jobs is the flour-egg-breadcrumb coating as it's impossible not to get yourself messy. It's worth it though; any skimping in this department and it's likely that the butter will escape during the cooking time, yielding nothing but disappointment when you cut into the chicken, instead of a satisfying (if potentially dangerous) molten spray of herby butter.

Serves 4

For the butter

100g unsalted butter, softened
4 garlic cloves, crushed
2 tbsp finely chopped parsley leaves
1 tbsp finely chopped tarragon leaves
juice of 1 lemon
sea salt and freshly ground black pepper

For the rest

4 skinless chicken breasts, butterflied (see page 11), mini fillets removed
2 tbsp plain flour
1 large egg, lightly beaten
50g panko breadcrumbs
vegetable oil, to deep-fry (optional)

First make the butter. Mash all the ingredients together, then divide into four pieces and roll into sausages. Wrap in cling film and chill until needed.

Put each chicken breast between two pieces of cling film and bash with a rolling pin until flattened to around 5mm thick. Make sure you do this evenly and gently; you don't want any holes to develop as that will be disastrous for keeping the butter within. Flatten all four mini fillets in the same way.

Lie a sausage of butter lengthways in the middle of each chicken breast. Place the flattened mini fillets over the butter. Fold the breasts over them, one side at a time, tucking the edges in. If you think the whole thing is likely to unravel, you can stick it together with a little egg and flour.

Wrap the rolled chicken breasts in cling film and freeze for at least 30 minutes. If you love chicken kiev, it's worth making a whole batch of them to this stage and leaving them in the freezer until you want them.

When you are ready to eat, remove the chicken breasts from the freezer and unwrap them. Put the flour, egg and panko crumbs in three shallow dishes. Dust the kievs first in flour, then dip in the egg, then into the breadcrumbs. Make sure that every bit of chicken is completely coated. Some people recommend a double dipping of egg and breadcrumbs; I don't think this is necessary and, besides, you will end up with a crust that is too thick.

To cook, either deep-fry at a temperature of 160°C/325°F for exactly eight minutes, or bake in an oven preheated to 190°C/fan 170°C/375°F/gas mark 5 for 40 minutes.

VARIATION: CHICKEN CORDON BLEU

Follow the instructions for Chicken kiev. When the chicken breasts are butterflied and flattened, put a slice of ham in the middle of each one and top with a slice of emmental or gruyère. Roll up in exactly the same way and proceed as before. Serve with a tomato sauce, such as the simple one I serve with *Chicken Parmigiana* (see page 120).

I love those croissants with the béchamel filling and like to replicate the same here, using chicken instead of croissant. If you are making béchamel for something else, it is worth adding a couple of tsp of it to this in the middle, before rolling the chicken up. You could also add a few cubes of very finely chopped tomato.

'Crispy pancakes'

You can do with these what you will. Either make the pancakes and serve with the filling just spilling out as you would with an open ravioli or an omelette, or go all out with the full crisp pancake treatment as suggested below. They'll taste good either way. There are several recipes in this book that provide good fillings, but I think that either the *Croquettes* or *Chicken and mushroom pies* (see pages 162 and 182) will work best.

Serves 4
For the pancakes
100g plain flour
sea salt
2 eggs, lightly beaten
250ml whole milk
15g unsalted butter

For the filling
50g chopped ham
50g grated cheddar or gruyère
½ *quantity* Chicken and mushroom pie filling, *or* Croquette filling *(see pages 182 and 162)*

To coat
50g plain flour
1–2 eggs, lightly beaten
75g fine breadcrumbs

To make the pancakes, whisk the plain flour with a pinch of salt. Make a well in the middle and gradually whisk in the eggs, then the milk until you have a smooth batter. Alternatively, whizz everything together in a blender or food processor. Leave to stand for 30 minutes. Melt the butter in a small crêpe pan then whisk it into the batter. Ladle the batter into the crêpe pan and cook: you need quite small (10–12cm in diameter) pancakes for these to work and the batter should give you around eight.

Preheat the oven to 200°C/fan 180°C/ 400°F/gas mark 6.

To assemble, add ham and cheese to your choice of filling. Place a couple of tbsp of filling on one side of each pancake, then fold over. Wet the edges and stick together. Put the flour, egg and breadcrumbs in three shallow dishes. Dust the filled pancakes in the flour, then dip in the egg and breadcrumbs and place on a baking tray. Bake in the oven for around 20 minutes until crisp and golden. (Alternatively, shallow-fry them in a little vegetable oil.)

I'm afraid I eat these on their own with ketchup. They would be good with a very simple tomato salad, though.

Chicken Parmigiana

This isn't exactly chicken Parmigiana, but a mash-up between that and melanzane Parmigiana (*photo on page 123*). It's quite a calorific dish, but when I used to make this in my 20s, I used to fry both the chicken and the aubergines in copious amounts of oil, so you come off much more lightly here!

If you are going to make this, consider making double the amount of chicken. It's fantastic in a sandwich and is also good used instead of regular chicken in a *Caesar salad* (see pages 129–130).

Serves 4

For the chicken and aubergines

2 chicken breasts, butterflied and flattened, lemon washed, salted and air-dried (see pages 11 and 22–23)
2 large aubergines, sliced into thin rounds
olive oil
2 tbsp plain flour
sea salt and freshly ground black pepper
2 eggs
75g fine breadcrumbs
75g finely grated parmesan
handful of basil leaves, very finely chopped
up to 2 balls of mozzarella, sliced

For the tomato sauce

1 tbsp olive oil
1 small onion, finely chopped
2 garlic cloves, finely chopped, plus 1 clove, halved, for the dish
100ml white wine
400g can of tomatoes
pinch of caster sugar
1 very meagre pinch of ground cinnamon
1 tsp dried Greek oregano
handful of basil leaves

Preheat the oven to 200°C/fan 180°C/400°F/gas mark 6.

Line two baking trays and arrange the aubergine slices over them. Brush with olive oil and bake in the oven until the centres have turned golden brown: this will take up to 30 minutes, but check on them regularly, turning once and removing any that turn too dark.

Pat the chicken dry. Put the flour on a plate and season with salt and pepper. Put the eggs in a shallow dish and beat lightly. Put the breadcrumbs, parmesan and basil on a third plate and combine.

Dip the chicken pieces in the flour, dust off any excess, then dip in the eggs, then coat thoroughly with the breadcrumb mix. Arrange on a baking tray and bake in the same oven as the aubergines for around 15 minutes.

Meanwhile, make the tomato sauce. Heat the olive oil in a saucepan. Add the onion and sauté until soft. Add the garlic and cook for a further couple of minutes, then pour in the wine. Allow the wine to bubble up for a couple of minutes, then add the tomatoes, along with the sugar and cinnamon. Season with salt and pepper. Simmer for around 20 minutes until well reduced, then stir in the oregano and basil.

Rub an oven dish over with the halved garlic clove. Arrange the chicken pieces over the bottom. Put one-third of the tomato sauce over the chicken, then follow with half the aubergines. Repeat this once more, then cover with the remaining tomato sauce. Dot slices of mozzarella on the top of the tomato sauce; it is up to you how much cheese you use, you can cover it entirely or space it out.

Bake in the oven for 10–15 minutes until the mozzarella is melted and bubbling.

Serve with a green salad to assuage the inevitable guilt.

Coronation chicken

When I was writing this, I was also reading Natasha Solomon's *Mr Rosenblum's List*, which has a brilliant description of a group of women preparing coronation chicken for their village's Coronation party. They work in a fugged-up kitchen, surrounded by mountains of plucked feathers, there are piles of herbs ready to be tied into bouquets garnis, the chickens are poached in vats of water and elderflower wine and at least three large jars of apricot jam go into the final

sauce. 'Fortunately the recipe was clear: the chicken must be made in advance and chilled.' The women thought this most considerate of Constance Spry, as it would mean that they would not have to miss the festivities in order to cook for the men. Spry recommends serving this with rice mixed with peas, cucumber, herbs and a French dressing, but that isn't my preferred way. I think it is a great sandwich filler, but is at its best when spooned into crisp chicory leaves. Don't forget that the poaching liquor will have an excellent flavour and should be used for anything that needs a light stock.

Serves 6
For the chicken
1 chicken
bouquet garni of thyme, bay, parsley
small bunch of tarragon
a few allspice berries
black peppercorns
1 carrot
1 onion
1 bulb of garlic, halved horizontally
250ml white wine

For the sauce
large knob of unsalted butter
1 small onion, finely chopped
2 garlic cloves, finely chopped
1 tbsp medium curry powder
juice of 1 lemon, plus more if needed
100ml white wine
1 bay leaf
sea salt and freshly ground black pepper
4 tbsp mango chutney (or the original apricot jam if you prefer)
100ml natural yogurt
100ml double cream

For the cucumber salad
1 tbsp white wine vinegar
1 tsp caster sugar
freshly ground white pepper
½ cucumber, peeled, deseeded and finely chopped
2 large heads of chicory, or Little Gem leaves
micro coriander if you can get it, or a few small leaves of coriander

Put the chicken in a large saucepan and poach (see pages 45–46), adding all the other poaching ingredients after skimming.

Meanwhile, make the sauce. Heat the butter in a saucepan and sauté the onion until soft and translucent, not browned. Add the garlic and curry powder and cook for a couple of minutes, then pour in the lemon juice, wine and 50ml of water. Add the bay leaf, season and simmer until reduced by half.

Stir the mango chutney or jam into the sauce and leave to cool. Remove the bay leaf, stir in the yogurt, then lightly whip the cream and add that, too.

To make the salad, mix together the vinegar, sugar, salt and white pepper and add a little water. Toss the cucumber in it and leave to sit, perhaps for as long as it takes to poach the chicken. Drain.

Remove the chicken from the stock and, when it is cool enough to handle, remove all the meat from the bones, discarding the skin. Use half the meat and reserve the rest for something else. Cut the meat into small pieces. Gently fold the chicken into the sauce, but be careful because you don't want it to shred. Taste for seasoning and add more salt, pepper and lemon juice as necessary.

To serve, spoon the chicken on to leaves of chicory or lettuce. Sprinkle with the lightly pickled cucumber and coriander leaves.

Chicken Veronique

Once, as a fairly young child (I'm not sure I was in double figures), I spent an entire afternoon peeling grapes for my perfectionist mother so she could serve chicken Veronique at a dinner party. Not one of my favourite memories, but I love the dish all the same as it's so gentle and understated. It's about the only time my mother used chicken breasts on their own and I do so here, but in very slim escalopes. It's entirely up to you whether you peel the grapes. (*Photo on page 126.*)

Serves 4
15g unsalted butter
3–4 chicken breasts, cut into thin escalopes
1 onion, finely chopped
250ml white wine (something light and floral)
300ml chicken stock
1 tsp finely chopped tarragon leaves
sea salt and freshly ground white pepper
50ml double cream
100g seedless green grapes, halved

Heat the butter in a shallow, lidded pan. Add the chicken and fry briefly on both sides until a very light golden brown. Remove and add the onion. Cook gently until very soft and translucent, then pour in the wine. Simmer until reduced by half, then add the chicken stock and tarragon. Season with salt and white pepper. Cover and simmer for a further five minutes, then taste; the wine should have mellowed nicely. Add the cream and simmer, uncovered, for another five minutes.

Return the chicken to the pan along with any juices and the grapes. Simmer until the chicken is cooked through.

Serve the chicken with the sauce spooned over, preferably with buttered new potatoes.

Coq au vin

This was the dish I used to make most often when I first starting having dinner parties. When I started writing this book I realised I hadn't made it since the 1990s, but I'm glad I've now revisited it as it's really very good. This is inspired by Simon Hopkinson's recipe in *The Prawn Cocktail Years*, a bible for anyone with a penchant for the type of food found in this chapter.

Serves 6
For the marinade/cooking liquor
1 bottle of full-bodied red wine
1 onion, chopped
1 leek, sliced
1 celery stick, sliced
1 bulb of garlic, halved horizontally
bouquet garni of parsley, thyme and 2 bay leaves
1 tbsp fruit jelly (redcurrant or anything apple-based is good)

For the chicken
1 chicken, jointed and skinned
sea salt and freshly ground black pepper
1 tbsp plain flour
1 tsp mustard powder (optional)
1 tbsp olive oil
25g unsalted butter
100g good-quality smoked bacon, cut into lardons
20 small onions or shallots, peeled
20 button mushrooms
50ml brandy

Put all the marinade ingredients into a saucepan. Bring to a fierce boil, then reduce the heat and simmer until the wine has reduced by about half. Allow to cool. Strain through a sieve and discard all the aromatics.

Put all the chicken pieces into a bowl or plastic container and pour over the marinade. Cover. Leave for a few hours if possible, or even overnight.

Remove the chicken from the marinade and brush off any stray pieces of vegetable matter. Dry thoroughly with kitchen paper if necessary, then season the flour, add the mustard powder, if using, and use to dust the chicken.

Put the olive oil and butter into a casserole over a medium heat. Fry the chicken pieces until golden brown. (You may have to do this in two batches.) Remove from the casserole and add the bacon. Fry until brown, then remove this as well. Fry the onions and mushrooms in the same way until the onions are also well-burnished in places. Return the chicken and bacon to the casserole.

Heat the brandy and set it alight: I find the easiest way to do this is in a ladle which I hold over the gas flame. When it is heated through, tip it slightly so the edge of the ladle catches the flame and the whole thing will ignite. Pour over the contents of the casserole.

Pour over the reserved marinade liquid and allow it to bubble. Gently move everything about, scraping anything up from the base of the casserole. Cover, and leave to simmer over as low a heat as you can manage for one hour.

I really like this with a potato and celeriac gratin. Butter an ovenproof dish, then arrange within 300g each of sliced potatoes and celeriac in layers. Pour over a mixture of 150ml double cream and 350ml whole milk. Grate over a little nutmeg and bake in an oven preheated to 200°C/fan 180°C/400°F/gas mark 6 for around one hour.

HUNTER'S CHICKEN, VARIOUS WAYS

There are several dishes here; stupidly, it didn't occur to me until writing this book that chicken cacciatore and chicken chasseur are just French and Italian versions of the same dish.

I then realised that practically every European country has their own variation. I've included a handful here, the common ground between them is tomatoes, but apart from that they are very different.

The French chassseur is more elegant, the Italian more pungent and earthier, while the bigos is hearty and uncomplicated and gets better and better the longer you keep it.

Pollo alla cacciatore

Clova, a rather glamorous friend of my parents, used to make this and I used to think it very sophisticated, mainly because it was made with wine, peppers and basil. She was the first person I knew who kept a pot of basil in her kitchen and I wasn't convinced by it; the scent seemed overwhelmingly intense to a small child.

In fact, I wasn't sure about the peppers either. Both seemed impossibly exotic to someone growing up in a very rural part of North Lincolnshire. I wanted to like them more than I actually did at that time.

Now I realise both Clova and my mother read and admired Elizabeth David, the difference being that Clova, who lived in Oxford as opposed to our rural North Lincolnshire, actually had access to most of the ingredients.

How things have changed!

Serves 4–6

8 pieces of skin-on bone-in chicken
2 tbsp olive oil
1 large onion, very thinly sliced
1 red pepper, thickly sliced
1 green pepper, thickly sliced
150ml white wine
1 bulb of garlic, halved horizontally
large sprig of rosemary
200g tomatoes, peeled, deseeded and roughly chopped
lots of torn basil leaves

Loosen the flesh from around the bone of the chicken and, if you are using thighs, flatten them out slightly to help them cook evenly.

Heat the olive oil in a large casserole. Put the chicken skin-side down in the oil and fry until crisp and brown. Cook on the other side, then remove from the casserole. Add the onion and peppers and sauté for several minutes until soft. Pour over the wine and allow to bubble up, then return the chicken to the pan, tuck in the garlic – cut-side down – and the rosemary, then pour over the tomatoes.

Cook for around 40 minutes, until the sauce has reduced and the chicken is tender. Keep an eye on it while it is cooking and add a splash of water when necessary.

Serve with plenty of torn basil, with perhaps some flat noodles (tagliatelle) or new potatoes. Or just a green salad.

Chicken chasseur

This also brings back memories, but not because I ever knowingly ate chicken chasseur, I didn't. I was always very curious about those packets of sauce, which a friend's mother always used to have, especially the version for this dish. It still bemuses me to this day why anyone would want to use a packet sauce for something so simple. Perhaps because it's cheaper than wine?

Serves 4–6

8 pieces of skin-on bone-in chicken
sea salt and freshly ground black pepper
1 tbsp plain flour
1 tbsp olive oil
25g unsalted butter
2 shallots, finely chopped
2 garlic cloves, finely chopped
300g chestnut mushrooms, finely sliced
200ml white wine
1 tbsp tomato purée
300ml chicken stock, or water
2 large very ripe tomatoes, peeled and chopped
2 tbsp finely chopped tarragon leaves

If you are using chicken thighs, loosen the flesh from around the bone a little, in order to help them cook more evenly. Season the flour and use to dust the chicken. Heat the olive oil in a large frying pan or large casserole and add the chicken. Fry on both sides for a couple of minutes until the skin is crisp and golden brown.

Remove the chicken from the pan and decrease the heat. Add the butter. When it has melted, add the shallots, garlic and mushrooms and sauté very gently, stirring regularly, until they have softened.

Pour in the wine and increase the heat. Allow the wine to bubble up, then stir in the tomato purée and stock or water. Add the tomatoes and tarragon and season with salt and pepper. Return the chicken to the pan.

Cook uncovered for around 40 minutes, keeping a regular eye on it; if it appears too dry, add a splash of water.

Bigos

This is made with all kinds of meat, but chicken is popular, second only to pork, and I love this version. There are all kinds of additions and flavourings you could add here, many recipes include prunes, some use Madeira instead of cider or wine, some go quite heavy on the sugar. (I even found one recipe including golden syrup, which I couldn't bring myself to try.)

Many recipes recommend making this dish two days in advance, cooking properly the first day, cooking for a further hour the second day, then cooking for another hour before serving on the final day. It does improve with age, but tastes pretty wonderful on the first day, too.

Serves 4–6
50g unsalted butter
1 onion, sliced
1 tsp crushed juniper berries
½ tsp caraway seeds
500g skinless boneless chicken thighs, chopped
1 tbsp brown sugar
500g sauerkraut
½ a white cabbage, shredded
10g dried mushrooms, soaked in warm water for 30 minutes
2 ripe tomatoes, peeled, deseeded and chopped
200ml cider or wine
300ml chicken stock
300g smoked sausage, such as kielbasa, sliced
1 eating apple, peeled and grated
sea salt and freshly ground black pepper

Melt the butter in a large casserole. Add the onion and sauté over a medium heat until the onion is softened and translucent. Sprinkle over the juniper and caraway, then add the chicken. Turn over and sprinkle with the brown sugar. Increase the heat to high for a couple of minutes, turning the chicken so it browns well.

Drain the sauerkraut well and rinse it if you want to lessen the vinegary flavour. The easiest thing to do is squeeze it out with your hands. Arrange this and the cabbage over the onion and chicken. Drain the mushrooms and add them along with the tomatoes. Pour over the cider or wine and stock.

Cover and simmer for 30 minutes, then add the smoked sausage and apple. Season with salt and pepper then cover and simmer for another hour.

You can eat this immediately, either on its own or with boiled or mashed potatoes. I like to serve it with lots of Dijon mustard.

Caesar salad

I love this salad, but I'm not so keen on the ritual of it being made tableside in restaurants. I can't remember exactly where this happened – it used to be quite common – but I do have a clear memory of being horror-struck when the trolley was wheeled over and I was asked about every single ingredient. It was tortuous and drawn-out. What I do like is the habit of making the dressing in the salad bowl, adding all the other ingredients and serving it with the yolk balancing in a shell on top of the salad. So that's what I've done here.

Use any leftover roast or poached chicken here, but what works best is either making some extra parmesan-coated chicken (see *Chicken parmigiana*, pages 120–122) and chop it up. Or it's a good way of using up any leftover grilled chicken breast (see pages 212–214), as flavour from the charring will add an extra dimension. Some crisp pieces of chicken skin would not go amiss either (see pages 21–22). (*Photo opposite.*)

Serves 4

For the croutons
4 tbsp olive oil
½ loaf of ciabatta or robust French sourdough, torn or cubed
1 garlic clove, crushed

For the dressing
6 anchovy fillets, finely chopped
1 garlic clove, crushed
sea salt
juice of ½ lemon
1 tsp white wine vinegar
1 tsp Dijon mustard
4 tbsp olive oil

For the salad
1 large cos lettuce, torn
handful of frisee (optional, to add a touch of bitterness)
2 cooked chicken breasts, chopped (see recipe introduction)
25g parmesan or Grana Padano, finely grated
some crisp chicken skin (optional, though good if you have it)
1 egg yolk

To make the croutons, drizzle the oil over the bread. Put in a hot frying pan and fry, turning regularly, until the bread is crisp and brown (this may take some time). Add the garlic towards the end and fry for another couple of minutes.

For the dressing, put the anchovy fillets and garlic in a large salad bowl with a large pinch of sea salt. Mash together until the anchovies have broken down. Add the lemon juice, vinegar and mustard, then whisk in the olive oil.

Put the lettuce, frisee, croutons and chicken in the salad bowl. Sprinkle over the parmesan and chicken skin, if using. Wash an egg thoroughly and plunge it into boiling water for a few seconds. Now break the egg. Save the white for something else, put the egg yolk in half the shell and balance on top of the salad.

To serve, tip the egg yolk over the salad and toss the salad until the dressing, parmesan and egg yolk combine to coat the remaining ingredients.

9. CHILLI CHICKEN

Like many people in this country, I had a few false starts with chillies and curry. The earliest I remember were once-a-year affairs, made by my mother on Boxing Day with leftover turkey, complete with pineapple and raisins. The strength of the curry depended on how far down the pot of Schwartz medium curry powder she was, so it would range from mildly spiced to tasting of stale dust. I remember taking over curry duty one year, shaking in 3 tbsp and just not being able to understand why there was absolutely no heat then I saw the use-by date on the pot. I've spared you this curry, and I've also spared you versions of my early tastings of what passed for Indian curry in North Lincolnshire. You know the sort: gloopy, fluorescent sauces which were either over-sweet or bitter with chilli and basmati rice multi-hued by unnatural colourings.

Fortunately, things picked up. A few years of travel culminated in a stint working in the Caribbean, which gave me a whole new repertoire of spicy chicken dishes. And these days I have a mother-in-law of Indian-Pakistani heritage who has passed to me many of her recipes and helped me develop many others. Of course, I have to temper them again afterwards, because neither I nor my husband can handle the same kind of heat his parents can, but a pot of sliced green chillies on the table solves the problem when serving them my milder concoctions.

My main focus here is Pakistan and the Caribbean, but I have included a few others along the way too, especially from South America, as it would be very wrong not to include a chilli dish from the place they hailed from. NOTE: all curries serve 4.

Butter chicken

This is one of the most popular chicken curries both in India and in the UK, only here we are more used to calling it chicken tikka masala. This is a far cry from the ready meal stuff, however, which I always find cloyingly sweet. I think it is much better made with grilled or tandoori chicken, I find otherwise that the sauce can verge on the sickly. So I recommend that you use a portion of *Tandoori chicken* (see page 220), or use the marinade in this recipe and grill the chicken.

For the chicken
1 chicken, jointed into 10, or 10 bone-in skinless chicken pieces
juice of 2 lemons
1 tsp sea salt

For the marinade
300ml full-fat natural yogurt
4 garlic cloves, crushed
2cm piece of root ginger, grated
1 tsp Kashmiri chilli powder
1 tsp garam masala (see page 136 or, if not making my own, I like Bart's)
½ tsp hot smoked paprika
½ tsp ground cumin
salt and freshly ground black pepper

For the sauce
1 onion, finely chopped
3 garlic cloves, chopped
2cm piece of root ginger, chopped
1 tbsp vegetable oil or ghee
8 large tomatoes, peeled, deseeded and puréed, or 700g tomato passata
1 tsp Kashmiri chilli powder
½ tsp garam masala
½ tsp ground coriander
½ tsp ground cumin
½ tsp ground fenugreek
pinch of ground cinnamon
pinch of ground cloves
50g unsalted butter
a pinch of caster sugar or ½ tsp red wine vinegar
2 tbsp double cream
chopped coriander leaves, to serve

Cut slashes all over the chicken, then rub it over with the lemon juice and salt. Leave to stand while you make the marinade: blitz all the ingredients, along with some salt and pepper, in a blender. Pour this over the chicken and leave to marinate for at least three or four hours.

Preheat your oven to its highest setting. Line a roasting tin with foil to catch any drips, then place the chicken on a wire rack over the tin. Bake for 20–25 minutes, turning at intervals, until the chicken is charred in places and a deep ochre colour.

Meanwhile, make the sauce. Blitz the onion, garlic and ginger together until smooth. Heat the oil or ghee in a large casserole, then fry the onion purée for a few minutes. If using fresh tomatoes, blitz them in a blender too, then push through a sieve to get them very smooth. Add this or the passata to the onions, and simmer for six to seven minutes until most of the liquid has evaporated away.

Mix the spices together, then mix this in. Whisk in the butter. At this point taste: if the tomatoes taste very acidic, add a pinch of sugar. If they are verging on too sweet, add a few drops of vinegar. Stir in the cream.

Add the chicken to the sauce and simmer for a few minutes, turning the chicken so it becomes completely covered. Serve with some coriander.

A mild, rose-scented curry

Some of the earliest curries recorded in this country are very pared-down affairs; I tried a version that had just white pepper, coriander and mace and was impressed by the delicate, minimalist flavour. This curry nods to that, but also to Moghul cooking.

I wanted a curry that was a far cry from the heat, bustle and vibrancy that we usually associate with India. This instead harks back to the time of Emperor Shah Jahan, builder of the Taj Mahal, and hopefully reflects the elegant and romantic White Banquets he held on moonlit nights.

The flavour is subtle and lightly scented with rose petals. It's a very good example of how a judicious use of spices brings out the flavour of chicken. (*Photo opposite.*)

For the curry paste
25g clarified butter or ghee
2 large onions, finely chopped
1 mild green chilli, deseeded and chopped
1 small piece of cinnamon stick
2 cloves
1 blade of mace
2 bay leaves

For the spice blend
seeds from 4 green cardamom pods
1 tsp fennel seeds
1 tbsp dried rose petals, plus more to serve (optional)

For the curry
25g unsalted butter or ghee
1 onion, sliced into crescents
2 garlic cloves, peeled
1 tsp finely chopped root ginger
1 small chicken, skinned and jointed into 8 (or 8 bone-in skin-on chicken pieces)
150ml full-fat Greek natural yogurt
200ml light chicken stock or water
sea salt
a few drops of rose water (optional)

Start with the curry paste: heat the butter in a frying pan and add the onions, chilli, cinnamon, cloves, mace and bay leaves. Cook for several minutes over a low heat until the onion is softened and translucent. Pour in 100ml of water and cook for a further five minutes. Remove from the heat, remove the spices and bay leaves, then tip the onions into a blender. Blitz until smooth.

While the onion mixture is simmering, grind everything for the spice blend together.

To make the curry, heat the butter in a casserole. Add the onion and cook for several minutes until softening, then add the garlic and ginger. Cook until softened, watching like a hawk as you do not want the garlic to brown. Push to one side and add the chicken pieces. Cook lightly on all sides, then pour over the curry paste. Sprinkle in the spice blend, then mix the yogurt with the stock or water and add that, too. Season with salt.

Stir, then cook gently for 25–30 minutes, checking regularly that the sauce isn't sticking. If it is, add a splash more water. The curry is ready when the chicken is cooked through and tender and the sauce is thick. Taste; if you think the curry needs a few drops of rose water, add them, but be very careful not to overdo it; some rose waters are much stronger than others!

Serve with basmati rice, sprinkled with a few extra rose petals if you like.

A pistachio korma

This is also quite a mild, delicate curry, but has slightly more complex spicing. It is similar to a recipe in Camellia Panjabi's *50 Great Curries of India*, bought for me by a friend years ago as he had a copy and was bowled over by the subtlety of some of her recipes. It's been my go-to book on the subject ever since.

I use pistachio nibs for this, as you get a brighter colour. I have also tried this using a combination of cashew nuts and almonds.

4–6 skinless boneless chicken thighs
1–2 skinless chicken breasts, halved horizontally (to get two thin pieces)
juice of 1 lime
1 tsp sea salt
100g shelled pistachios or cashew nuts, finely ground
4 green chillies
6 garlic cloves, crushed
3cm piece of root ginger, grated
50ml single cream
2 tbsp vegetable oil
2 onions, finely sliced
1 tsp garam masala (see right)
½ tsp ground white pepper
2 tsp fennel seeds, ground
1 tomato, finely chopped
50ml natural yogurt
500ml chicken stock or water
seeds from 1 tsp green cardamom pods, ground
a few coriander leaves, to serve
sliced green chillies, to serve

Rub the chicken with the lime juice and sprinkle with the salt. Leave to stand until you are ready to use it.

Blend the pistachios with the chillies, garlic, ginger and cream. Add a little water if it is proving tricky. Season with salt.

Heat the oil in a large casserole. Fry the onions until soft and starting to turn a light golden brown. Add all the spices and the pistachio mixture and fry for a couple of minutes. Add the chicken and sauté for five minutes, then add the tomato and yogurt and pour over the stock. Cover and simmer until the chicken is cooked through (around 10 minutes). Add a splash of water if you need to, but it should be OK.

Serve sprinkled with the ground cardamom seeds, coriander leaves and green chillies. (Or you can serve the chillies in a bowl at the table.)

Coriander chicken

If the holy trinity of most curries is ginger, garlic and chilli, then coriander has to be a close fourth. There are few curries not improved by it and, in this dish, it takes centre stage with superb results. This is actually very good without any spices at all, but I do like to sprinkle in some garam masala at the end. You can miss it out, or just use a ready-made garam masala instead. (*Photo opposite.*)

For the garam masala
1cm piece of cinnamon stick
1 tsp black peppercorns
seeds from 2 tsp green cardamom pods
1 black cardamom pod
1 tsp coriander seeds
½ tsp fennel seeds
½ tsp cloves
½ tsp turmeric
1 bay leaf (if you can't find a cinnamon leaf which is preferable)

For the chicken and marinade
8 bone-in skinless chicken thighs
5cm piece of root ginger, chopped
6 garlic cloves, chopped
juice of ½ lemon or lime
1 tsp sea salt

For the sauce
1 tomato
large bunch of coriander (reserve some leaves for garnish)
3 green chillies, deseeded if you like

For the rest
2 tbsp olive oil or ghee
200ml natural yogurt
green chillies, sliced, to serve (optional)

Grind together all the ingredients for the garam masala, in a spice grinder or coffee grinder kept for the purpose.

Cut slashes at intervals in the chicken thighs. Blitz together the ginger, garlic, lemon or lime juice and sea salt with a little extra water until you have a smooth paste. Rub this into the chicken, then cover and leave to marinate in the fridge for at least one hour, preferably overnight.

For the sauce, blitz together the tomato, coriander and chillies with a little water and some seasoning until smooth. Add all of the spice mix, if using.

When you are ready to cook, heat the oil in a large frying pan. Brush the marinade from the chicken and pat dry. Fry the chicken until browned on all sides, this should take around 10 minutes. Pour over the sauce and continue to cook for 10 minutes more over a medium–low heat. Stir regularly. When the sauce is cooked, it will separate from the oil.

Stir in the yogurt and cover. Simmer for a further 10 minutes over a very low heat until the chicken is tender and completely cooked through. Sprinkle with the reserved coriander leaves and a few slices of green chilli for extra heat, if you want it.

A hot and sour curry

This is a particularly pungent curry. It's a classic, but this version comes to me via my mother-in-law who has a knack for simplifying curries without sacrificing any complexity of flavour. To turn it into a completely different curry, add coconut milk. I sometimes do this if I want to make it more child-friendly.

2 tbsp mustard oil or 2 tbsp vegetable oil and 1 tbsp mustard seeds (preferably yellow)
4 cloves
4 cardamom pods
½ cinnamon stick
15 curry leaves
1 large onion, finely sliced
4 garlic cloves, crushed
2cm piece of root ginger, finely grated
4 green chillies, sliced on the diagonal
1 tsp turmeric
1kg bone-in skinless chicken pieces
2 very ripe tomatoes, chopped
2 tbsp tamarind paste, diluted in 100ml just-boiled water
200ml chicken stock or water
sea salt and freshly ground black pepper

Heat the oil in a large casserole (if using mustard oil, heat it to smoking point first, then reduce the heat and continue). Add all the whole spices and the curry leaves and leave until the mustard seeds start popping. Add the onion and sauté over a medium heat for several minutes until starting to soften. Add the garlic, ginger, chillies and turmeric. Cook for a further couple of minutes, then add all the chicken.

Cook the chicken for a couple of minutes on both sides, then add the tomatoes, tamarind water, stock or water. Season with salt and pepper then simmer for around 30 minutes, until the chicken is cooked through. Add a drop more water if it starts to get dry.

Serve with basmati rice.

Chicken colombo

This is a French Caribbean curry; the spicing is quite complex and reflects a number of different origins: there is *quatre epices* from France, a Sri Lankan influence from the Colombo powder – the main type of curry powder used throughout the French Caribbean, which helps to thicken the dish slightly thanks to the inclusion of toasted rice – and flavours you would expect from the Caribbean: hot sauce made with scotch bonnet chillies, allspice and 'cieve n thyme' always sold together in the Caribbean and translated to us as bunches of long-leafed spring onions tied up with little bundles of woody, pungent thyme.

It all makes for a fragrant and complex curry, best served simply with some coconut rice. You can also use it in *Bokits*, a type of French Caribbean sandwich (see page 238).

For the chicken and marinade
1 tbsp coconut oil or butter
4 garlic cloves, crushed
½ tsp allspice berries, ground
1 tsp quatre epices (see right)
1 tsp dried thyme
1 tsp sea salt
1 tsp hot sauce
finely grated zest and juice of 1 lime
1 chicken, jointed, or 8–10 bone-in skin-on chicken thighs

To cook
1 tbsp coconut oil
2 onions, sliced into crescents
2cm piece of root ginger, finely chopped
1 tbsp tamarind paste
300ml chicken stock
1 tomato, finely chopped
2 tsp Colombo powder *(see page 140), optional*
spring onions, finely sliced, to serve

Mix together the oil or butter with all the rest of the marinade ingredients. Rub this over the chicken, getting as much of it under the skin as possible. Cover and leave to marinate for a few hours, or overnight.

When you are ready to cook the chicken, heat the oil in a large casserole or lidded frying pan. Brush off the chicken pieces and fry until well-browned on all sides. Remove from the pan and add the onions. Sauté until softened. Add the ginger and cook for a further minute.

Add the tamarind, then pour in the stock and add the tomato. Bring to the boil, then return the chicken to the pan, reduce the heat and simmer gently, part-covered, for around 45 minutes until the chicken is tender.

Mix the Colombo powder, if using, with a little water, then stir this into the curry. Continue to simmer for a few minutes, uncovered, until the sauce has reduced and thickened slightly. Serve sprinkled with finely sliced spring onions.

For the *quatre epices*
2 tbsp white peppercorns
1 tbsp cloves
1 tbsp freshly grated nutmeg
1 tbsp ground ginger

Grind the peppercorns and cloves together then mix with the nutmeg and ginger. Store in a jar until needed.

For the Colombo powder
(poudre de Colombo)
2 tbsp uncooked white rice
2 tbsp coriander seeds
2 tbsp cumin seeds
2 tsp mustard seeds
2 tsp white peppercorns
1 tsp fenugreek seeds
1 tsp fennel seeds
2 tsp turmeric

Toast the rice in a frying pan, shaking constantly until it starts to lightly brown and is giving off a nutty aroma. Remove immediately and cool. Add the rest of the whole spices and toast in the same way. Remove as soon as the mustard seeds start popping. Grind the rice with the spices to a fine powder, then mix in the turmeric. Store in a jar until needed.

Coconut rice

To make coconut rice, heat 2 tbsp coconut oil in a saucepan. Add 400g well-rinsed long-grain rice and cook for a couple of minutes until it is starting to look very glossy. Pour over 700ml water along with 100ml coconut cream. Season with salt and pepper and squeeze in some lime juice. Bring to the boil, then cover, reduce the heat to a low simmer and cook for 20 minutes until all the liquid has been absorbed. Remove from the heat but leave, covered, to steam in its own heat for another 10 minutes to make it fluffier.

Coconut Caribbean curry

This is a recipe I devised when working in Dominica. It is very mildly spiced – the scotch bonnet is there for flavour more than heat – and the most important flavours besides the chicken are coconut and lime. Regular citrus lime leaves have a very delicate perfume so if you can't find them don't be tempted to replace with kaffir, just omit.

1 large chicken, jointed into portions, or 8–10 bone-in skin-on chicken pieces
juice and finely grated zest of 1 lime, plus 1 tbsp lime juice to serve
sea salt and freshly ground black pepper
2 tbsp coconut oil
1 onion, sliced
½–1 scotch bonnet, deseeded, deveined and finely chopped
4 garlic cloves, finely chopped
1cm piece of root ginger, sliced into slivers
1 tbsp very mild curry powder
½ tsp ground allspice
1 tsp soy sauce
1 tsp Pickapeppa sauce
400ml can of coconut milk
a few lime leaves (not kaffir)
100g finely grated fresh coconut, or dried coconut
1 tsp soft light brown sugar
1 tbsp rum

Preheat the oven to 180°C/fan 160°C/350°F/ gas mark 4.

Put the chicken in a bowl. Mix the lime

juice with the same amount of water, then pour it over the chicken. Rub it in well and season with salt and pepper. Leave for at least one hour.

Heat the oil in a large casserole. Fry the chicken pieces until brown on all sides. Remove and drain off any excess fat that has rendered out, then add the onion. Sauté until softening, then add the scotch bonnet, garlic, ginger and lime zest. Sauté for another minute or two, then add the spices, the sauces, coconut milk and lime leaves. Season. Return the chicken pieces to the casserole.

Bring to the boil and put in the oven, uncovered, for around 30 minutes or until the chicken is cooked through and tender.

Meanwhile, put the coconut in a small saucepan with 2 tbsp of water and the sugar. Cook over a low heat to begin with, just to allow the coconut to soften a little, then increase the heat. Stir constantly until the coconut has started to brown and caramelise around the edges.

Remove the chicken from the casserole and keep warm in the oven. Add the toasted coconut to the casserole and simmer for a few minutes to reduce the sauce a little. Taste for seasoning and add the rum and 1 tbsp of lime juice. Serve spooned over the chicken. This is good with green salad and perhaps some rice.

A dry Caribbean chicken curry

I do not refer to the chicken here, but to the fact that this is a gravy-less curry; the liquid is deliberately reduced down to a rich, dark coating. This makes it perfect for filling rotis (see pages 235–236).

The coriander leaves are quite inauthentic for most of the Caribbean but I like them!

For the chicken and marinade
1kg skinless boneless chicken thighs, chopped
juice of 1 lime, plus more to serve
1 tsp sea salt
2cm piece of root ginger, grated
4 garlic cloves, crushed or grated
1 onion, finely chopped
1 scotch bonnet, deseeded and finely chopped
2 tsp thyme leaves

For the spice mix
4 cloves
1 tsp allspice berries
2 tsp fennel seeds
3cm piece of cinnamon stick
1 tsp black peppercorns
½ tsp fenugreek seeds
½ tsp turmeric
½ tsp chilli powder

For the curry
200ml coconut milk
2 tbsp coconut oil
1 large onion, sliced
2 spring onions, sliced into rounds
a few coriander leaves (optional)

Put the chicken in a bowl and add the lime juice and salt. Turn over with your hands so the chicken is covered with the lime, then add the ginger, garlic, onion, scotch bonnet and thyme. Combine thoroughly.

For the spice mix, toast all the whole spices in a dry frying pan, then cool. Grind to a powder then mix with the turmeric and chilli powder. Pour the lot over the chicken and again combine thoroughly. Leave for at least one hour to marinate.

Put the chicken and its marinade in a large casserole or saucepan. Pour over the coconut milk. Bring to the boil, then reduce the heat, cover and simmer for five minutes. Now remove the lid and put over the lowest heat. Cook slowly, stirring regularly, until the liquid has almost completely evaporated. The sauce will gradually become darker. When you can't reduce any more without the curry catching, remove from the heat.

Allow to cool and, if possible, leave overnight, or even freeze, as the flavour will be so much better.

When you are ready to eat the curry, heat the coconut oil in a frying pan or casserole and add the onion. Fry over a medium heat until the onion is golden brown and starting to soften. Add all the chicken and fry for a few more minutes, keeping stirring to a minimum as you don't want to break the chicken up and it may shred if you handle it too roughly. When the chicken has started to brown round the edges, remove from the heat. Serve in roti bread or with rice, the spring onions, a few coriander leaves and a squeeze of lime juice.

Mussaman curry

Over a relatively short period of time, Thai curries have become ubiquitous to the point of becoming part of our cuisine. They have this in common with chicken tikka masala. However, of course, there is more to them than the red, green and yellow we most commonly see. This is a fusion of North Indian and Muslim curries (Mussaman is the Thai word for Muslim) with Thai flavours. You will see from the list of ingredients that it's a real mix of the two. The other thing about it is that it has quite a soupy texture, in line with Thai curries, but very unlike anything I've eaten from Pakistan.

For the paste
1 tbsp coriander seeds
2 tbsp cumin seeds
seeds from 1 tsp green cardamom pods
5cm piece of cinnamon stick
1 blade of mace
1 tsp cloves
1 tbsp vegetable oil
12 Kashmiri chillies, deseeded and soaked in just-boiled water for 20 minutes
2 shallots or 1 onion, finely chopped
1 bulb of garlic, cloves finely chopped
5cm piece of root ginger or galangal, finely chopped
4 lemon grass stalks, tender part only, finely sliced
2 tbsp coriander stems (or root, if you can get it), finely chopped
1 tsp shrimp paste

For the curry
8–10 bone-in skinless chicken thighs
400ml coconut milk
400ml chicken stock or water
2 black cardamom pods
5cm piece of cinnamon stick
1 tsp sea salt
500g baby new or waxy potatoes
2 large onions, thickly sliced
2 tbsp fish sauce
2 tbsp tamarind paste (not concentrate)
1 tbsp palm sugar
coriander leaves or Thai basil

First make the paste. Dry-roast all the whole spices in a frying pan, shaking constantly until they become aromatic. Remove immediately and, when they are cool, grind to a fine powder.

Heat the oil in a frying pan. Add the chillies, shallots, garlic, ginger or galangal, lemon grass and coriander stems and fry until everything is softening and a light brown. Cool, then add to the spices. Purée with the shrimp paste, adding a little water if necessary, until you have a reasonably smooth paste.

Put the chicken pieces in a large casserole with the coconut milk and stock. Add the spices and salt. Bring to the boil, then immediately reduce the heat and simmer, partially covered, for about one hour. Alternatively, cook in a pressure cooker for 20 minutes, then release the pressure naturally. Add the potatoes, onions, curry paste, fish sauce, tamarind paste and sugar. Simmer for another 20 minutes or so until the potatoes and onions are tender.

Serve sprinkled with coriander or Thai basil, with steamed jasmine rice.

Red mole chicken

The sauce for this dish was given to me by Ben Jackson, an expert on Mexican chillies and proprietor of the Capsicana Chilli Company www.capsicana.co.uk. It's much less labour intensive than many mole sauces, but I promise the flavour doesn't suffer because of it. (*Photo on page 144.*)

It also makes twice as much as you need, but it freezes very well and is also useful for using up cooked chicken (see my variations, page 145).

For the sauce
1½ tbsp sesame seeds
10g dried mulato chillies
10g dried guajillo chillies
5cm piece of cinnamon stick
½ tsp black peppercorns
1 tsp anise seeds
3 cloves
3 tbsp vegetable oil, lard or schmaltz
½ small onion, coarsely chopped
5 garlic cloves, finely chopped
2 small ripe tomatoes, coarsely chopped
¼ very ripe plantain or 1 medium ripe banana, peeled and finely chopped
2 bay leaves
1 tbsp thyme leaves
1 tsp dried oregano
25g raisins
50g blanched almonds
750ml chicken, pork or vegetable stock
50g very fine breadcrumbs, ideally made from stale brioche
20g dark chocolate (70 per cent cocoa solids), grated or finely chopped
½ tsp sea salt, or to taste
1 chicken, jointed, or 8–10 bone-in skin-on chicken pieces

Put the sesame seeds in a small heavy-based frying pan over a medium heat. Shake the pan constantly until they start to turn a golden colour, then immediately remove from the pan and leave to cool.

Wash the chillies, break them open and remove the seeds and veins. Dry-roast in the frying pan for a minute or two, being careful not to burn them. Remove and put in a bowl, then cover in just-boiled water and leave to stand for 20 minutes.

Grind the cinnamon, black peppercorns, anise and cloves together.

Heat 1 tbsp of the oil (or alternative) in the frying pan. Add the ground spices and cook for a minute or two, stirring constantly.

Add the onion, garlic, tomatoes, plantain or banana, herbs, sesame seeds, raisins and almonds. Fry these gently together for around 15 minutes, stirring regularly, then remove from the heat and cool.

Put the contents of the frying pan in a blender with a ladleful of the stock and the drained chillies. Blend until very smooth.

Heat another tbsp of the oil in a large casserole. Add the contents of the blender, then gradually stir in the rest of the stock. Simmer uncovered for five minutes, then stir in the brioche crumbs. Cook, stirring regularly, for around 10 minutes, until the sauce has lightly thickened. Stir in the chocolate and stir until well dissolved. Season with the salt.

Preheat the oven to 180°C/fan 160°C/350°F/gas mark 4.

Heat the remaining oil, lard or schmaltz in a large casserole, then fry the chicken in batches until well-browned on all sides. Spoon off some of the fat if there is more than around a couple of tbsp left in the casserole and return all the chicken. Pour over half the sauce and put in the oven, covered, for 30–40 minutes until cooked through. (Freeze the remaining sauce.)

Serve with the coriander rice that I suggest to accompany the chilli (see right).

VARIATION FOR LEFTOVER SAUCE

If you have any cooked chicken to hand, shred it, skin and all, and fry with a little oil or schmaltz in a frying pan. Ladle over some sauce – enough to coat the chicken, but it definitely should not be swimming in it – and keep cooking until the chicken crisps up and the sauce is very glossy.

Serve in warm tortillas with lots of coriander and mint leaves, slices of avocado and, if you like, a zesty salsa, made from a couple of finely chopped tomatoes or tomatillos, finely chopped red onion and the juice of a lime.

A sweet, smoky chilli

I put these flavours together a while ago when I was adding fennel seeds to absolutely everything and it stuck here, because it complements the chipotle so brilliantly. If you are asking your butcher to mince the chicken for you, make sure he doesn't trim off the fat; you need it here.

I like serving this with coriander rice, an American easy-cook or short-grain rice (plumper than basmati) cooked with finely chopped coriander stalks, with the coriander leaves stirred in at the end. But you can serve it with regular rice and use the coriander sprinkled over the chilli instead, if you prefer.

Serve this with the works – grated cheese, sour cream, lime wedges, avocado – and with a tomatillo salsa which gives a good contrast to the rich chilli.

1 tbsp olive oil
1 tbsp schmaltz or unsalted butter
1 large onion, finely chopped
1 red pepper, deseeded and finely chopped
3 garlic cloves, finely chopped
1 tbsp fennel seeds
1 tsp cumin seeds
1 tsp ground coriander
1 tsp ground chipotle (or any other chilli powder of your choice)
¼ tsp ground cinnamon
500g minced chicken thighs
250g tomato passata
100ml chicken stock
1 large sweet potato, peeled and finely chopped
250g cooked pinto beans
sea salt and freshly ground black pepper
1 small square of dark chocolate (optional)
1 tbsp sherry
juice of ½ lime

Heat the oil and fat and add the onion and red pepper. Sauté for several minutes, then add the garlic, spices and chicken. Stir over a high heat, breaking the meat up with the wooden spoon, until the chicken has browned, then pour over the passata and stock. Add the sweet potato and beans and season with salt and pepper.

Simmer for around 20 minutes covered, then stir in the chocolate, if using. Leaving uncovered now, simmer for a further 10 minutes, until the vegetables are tender and the sauce has thickened. Add the sherry and lime juice to taste.

Alternatively, cook in a pressure cooker for 10 minutes, allowing the pressure to release naturally.

Gung pao chicken

This has a real triple-whammy of fire to it, containing as it does chillies, Szechuan peppercorns and regular black peppercorns.

The cut of meat here is quite finely chopped, which isn't the easiest of things to do with the skin on. To make it easier, you could lie the chicken thighs flat and freeze them. You can then slice and chop them when they are still fully or partially frozen, when the skin is easier to cut. (*Photo opposite.*)

For the chicken
400g skin-on boneless chicken thighs
1 tbsp light soy sauce
1 tbsp rice wine vinegar
2 tsp cornflour or potato flour
½ tsp sea salt
2 tbsp vegetable oil
10 dried red Kashmiri chillies (or any other fairly mild red chilli)
1 tsp whole Szechuan peppercorns, lightly crushed
1 tsp black peppercorns, lightly crushed
4 garlic cloves, finely sliced
2cm piece of root ginger, peeled and finely chopped
6 spring onions, sliced into rounds
50g roasted peanuts

For the sauce
1 tbsp caster sugar
1 tsp cornflour or potato flour
1 tbsp dark soy sauce
1 tbsp light soy sauce
1 tbsp rice wine vinegar
1 tsp sesame oil
50ml chicken stock

Chop the chicken into around 1.5cm pieces. Mix together in a bowl the soy sauce, rice wine vinegar and cornflour or potato flour, with the salt and 1 tbsp of water. Whisk until smooth, then add the chicken. Leave to marinate for around 30 minutes. Combine together all the sauce ingredients.

Heat the oil in a large wok or frying pan. Cut the chillies into rounds, discarding the seeds as you go; it's easier to use a sharp pair of scissors for this rather than a knife. Add the chillies and both types of peppercorns to the oil and stir-fry for a few seconds. Add the chicken and its marinade. As soon as the chicken has started to cook and is no longer clumping together, add the garlic, ginger and spring onions. Cook, stirring constantly, until the chicken is cooked through.

Pour over the sauce and continue to stir while it cooks. As soon as the sauce has thickened and the chicken is well coated, add the peanuts. Give them a thorough toss too, then serve immediately, preferably with some steamed rice and greens.

10. FRIED CHICKEN

This chapter does contain a recipe for the properly calorific Southern-fried chicken. You know, the one you bought the cast-iron skillet for; the one you cook once, maybe twice a year, supposedly because it stops your husband visiting a takeaway, but really because you love it just as much as he does. You just need the memory of lingering cooking oil odour and the oil-spattered hob to recede before you can bear to cook it again.

Once upon a time, frying up some chicken seemed like a simple thing to do. I would make it every so often, and used one recipe, out of habit, which I was very happy with.

Then the subject started niggling away at the back of my brain and I started to worry, even obsess about it. Because suddenly, fried chicken was everywhere. Every newspaper, magazine, blog, restaurant, or celebrity chef had a version, and everyone takes it Ever So Seriously and thinks theirs is The One. It made a truism of what American food writer Laurie Colwin says on the subject: 'As everyone knows, there is only one way to fry chicken correctly. Unfortunately most people think their method is right and most people are wrong.'

There are even books devoted to the subject. I know, because I discovered and own *Fried and True*, by Lee Brian Schrager and Adeena Sussman. It is a great book, but it confused me further. After I'd tried a few recipes, I still didn't feel as though I was any the wiser about whether to brine, marinate in buttermilk, keep the skin on or off, stick to a flour coating or add more texture, even whether to shallow-fry, deep-fry, bake or a combination of all three. In the end, I got ruthless when deciding what to try. I want crisp, lightly floured skin, not batter or crumbs. I also want seasoning that lightly enhances the chicken, not something that becomes dominant. Out went anything too insanely complicated, such as the recipe which required a lengthy brine, then air-dry, then buttermilk marinade; that was three days right there and then. The flavour and texture might be very slightly better. Enough to go to all that trouble? No.

Of course, I ended up with a recipe not too far away from the one I started with. And it took me about six months to get there, see opposite.

Things do get healthier after *Classic Southern-fried chicken*. The recipes are split mainly between European-style sautés, which are a slower and more gentle way of frying, and the almost-instant style of wok frying popular throughout Asia.

I wanted these recipes to be a faster proposition than the bakes and braises, so they all use filleted meat. If you would rather fry the meat on the bone, you can do so, but increase the cooking time more in line with the cooking times you will find in the braising chapter of this book. I also use thigh meat more than breast meat, for all the reasons I've already mentioned. If you really want to use breast meat instead, you will have to reduce the cooking time slightly.

There are a few other recipes dotted around the book which rely on a fast and fierce cooking and so are very quick and easy; try, for example, some of the spicier minced chicken dishes.

Classic Southern-fried chicken

So here is my preferred method of frying chicken. And in a world where everyone professes that their version is the best, all I can say is that this recipe makes everyone who eats it happy and that is good enough for me. If you haven't got any buttermilk, you can mix 750ml of whole milk with the juice of a lemon. Leave it to stand until thickened. (*Photo overleaf.*)

juice of 1 lime
1 chicken, jointed into 10 pieces, or 10 skin-on bone-in chicken pieces
3 tbsp sea salt
2 x 284ml pots of buttermilk
150ml whole milk
200g plain flour
2 tsp ground white pepper
2 tsp garlic powder
1 tsp sweet smoked paprika
groundnut oil and, if you have it, lard, to fry

Rub the lime over the chicken, then pat it dry. Mix the salt with the buttermilk and milk. Pour this over the chicken and mix thoroughly. Lay the chicken out on a rack or baking tray and put in the fridge, preferably overnight, reserving the buttermilk marinade. Baste once or twice with the leftover marinade if you have time, but don't worry if you don't. The aim is for the buttermilk to tenderise the chicken without it getting too soggy. When you're ready to fry, remove the chicken from the fridge and allow it to reach room temperature.

Mix the flour with the white pepper, garlic powder and paprika, then season well with fine salt. Dip the chicken pieces in the flour, a few at a time, dusting off any excess flour as you go.

Heat a 2cm depth of oil in a large, deep-sided skillet. You need the chicken to fit into it in a single layer, with just a little room to breathe; you don't want them touching. Don't overcrowd the pan; if necessary, use two. Add a thick slice of lard or bacon drippings to the pan if you have it, it will help the flavour by making it very slightly sweeter.

Test the oil with the end of a drumstick, or a cube of bread speared on a fork. Hold in the oil, it should immediately bubble and start frying.

Add the chicken pieces and cover. You should be able to maintain the frying over a medium heat. You don't want the oil too hot, or the chicken to brown too quickly, as the

outside will cook long before the inside is done. Cook for six to eight minutes on each side, depending on how thick the pieces of chicken are. I test for doneness with a probe thermometer, it should read 75°C (167°F). Otherwise, if you pierce with a skewer, it should come out too hot to touch for more than a millisecond. This is the first stage..

Remove the lid and increase the heat. Continue to fry for another minute or so (perhaps longer) on each side until the outside is mid brown. Drain on kitchen paper then keep warm in the oven until you are ready to eat.

If you prefer to bake in the oven, preheat the oven to 200°C/fan 180°C/400°F/gas mark 6. Put the chicken on a baking tray and bake for 45–50 minutes. It should still be lovely and crisp. Sounds a bit simpler, too, doesn't it?

VARIATION: CHICKEN MARYLAND

This is an oddity, and one I approached with trepidation until a passage in Jane Grigson's *Vegetable Book* reassured me it was a winner and so it proved to be, with the children at least. It is fried chicken with gravy, sweetcorn fritters, fried bananas and bacon. So, make a gravy by simmering 200ml chicken stock until reduced by half and mixing with 25ml double cream and a squeeze of lemon juice. Make sweetcorn fritters by whisking 3 eggs with 1 tbsp soy sauce and stirring in 300g drained sweetcorn and 75g plain flour. Lightly oil a frying pan and fry dollops of the sweetcorn batter for a couple of minutes on each side. Keep warm. Fry bacon, then remove and add quartered bananas to the pan with a knob of unsalted butter and 1 tbsp light brown sugar. Fry. Serve everything together with *Classic Southern fried chicken* (see page 149), with gravy drizzled over.

Mustard chicken

This is based on a French dish I absolutely adore. I eat it with new potatoes and a floppy green salad, but could imagine it being very good in a sandwich too. The vinegar really packs a punch; you could soften the overall effect by using verjuice instead, which is less astringent and slightly sweeter.

8 skin-on boneless chicken thighs, flattened slightly
4 tbsp olive oil
sea salt and freshly ground black pepper
sprigs of tarragon (optional)
3 tbsp red wine vinegar
4 tbsp Dijon mustard

Preheat the grill to its highest setting. Heat 1 tbsp of the olive oil in a shallow ovenproof dish. Fry the chicken, skin-side down, for a couple of minutes, just to get it started. Season the flesh side of the chicken with salt and pepper, then leave it skin-side down and tuck a few sprigs of tarragon underneath, if using. Whisk the remaining olive oil, vinegar and the mustard together and then pour over the chicken.

Put under a hot grill for around 10 minutes. Turn the chicken so it is skin-side up and baste with the cooking juices. Grill for 10 minutes more until the skin is well browned and the flesh cooked through.

Chicken with red peppers and green olives

There are lots of recipes in this book that contain both chicken and red peppers, but this quick sauté puts both centre stage. It doesn't really need much adding to it beyond a splash of sherry, but I like the saltiness of the green olives.

I often have roasted red peppers to play with as I will make a large batch of them and either store in oil in the fridge or in the freezer. There are two easy ways to roast peppers: either halve them and roast in a hot oven until the skins start to blister and blacken, then transfer to a sealed container, leave to cool, then slide the skins off. Even faster is throwing them in a pressure cooker with some oil. Fry for five minutes to get them going then add a splash of water, bring up to high pressure, then remove from the heat. By the time the pressure has dropped, the skins will slip off easily. (*Photo opposite.*)

2 tbsp olive oil
1 red onion, cut into wedges
8 skin-on boneless chicken thighs, flattened out a bit
2 garlic cloves, finely chopped
100ml fino sherry or white wine
a few sprigs of rosemary
4 roasted red peppers, sliced
100g green olives, pitted and halved
handful of basil leaves

Heat the oil in a frying pan. Add the onion and cook briskly for a few minutes until it starts to brown around the edges. Push to one side, then add the chicken skin-side down and cook until very well browned. Turn over and continue to cook. Add the garlic and sauté it very slightly, then pour over the sherry or wine. Add the rosemary and red peppers.

Partially cover and cook over a fairly low heat for around 10 minutes, adding a splash of water if necessary. Add the olives, warm though, then serve with basil leaves strewn over.

Chicken with lemon, basil and capers

This is a very simple supper dish which is infinitely adaptable, it's really a slightly mellower version of *Mustard chicken* (see page 151). Again, it needs nothing more than a green salad (the floppy butterhead sort is best) and perhaps some steamed new potatoes. I will sometimes eke it out more by adding 200g whole small button mushrooms or sliced chestnut mushrooms when the chicken is returned to the pan.

1 tbsp olive oil
25g unsalted butter
8 skin-on boneless chicken thighs, flattened slightly
1 small onion, finely chopped
4 garlic cloves, finely chopped
finely grated zest of 1 unwaxed lemon or lime
100ml white wine
1 tbsp Dijon mustard
sea salt and freshly ground black pepper
1 tbsp capers, well rinsed (optional)
large handful of basil leaves, roughly torn

Heat the olive oil and butter in a wide, shallow frying pan, preferably one with a lid. Add the thighs, skin-side down and fry until they are well browned, then turn over and fry for a couple of minutes on the other side. Remove, add the onion and fry until starting to soften. Add the garlic and lemon or lime zest, cook for a further minute, then return the chicken to the pan, skin-side up.

Pour over the wine, then stir in the mustard. Stir to make sure you have got any brown bits from the base and season well with salt and pepper.

Cook, half-covered, for around 10 minutes, until the thighs are cooked through. Keep an eye on it and add a splash of water if it looks as though it is drying out.

When you are ready to serve, stir in the capers (if using) and basil. Serve with a green salad or perhaps some new potatoes.

Chicken escalopes in a sage and marsala sauce

There are two main ways to serve escaloped chicken. There is the breaded version, similar to a schnitzel, or this way, which has just a light dusting of flour. I have found that the chicken and ham tends to glue together without the necessity of a cocktail stick, so I haven't bothered using them.

2 chicken breasts, butterflied, halved and flattened (see pages 11–14)
1 tbsp plain flour
finely grated zest of 1 unwaxed lemon, very finely chopped, plus a squeeze of juice
4 slices of parma ham or prosciutto
4 sage leaves, plus 1 tsp dried sage
1 tbsp olive oil
slice of unsalted butter
1 onion, finely chopped
150ml marsala
100ml chicken stock or water
lemon wedges, to serve

Take each chicken escalope and dust it with flour. Pat off any excess, then sprinkle lemon zest on one side.

Put a sage leaf firmly in the middle, then top with a slice of parma ham or prosciutto. Press down evenly all over and tuck any edges of the ham underneath. Repeat with the other escalopes.

Heat the olive oil and butter in a large frying pan. Add the onion and cook until very soft and translucent; if you have chopped it finely enough this shouldn't take too long. Push to one side while you fry the chicken. If your pan isn't large enough to hold all the escalopes (it's unlikely to be), cook them two at a time, for just a couple of minutes on each side. Remove the escalopes and keep warm on a plate covered with foil, or in a very low oven.

Deglaze the frying pan with the marsala, allowing it to bubble up. Add the dried sage, then pour in the stock or water. Simmer for a couple of minutes to reduce; you don't need a lot of liquid here but you do want a good syrupy consistency. Add any juice which may have collected under the resting chicken, check the seasoning and add a squeeze of lemon juice. Serve with the sauce spooned over and lemon wedges.

VARIATION For a zestier version, add a few anchovies along with the onion, mashing them up with a back of a spoon as you fry them. Then use white wine instead of marsala and add 1 tbsp of capers towards the end.

Gin-soaked chicken

I take poetic licence with the recipe title, as the chicken isn't really soaked at all, rather it's flambéed in gin. I have included this for all the many gin lovers I know, especially Fiona Kirkpatrick, who will rarely say no to a martini, but strangely needs more convincing when it comes to eating chicken.

8 skin-on boneless chicken thighs, flattened slightly
sea salt and freshly ground black pepper

1 tbsp olive oil
thick slice of unsalted butter
1 onion, finely chopped
1 garlic clove, finely chopped
75ml gin or genever
2 tsp juniper berries, lightly crushed
up to 75ml chicken stock, as needed

Season both sides of the chicken with salt and pepper.

Heat the oil and butter in a large, shallow pan which is wide enough to hold all the thighs. If you don't have one, you will have to cook them in more than one batch. Add the chicken thighs, skin-side down and cook for several minutes until the skin is crisp and brown. Turn over and cook for a couple more minutes. Remove.

Drain off a little of the rendered chicken fat if there is a lot, you will still be left with plenty of buttery flavours there. Add the onion and sauté until softened, then add the garlic. Return the chicken to the pan, along with any liquid that has drained out of it. Reduce the heat to low and cover until the meat has completely cooked through; this should not take long, around 10 minutes at most. Baste a couple of times with pan juices while it is cooking.

Put the gin or genever in a small saucepan or ladle and heat. Either ignite by slightly tipping towards the flame or – the safer method – use a long kitchen match. Pour this over the chicken. When the flames have died down, add the juniper berries to the pan. Increase the heat and turn the chicken pieces so they are completely covered in the pan juices. If it seems a bit dry, add some or all of the chicken stock and simmer for a further couple of minutes.

VARIATION WITH BLACKBERRIES I tried this after a blackberrying session and it works really well. Add 1 tbsp crème de mûre after the gin and a handful of blackberries with the juniper. I see no reason why sloe gin wouldn't work either.

STIR-FRIES

Just about everyone has a standard stir-fry, often using chicken. I admit to using them to mop up any leftover vegetables but, really, I prefer quite minimalist versions and don't like to use the packs of stir-fry vegetables available in most supermarkets. It's much better to focus on the chicken with two or three vegetables and cook those really well.

A summery chicken stir-fry

I have lost count of the times I have made a variation on this, it's the sort of food I make when I have only myself to please. It's particularly wonderful if you have a glut-producing vegetable patch, or if you can take advantage of cheap and plentiful summer vegetables from a market, as you can add anything you like to it and it will still work. It also means it will never be the same dish twice. I sometimes make it without chicken flesh, just adding crisp strips of chicken skin at the end. It adds interest, without being at all obtrusive.

You can add as many or as few of the vegetables as you like, or swap them for others. For example, runner beans would be lovely shredded, blanched for one minute, then added in place of the French beans.

1 tbsp olive oil
4 skinless boneless chicken thighs, chopped (or remove the skin yourself and fry it separately if you like)
a few baby leeks cut into 4cm lengths, or 2 large leeks cut into rounds
large bunch of chard, leaves and stems separated and shredded
1 small fennel bulb, halved and shredded widthways
1 courgette, or several small courgettes, sliced diagonally
100g French beans, blanched for one minute
100g baby broad beans, blanched for one minute and podded, or peas
2 garlic cloves, finely chopped
finely grated zest of 1 unwaxed lemon, finely chopped
sea salt and freshly ground black pepper
handful of cherry tomatoes

To serve
a squeeze of lemon juice or a drizzle of balsamic/sherry vinegar
a selection of summer herbs: basil, bronze fennel, chervil, tarragon, mint
a few edible flowers if you have them; borage is particularly good, or any herb flowers
a few shavings of parmesan
some crisp strips of chicken skin

Heat the olive oil in a wok. Add the chicken and cook over a high heat, stirring regularly, for a couple of minutes, until the meat is browned on all sides. Add the leek, chard stems, fennel, courgette and French beans. Stir-fry over a high heat for around three minutes, then add the broad beans or peas, garlic and lemon zest. Season with salt and pepper and pour over 50ml of water. Simmer for a couple of minutes, then add the chard leaves and cherry tomatoes.

When the chard leaves have wilted down and the cherry tomatoes have softened and burst a little, remove from the heat. Squeeze over a little lemon juice. Alternatively, if you want something more peppery you could instead drizzle over a sweet balsamic or sherry vinegar.

Serve with lots of summery herbs and flowers if you have them and perhaps a few shavings of parmesan and/or strips of chicken skin.

A very fast Mexican stir-fry

The inspiration for this came from a Peruvian stir-fry, when chicken is cooked using Chinese methods but with a mixture of Peruvian and Chinese flavours. I've adapted this with Mexican flavours. It can be served with rice or noodles (I prefer the latter), but it's also the sort of thing you can put into fajitas or burritos. I will also put it on top of tacos or tostadas (see page 240).

1–2 tsp chipotle paste, according to how hot you want it
1 tbsp tomato paste or purée
dash of soy sauce
50ml chicken stock
1 tbsp groundnut oil
1 onion, sliced into crescents
1 red pepper, sliced
2 skinless boneless chicken thighs, sliced
2 skinless chicken breasts, sliced
4 garlic cloves, finely chopped
2 tsp ground cumin
1 tsp dried oregano
squeeze of lime juice
a few coriander leaves, to serve

Mix together the chipotle paste, tomato paste, soy sauce and stock. Set aside.

Heat the oil in a wok or frying pan. Add the onion and pepper and cook over a high heat, stirring constantly, until they start to take on some colour. Add the chicken and cook until browned on all sides. Add the garlic and cook for another minute. Reduce the heat to medium, then sprinkle in the cumin and oregano.

Pour in the chipotle paste mixture and simmer for a couple of minutes. Check the seasoning and squeeze over some lime juice. Serve with rice or noodles, with the coriander leaves strewn over.

An Indian curry-inspired chicken stir-fry

I would happily eat just a big bowl of this on its own, but serve it with rice if you prefer. What is good with it is a simple tomato salad: just slice very ripe, sweet tomatoes and sprinkle them with salt and pepper. Leave to stand until you are ready to eat, making sure they are kept at room temperature – never chilled.

1 tsp garam masala (see page 136)
¼ tsp turmeric
100ml chicken stock or water
1 tbsp groundnut or coconut oil
2 garlic cloves, finely sliced
2cm piece of root ginger, finely chopped
1 mild green chilli, finely chopped
4 skinless boneless chicken thighs or 2 chicken breasts, chopped
1 cauliflower, broken into the smallest of florets, blanched for 1 minute
sea salt and freshly ground black pepper
1 tsp nigella seeds
½ tsp cumin seeds
½ tsp fennel seeds
handful of coriander leaves, to serve

Combine the garam masala and turmeric and whisk into the chicken stock. Set aside.

Heat the oil in a wok. When the oil is shimmering, add the garlic, ginger and chilli. Cook for no more than 30 seconds, then throw in the chicken and continue to stir-fry until the chicken has taken on some colour. Throw in all the cauliflower and stir to combine, then pour in the spice-laden stock. Season with salt and pepper, then sprinkle over the seeds. Simmer for a few minutes, until the chicken is cooked through and the cauliflower is tender. Serve with a tomato salad and coriander leaves.

Chinese lemon chicken

Most of my memories of this are of breadcrumbed chicken breasts drowning in neon yellow sauce so, when I tried this version, I couldn't believe it was based on the same dish. It's truly wonderful. (*Photo overleaf.*)

For the chicken
2 tsp cornflour, plus 1 tsp, mixed to a paste with some water (optional)
1 egg white
2 skinless chicken breasts, sliced
2 skinless boneless chicken thighs, sliced
2 tbsp vegetable oil
1 onion, cut into wedges
sea salt and freshly ground black pepper
1 tsp sesame oil
2 tsp sesame seeds, lightly toasted (see page 143)
2 spring onions, shredded

For the sauce
150ml chicken stock
juice of 3 lemons
2 tsp caster sugar
2 tbsp light soy sauce
2 tbsp rice wine or mirin
4 garlic cloves, finely chopped
½ tsp chilli flakes

Put the cornflour and egg white into a large bowl. Whisk together until it is lump free, then add the chicken. Mix thoroughly so all of the chicken is coated, then leave in the fridge for around 30 minutes, or until you are ready to cook.

Mix all the sauce ingredients together and have them ready by your wok.

Heat the oil in the wok. When it starts to shimmer, add the onion and chicken. Stir-fry quickly until the chicken has browned on all sides – no more than a minute or two – some of the breast will cook completely in this time. Pour over the sauce and season with salt and pepper. Bring to the boil, turn the heat down and simmer for a minute.

If you want to thicken this slightly, add the cornflour paste and continue to cook until thickened. Sprinkle over a few drops of sesame oil, the sesame seeds and the shredded spring onions. Serve with some Chinese greens and steamed rice.

A mellow coconut and lemon grass stir-fry

This uses fresh coconut; if you don't want to buy a whole coconut, you can use the packets of coconut found in the chiller cabinets in supermarkets. Scrape off any brown membrane, then grate or slice with a peeler.

75g coconut flesh, coarsely grated
100ml chicken stock or water
1 tsp ground cumin
1 tbsp vegetable oil
3 lemon grass stalks, tender part only, finely sliced
2 garlic cloves, sliced
1 green chilli, chopped
4–6 skinless boneless chicken thighs, cut into thin strips
150g green beans (long beans or French), cut into 3–4cm lengths
sea salt and freshly ground black pepper
large handful of coriander
large handful of Thai basil (or regular basil if you can't find that, it still works)

Mix the coconut with the chicken stock or water and cumin. Heat the oil in your wok. When it is shimmering, add the lemon grass, garlic and chilli. Fry for 30 seconds to one minute, keeping a close eye on the garlic. As soon as it looks like it is starting to brown, add the chicken and the green beans. Stir-fry for a minute or two and season with salt and pepper.

Add the coconut, then simmer until the chicken and beans are cooked. Sprinkle over the herbs, then serve immediately, perhaps with some flat rice noodles.

Chicken and noodle stir-fry with cucumber kimchi

I've got slightly addicted to the flavour of kimchi and I really love its cooling effect against this hot, savoury stir-fry.

If you don't want to make kimchi, it can be bought in Oriental supermarkets, or you could also just marinate crisp, cold cucumber

by sprinkling it with tablespoons of salt, sugar, finely chopped garlic and ginger. (*Photo opposite.*)

For the chicken
4–6 skin-on boneless chicken thighs, sliced
1 tbsp groundnut oil
1 carrot, cut into matchsticks
1 red pepper, finely sliced
½ Chinese leaf cabbage, shredded
2 portions of egg noodles, cooked according to packet instructions

For the sauce
1–3 tbsp Korean red chilli paste (gochujang)
4 tbsp soy sauce
1 tbsp mirin
2 tsp sesame oil
1 tbsp light soft brown sugar
2 garlic cloves, crushed
3cm piece of root ginger, grated

To serve
100g cucumber kimchi, well chilled (or just some thick slices of cucumber)
sesame seeds

Pound the chicken pieces under some cling film to get them very thin. Combine all the sauce ingredients, stirring until the sugar has dissolved. Add the chicken to the sauce and leave to marinate for a few minutes.

Heat the oil in a wok. When it is shimmering, add the carrot and red pepper. Stir-fry for a couple of minutes. Drain the chicken, reserving the sauce. Add the chicken to the wok and continue to stir-fry for a couple of minutes, until it looks crisp and brown. Add the cabbage and continue to cook for a minute, then pour over the reserved sauce. Leave to simmer for a minute or two, just until the cabbage has wilted, then add the noodles. Toss until everything is well combined. Sprinkle with sesame seeds and serve with the cucumber.

FOR THE CUCUMBER KIMCHI

This is instant kimchi. It has all the flavour without the long fermentation. If you do want to ferment it, store it in the fridge and mix it daily. It will be very good to eat for at least a couple of weeks. I always grate ginger over a small bowl, so I can add both its juice and the fibres themselves.

500g small pickling cucumbers, halved and cut into chunks
3 tbsp finely ground sea salt, plus 2 tsp
1 tbsp light soft brown sugar
3cm piece of root ginger, grated (make sure you keep all the juice)
4 garlic cloves, finely sliced
4 spring onions, very finely chopped
1 tbsp light soy sauce
1 tbsp fish sauce
½ tsp dried shrimp paste (unless you have jarred salted shrimp, in which case use this instead)
1 tbsp mild red chilli powder (preferably Korean)

Cover the cucumbers with the 3 tbsp of salt and leave to stand for up to 30 minutes, until they have released liquid. Rinse thoroughly and pat dry.

Mix all the other ingredients together, not forgetting the 2 tsp of salt, then add the cucumbers. Toss well so the cucumber is completely coated with the rest of the ingredients, then leave it to stand for 15 minutes. You can start eating it at this point. To keep it, store in the fridge; it will keep for several weeks.

11. CHOPPED CHICKEN

The recipes in this chapter are testament to how home cooks over the years have eked out their chicken and other leftovers, as they are all very good at absorbing any stray vegetables you may have lying around.

I've left out one or two traditional uses for leftover chicken; for instance, I didn't see any need for a rissole recipe. Tracing recipes for these over the decades, they seem to have morphed into something made from chicken mince, so have really become just like meatballs or patties and you will find plenty of recipes for these below. Going back to the original seemed unnecessary, as there are far better things to do with chicken and breadcrumbs. Instead I suggest you try the *Croquettes* opposite.

Many of the more fiddly recipes in this chapter – including the *Croquettes* and the various dumplings, in particular – are made in quite large quantities. This was deliberate on my part. They can take a while to make, but all freeze very well, so it makes sense to make more than you need and freeze the rest for another time. If doing so, open-freeze on a lined baking tray until solid. You can then decant them to a bag or container and just shake out a few at a time. This method of freezing will work with the croquettes, meatballs and dumplings.

A note about minced chicken: I always use chicken thighs, rather than breast, or a combination of the two, never just breast. This is because I find thigh meat is more robust and also has that seam of fat under the skin, which you should leave on; the little bit of extra fat can make a big difference to the end result.

A good butcher should be happy to mince the meat for you, otherwise it can be done by hand or in a food processor. I own a mincer, but don't often bother using it as I find the food processor does just as well. If you decide to finely chop the meat by hand – unless you are using a very sharp and sturdy chef's knife or cleaver – it is easier to work with very well chilled or semi-frozen chicken.

Croquettes *(croquetas)*

These are popular all over Europe. Belgian friends always used to make them with brown shrimp, the Spanish prefer *jamón*; here I use chicken. You could also try making them with smoked chicken (see pages 24–26). (*Photo opposite.*)

For the croquettes
400ml whole milk
1 slice of onion, or a few slices of leek
2 bay leaves
½ tsp lightly crushed allspice berries

blade of mace
75g unsalted butter
100g plain flour
300ml chicken stock
sea salt and freshly ground white pepper
175g cooked chicken, finely chopped
a little flavourless vegetable oil, plus more to deep- or shallow-fry (optional)

For the coating
plain flour
2 eggs, lightly beaten
100g very fine breadcrumbs

Put the milk in a small saucepan and add the onion or leek, bay leaves, allspice berries and mace. Heat gently until almost at boiling point, then remove from the heat and leave to infuse. When cool, strain into a jug.

Melt the butter in a saucepan. Add the flour and stir until completely combined. Continue to stir over the heat for a few minutes to give the flour a chance to cook, then gradually add all the milk and stock, stirring between each addition until you have a thick sauce. Season with salt and white pepper, then mix in the chicken.

Line a shallow container with lightly oiled cling film and pour over the mixture. Then cover with another layer of oiled cling film, pushing it down so it comes into contact with the mixture; this will prevent a skin forming. Chill for several hours or overnight.

When you are ready to make the croquettes, either heat oil in a deep-fat fryer to 180°C (350°F), or coat the base of a frying pan with vegetable oil, or preheat the oven to 220°C/fan 200°C/425°F/gas mark 7. Remove the chicken mixture from the fridge and carefully pull it out of the container, holding the sides of the cling film, and put on a work surface. Cut the béchamel into thick fingers (easiest done with a knife blade heated in hot water); you should make around 30 with this amount of mixture. Put half of the flour, egg and breadcrumbs on to three separate shallow dishes. Take each finger and form it into a sausage (smooth off the corners). Dip it in flour, then egg, then breadcrumbs. So you don't get really messy, it's worth doing a few in each coating at a time. When you have used up the coatings, add the rest.

Either fry the croquettes a few at a time in your deep-fat fryer, this will take around three minutes, or a frying pan (this is the trickiest because they need constant attention, it's harder to get them browned evenly, and the more you move them, the higher the risk of them breaking) or place on a baking tray and bake for 15–20 minutes. Eat while piping hot.

MEATBALLS, SLIDERS AND BURGERS

These are all pretty much the same thing, the difference being the shape and size the minced chicken mixture is formed into. Of course, you can vary the mix enormously, keeping them quite plain or adding lots of different aromatics, though keep a light touch as you don't want anything to dominate the flavour of the chicken. Also, be careful about seasoning; it's easy to under-season meatballs, they probably need slightly more salt than you would think.

The basic chicken meatball

I originally assumed that when it comes to meatballs the higher the meat ratio, the better the end result. However, adding breadcrumbs and moisture – usually dairy such as milk, cream or a soft cheese – makes for a softer, more palatable texture. This was quite revelatory for me and transformed how I made meatballs; no longer did I make hard little bullets that stuck in the craw. It is also much easier to steam or bake the balls than fry them. Shallow-frying meatballs is a pain, you constantly have to keep an eye on them and keep turning them to make sure they brown evenly. Baking or steaming them takes away this particular kitchen headache. My basic formula is 500g meat + 75g breadcrumbs (or other filler) + 50g liquid + 1 egg.

Allowing for the extras – onion, herbs, spices or cheese – this will give you 20 meatballs of around 35g each, or 12 sliders of around 60g each, or 6 burger patties of around 120g each. Each option will serve around six people.

Baked Italian meatballs

These are versatile. I like the meatballs sliced into a sandwich, but usually serve them with this simple tomato sauce and spaghetti.

For the meatballs
1 tbsp olive oil
100g smoked bacon, finely chopped
1 onion, very finely chopped or grated
2 garlic cloves, finely chopped
500g minced chicken thighs
1 tsp dried oregano
75g breadcrumbs
25g parmesan, finely grated
50ml single cream
finely grated zest of 1 unwaxed lemon
grating of nutmeg
1 egg, lightly beaten

For the tomato sauce
3 tbsp olive oil
1 onion, finely chopped
2 garlic cloves, finely chopped
400g can of tomatoes, or 4 large tomatoes, cored and peeled
sea salt and freshly ground black pepper
a few sprigs of rosemary or thyme
handful of basil leaves, torn

Preheat the oven to 220°C/fan 200°C/425°F/ gas mark 7.

Start with the meatballs. Heat the olive oil in a frying pan. Add the bacon and fry until crisp and brown. Remove, then add the onion. Cook for several minutes over a medium–high heat until taking on some colour and softened. Add the garlic and cook for a minute longer.

Put the chicken in a large bowl, then add the contents of the frying pan, the bacon and all the other ingredients. Mix thoroughly, then form into 20 meatballs of around 35g each. Place on a baking tray.

Bake in the preheated oven for around 15 minutes until well browned.

To make the tomato sauce, heat the olive oil in a saucepan and add the onion. Sauté over a medium–low heat for up to 10 minutes until the onion is very soft and translucent. Add the garlic and cook for a minute or two longer, then pour in the tomatoes. Season with salt and pepper and add the herbs. Bring almost to the boil. Cover and simmer for around 20 minutes. (For a more concentrated, richer sauce, reduce for longer.) Remove the sprigs of herbs, add the torn basil and serve with the meatballs.

A light, summery meatball

From the previous recipe, take out the onion, bacon, oregano and parmesan. Finely chop 1 small fennel bulb and sauté in olive oil and unsalted butter until soft. Add this with 25g ground pine nuts, 1 tsp lightly crushed fennel seeds and 1 tbsp finely chopped tarragon leaves.

Serve with a lemon sauce: melt a knob of unsalted butter in a small pan and add a finely chopped garlic clove. When soft, pour in 150ml chicken stock and 100ml white wine. Reduce by half, then add the juice of 1 lemon. Season with salt and freshly ground black pepper, then add 50ml cream. Stir in a large handful of basil leaves. Serve with the meatballs on their own, with salad or over pasta.

A MEATLOAF VARIATION

This is inspired by a dish from Josceline Dimbleby's *Marvellous Meals with Mince*, the earlier form of which has been a favourite in my family for years. I didn't really expect the children to enjoy the blue cheese centre, but they couldn't get enough of it.

Use the meatball recipe on page 165, but increase the amount of chicken to 600g and leave out the parmesan. There is no need to precook the bacon and onion for this recipe, just make sure it is all very finely chopped.

Preheat the oven to 180°C/fan 160°C/350°F/gas mark 4. Butter a 1kg loaf tin with butter (or line it instead, if you prefer). Put half the mixture in the base of the loaf tin, making sure it is evenly spread. Take 100g of soft blue cheese and crumble over. Add the final layer of chicken. Cook in the oven for around 45 minutes until well browned. Make sure it is piping hot.

Serve in slices with the same tomato sauce as the Italian meatballs.

If you don't want to use blue cheese, grated cheddar or a smoked cheese will also work well.

Steamed chicken meatballs

There are lots of ways to eat these; serve as they are or with a dipping sauce, or drop them into *Thai chicken and galangal soup* (see page 41) or broth, or with noodles.

Pandan leaves are available from all Oriental supermarkets. They aren't essential here as the flavour is very subtle, but in my blind tasting everyone preferred those wrapped in the leaves to those left naked.

You can obviously vary these considerably. If you want a gluten-free version, the breadcrumbs aren't essential and the meatballs will be firmer. Or you could replace the breadcrumbs with quinoa; these will be particularly light. And if you want more heat than that given by the ginger, you can always add a couple of chopped green chillies when making the paste.

For the meatballs
½ small onion, or 1 shallot, chopped
2 garlic cloves, chopped
3cm piece of root ginger, chopped
2 lemon grass stalks, tough outer layers removed, sliced
finely grated zest and juice of 1 lime
2 tbsp chopped coriander stems
2 tbsp fish sauce
500g minced chicken thighs
75g breadcrumbs
1 egg, lightly beaten
sea salt and freshly ground black pepper
10 fresh pandan leaves

For the dipping sauce
1 tbsp tamarind paste (not concentrated)
2 tbsp soy sauce
1 tbsp lime juice
1 tsp palm or soft brown sugar, or more to taste
2 chillies, sliced into rounds
1 garlic clove, very finely sliced

For the meatballs, put the onion, garlic, ginger, lemon grass, lime zest and juice, coriander stems and fish sauce in a food processor or blender. Blitz until you have a paste, but don't go too far; you don't want this completely smooth.

Put the chicken in a bowl and add the paste, breadcrumbs and egg. Season with salt and pepper. Mix thoroughly (this is easiest with the hands). Form the mixture into about 20 walnut-sized balls (around 35g each).

Take the pandan leaves and cut in half. Using the thickest parts, wrap the chicken balls. There is no need to do anything too fancy, I just encircle the ball, then twist the leaf slightly so it will encircle the remaining sides and tuck the end underneath. You can angle these slightly differently and do an extra turn if you like.

Put the balls in a steamer – these will fill two layers of a bamboo steamer – and steam over simmering water for 15–20 minutes.

To make the dipping sauce, whisk all the ingredients together until the sugar has dissolved.

Serve the meatballs on their own, with the dipping sauce or dropped into a chicken broth.

VARIATION You can replace 150–200g of the chicken with minced prawns here; they will complement one another well.

Paprika-scented patties with yogurt

This is a Bulgarian dish which I have adapted from Elisabeth Luard's *European Peasant Cookery*. The combination of savoury, smoky, sharp and mellow is quite perfect, with the smokiness of the patties and the creaminess of the yogurt working hard to mellow out both the lemon and tomato. You can add all kinds of vegetables to the sauce, including carrots, pumpkin and cucumber, but I've kept things simple here.

These little patties are quickly browned, then the cooking is finished off in the sauce. If you would rather oven-bake them, treat them in the same way as the *Baked Italian meatballs* (see page 165). The advantage to this is that you can prepare them ahead and simply add to the sauce to reheat when you are ready to eat.

For the patties
500g minced chicken thighs
75g breadcrumbs
2 garlic cloves, finely chopped
1 tsp ground cumin
1 tbsp smoked paprika (sweet or hot, up to you)
finely grated zest and juice of 1 unwaxed lemon
3 tbsp olive oil
sea salt and freshly ground black pepper

For the sauce
1 tbsp olive oil
large knob of unsalted butter
2 leeks, finely sliced
1 green pepper, finely chopped
400g tomatoes, peeled and deseeded, or 400g can of chopped tomatoes

To serve
150ml Greek-style natural yogurt
handfuls of parsley and mint leaves

Make the patties by mixing all the ingredients together with just 1 tbsp of the olive oil, then seasoning with salt and pepper. Shape into 12 small patties or burgers.

Heat the remaining 2 tbsp of olive oil in a non-stick pan, and fry the patties for a couple of minutes on each side until well browned. You will probably have to do this in more than one batch.

To make the sauce, heat the olive oil and butter in a casserole until the butter foams. Add the leeks and green pepper and cook over a low heat until the leeks have softened. Add the tomatoes, bring to the boil, then add all the patties. Simmer for around 20 minutes, covered, then for another five, uncovered, to allow the sauce to thicken a little. Serve with thick yogurt spooned over and sprinkled with mint and parsley.

A pad Thai-inspired omelette

This is very light and one of my favourite summer lunches. You can throw any vegetables in here, really: shredded courgette is good, so are fine green beans cut into thin rounds. There is enough here to serve two, so you can either make one large omelette and cut it in half, or make two separate smaller omelettes. You also don't have to roll the omelette completely, I often just turn one side over and serve it as is in the frying pan.

Serves 2
For the omelette
1 tbsp vegetable oil
1 shallot, sliced
1 carrot, cut into matchsticks
¼ white cabbage, shredded
5g root ginger, finely chopped
1 thin red chilli, sliced
2 garlic cloves, sliced
200g finely chopped or minced chicken
100g beansprouts
slice of unsalted butter
4 eggs, lightly beaten

For the sauce
1 tbsp tamarind water (not concentrated)
1 tbsp fish sauce
1 tsp palm sugar or caster sugar
¼ tsp shrimp paste (optional)
sea salt and freshly ground black pepper

To serve
2 spring onions, shredded
handful of coriander, roughly chopped
1 tsp finely chopped or ground peanuts

Heat the vegetable oil in a frying pan. Add the vegetables, ginger and chilli. Fry over a high heat for two or three minutes until starting to soften, then add the garlic and chicken. Continue to cook, stirring constantly, until the chicken is completely cooked through.

Combine together the sauce ingredients and season with salt and pepper. Pour this over the chicken and vegetables and allow to bubble up, then add the beansprouts and stir for a minute.

Melt the butter in a large, non-stick pan. Add the eggs and swirl around so the base is completely covered. Cook for a couple of minutes until the eggs are almost set, then reduce the heat. Put the chicken and vegetable mixture in a line slightly to one side of the centre of the omelette and sprinkle with the spring onions, coriander

and peanuts. Fold one side of the omelette over the filling, then do the same with the other side. Roll the whole thing over so the filling is completely encased. Cut in half and divide between two plates.

A large pancake or several small fritters, ideal for leftover chicken

The same flavours in the Thai omelette make really good fritters. Use the same ingredients as on page 168, but omit the beansprouts, add around 100g sweetcorn and replace the raw chicken with cooked (the vegetables will all be raw; it's supposed to be really crunchy). Mix the sauce ingredients with 1 tbsp plain flour (this isn't essential, but will help) and 3 eggs, then add all the other ingredients along with lots of coriander leaves. Heat oil in a frying pan and either make one big pancake or lots of small fritters. Serve with a sweet chilli sauce, or whisk together some soy sauce with a few drops of sesame oil.

Circassian chicken with beetroot and chickpeas

This can be made with leftovers, but it's probably best made with chicken thighs. It's a dish best served at room temperature as part of a mezze. As it's quite rich, you don't need anything elaborate with it. If you don't want to make the beetroot, serve it simply with some toasted pitta fingers, grilled red peppers and artichokes. (*Photo opposite.*)

For the chicken
6 skin-on bone-in chicken thighs
500ml well-flavoured chicken stock
2 bay leaves
1 tsp black peppercorns
sea salt
100g walnuts
2 garlic cloves, crushed
1 tsp hot smoked paprika, plus more to serve
juice of ½ a lemon
olive oil, to drizzle

For the beetroot and chickpeas
2 tbsp olive oil
1 tsp cumin, ground or seeds
3 fat, cooked beetroot, skins rubbed off, finely chopped
200g cooked chickpeas (see page 100)
freshly ground black pepper
squeeze of lemon juice
handful of parsley leaves, chopped, to serve

Put the chicken thighs in a saucepan with the stock, bay leaves and peppercorns. Season with salt. Bring to the boil, then reduce the heat and poach gently for 30 minutes until tender. Strain, reserving the stock, then when cool enough to handle, remove the skin and bones and chop up the meat.

Put the walnuts in a food processor and blitz until fine but do not overwork them, as they can turn oily in an instant. Add the garlic and paprika, then drizzle in the chicken stock until you have a smooth sauce.

Mix the sauce and the chicken together and squeeze over the lemon juice. Drizzle over some olive oil and add a sprinkle more paprika.

To make the beetroot, heat the olive oil in a frying pan and add the cumin. Stir for a minute or two, then add the beetroot and chickpeas. Season with salt and pepper. Heat for a minute or two, then squeeze over the lemon juice. Serve at room temperature with parsley sprinkled over.

Larb or Laab

This is lightly spiced minced chicken served over salad leaves, so I normally pile small mounds of it into the cup of Little Gem or endive leaves. This is something I like to vary quite a lot, depending on what I have to hand in the fridge. Hence the Mediterranean version opposite. (*Photo opposite.*)

1 tbsp rice, preferably jasmine
juice of 2 limes, plus lime wedges to serve
50ml chicken stock
2 tbsp fish sauce
2 kaffir lime leaves, bruised
1 green chilli, bruised, plus more, finely sliced, to serve
1 lemon grass stalk, bruised
1 tbsp vegetable oil
300g minced chicken
4 spring onions, finely chopped
sea salt and freshly ground black pepper
handful of green beans, cut into rounds, blanched for one minute
1 tsp caster sugar
leaves from 2–3 large endive or Little Gems
handful of coriander or Thai basil leaves
a few radishes, finely sliced

Toast the rice in a dry frying pan for a couple of minutes, shaking until it is brown. Remove from the pan, cool, then roughly grind.

Put the lime juice, chicken stock and fish sauce in a saucepan with the lime leaves, chilli and lemon grass. Bring to the boil, then remove from the heat and leave to infuse at least for the time it takes to cool down.

Heat the oil in a frying pan and add the chicken and spring onions. Season. Fry quickly until the chicken is browned. Add the blanched green beans. Strain the infused liquid and pour this over the chicken. Simmer for a minute until the chicken is completely cooked through. Sprinkle over the toasted rice. Allow to cool a little, then spoon on to the leaves. Garnish with sprigs of coriander, finely chopped green chilli and slices of radish. Serve with wedges of lime.

MEDITERRANEAN VERSION
This was the happy result of a fridge forage. Fry chicken in olive oil with 1 finely chopped onion, 2 garlic cloves and 1 grated courgette. Add salt, freshly ground black pepper and a large pinch of sweet smoked paprika. Pour over 1 shot of vermouth and let it all bubble down; it should be very creamy, thanks to the courgette. Add lots of shredded basil or mint leaves and a squeeze of lime juice. Cool a little and pile into lettuce or chicory leaves.

Chicken custards

I adore these little savoury custards. They're perfect for a light lunch and brilliant for soaking up leftovers. The texture very much depends on how you cook them. I like them cooked to a very slight wobble, so they are silky smooth; the longer you cook them, the more they will firm up into something more like the texture of omelette.

These are based on *chawanmushi*, which is the Japanese way with savoury custards and is also very similar to the way the Chinese make them. When I use more traditionally British flavours – bacon, herbs, perhaps a little chopped tomato – I reduce the stock by half and melt in some cheese.

4 eggs, lightly beaten
500ml light chicken stock
100ml single cream

1 tsp tamari or light soy sauce
1 tsp mirin
sea salt and freshly ground white pepper
150g cooked chicken meat, chopped
handful of peas
50g shiitake mushrooms
4 spring onions, sliced

Mix together the eggs, stock, cream, tamari and mirin. Season with a little salt and white pepper. Divide the chicken, peas, mushrooms and spring onions between four large ramekins or heatproof bowls. Strain the egg mixture into a jug and then divide it between the ramekins.

Cover each ramekin with cling film and put in a steamer. Steam over a high heat for two minutes, reduce the heat and leave for 20 minutes. When the custards are done, a skewer will come out clean when inserted.

DUMPLINGS

There are zillions of different dumpling recipes, so I've just selected my absolute favourite here. These are worth making huge batches of; you can then open-freeze them until solid, decant into a bag and shake a few out every time you fancy a quick meal.

Chicken gyoza

I very rarely bother making my own wrappers, but have included the recipe anyway in case you find it hard to get hold of them. They're available from any Oriental or Japanese supermarket, usually sold frozen. This mixture will probably give you 50–60 dumplings. If that's too many for one sitting, you can either make them up and open-freeze some of them, or just freeze leftover filling for another time. You could also fry the ingredients as for *Larb* (see page 172), giving you another variation.

For the dipping sauce, I prefer to use a good chilli oil – there are lots of good brands available online. You can instead use a mixture of vegetable and sesame oils with some finely chopped garlic and chilli flakes mixed in. (*Photo on page 176.*)

For the wrappers
150g strong white flour (bread flour), plus more to dust
150g plain flour
½ tsp sea salt
200ml just-boiled water

For the filling
350g minced chicken thighs
150g finely chopped prawns (or increase the chicken to 500g if you don't want to use prawns)
½ pointed green cabbage, very finely shredded and chopped
4 spring onions, very finely chopped
2 tbsp coriander stems, very finely chopped
2 garlic cloves, crushed
2cm piece of root ginger, grated
1 tbsp soy sauce
1 tbsp mirin
1 tsp sesame oil, plus more to serve
sea salt and freshly ground black pepper
1–2 tbsp vegetable oil

For the dipping sauce
2 tbsp chilli oil
2 garlic cloves, finely sliced (if the chilli oil doesn't have garlic)
2 tbsp soy sauce
1 tbsp mirin

For the wrappers, put the flours in a large bowl and whisk to remove any lumps. Add the salt to the just-boiled water. When it has dissolved, make a well in the centre of the flour and gradually incorporate the water, cutting in with a knife until all is combined, then switch to your hands. Flour a work surface and turn the dough out. Knead lightly until smooth. Add more water if the dough is too dry and crumbly or more flour if it's too sticky. Put the dough back in the bowl and cover with a damp cloth or cling film until you are ready to use it.

For the filling, mix all the ingredients together except the vegetable oil and season with salt and pepper.

To make the dipping sauce, mix together all the ingredients.

To assemble the gyoza, divide the dough into four pieces; this will make it more manageable. Dust your work surface and dough with flour, then roll out as thinly as you can. Using an 8cm cutter, cut out rounds. To fill, hold a wrapper in one hand and put 1 tsp of the filling mixture in the centre. Wet around the edges and close them firmly together, making little pleats on the top side as you go. Make sure it is completely sealed. Continue until you have used up all your dough and filling.

To cook, heat the vegetable oil in a large, well-seasoned or non-stick frying pan that has a lid. Put the first batch of dumplings in, being careful not to overcrowd the pan, then pour in around 100ml water. Cover and cook for five minutes until all the water has evaporated, then remove the lid and cook for a further minute for the bottom of the gyoza to crisp up. You should be left with lovely soft, plump dumplings with a crisp underside.

Drizzle the dumplings with a little sesame oil and serve with the dipping sauce.

CHICKEN AND SWEETCORN

This is a combination I love, particularly when they are flavoured with the smoky, spicy notes so popular in South America. The following two dishes are both family favourites and I find they are very good for getting children used to slightly spicy food, as the heat is offset by the sweetness of the corn. Choclo really refers to a variety of corn which has a larger, starchier kernel than sweetcorn. It is hard to get hold of and, really, I prefer sweetcorn anyway.

Pastel de choclo

This is a bit like shepherds or cottage pie, just with a spicier filling and a sweetcorn topping in place of mashed potato.

In South America, it's usually made with a combination of a spiced beef ragu and pieces of roast chicken, but I like making it simply with minced chicken.

For the topping
500g sweetcorn kernels
50g unsalted butter
1 tbsp hasa marina, if you have it, or plain flour
1 tsp baking powder
sea salt
50g cheddar, grated

For the filling
2 tbsp capers, rinsed
2 tbsp green olives, pitted and chopped
1 quantity A sweet, smoky chilli *(see pages 145–146), preferably without the beans*

Preheat the oven to 180°C/fan 160°C/350°F/ gas mark 4. To make the topping, take half the sweetcorn and blitz it in a food processor until quite smooth. Add the butter, hasa marina or flour and baking powder, then season with salt. Blitz again, then add the rest of the sweetcorn and give one final blitz until you have a paste with a dropping consistency.

Add the capers and green olives to the chilli and spoon it into a shallow gratin dish. Top with the sweetcorn mixture, smoothing it out with a palette knife and making sure any gaps are filled. Sprinkle over the cheese and bake in the oven for around 30 minutes until deep golden brown.

Chicken and corn pudding

This is a bit like the sweetcorn and cheese pudding I used to eat as a child, but with a layer of chicken in the middle. It's a brilliant lunch dish as it isn't remotely heavy, thanks to the eggs. I like to use shredded chicken in this, preferably some of the *Pulled chicken* (see page 232).

For the corn
500g sweetcorn kernels, cut from the cob or frozen
50g fine cornmeal or polenta
3 eggs, lightly beaten
100ml double cream
50g cheddar, grated
50g mozzarella, torn into small pieces
knob of unsalted butter

For the filling
250g leftover chicken (either Pulled chicken *(page 232),* A dry Caribbean chicken curry *(page 141), or any of the other curries, as long as there is some sauce)*
large handful of coriander leaves, finely chopped

Preheat the oven to 180°C/fan 160°C/350°F/ gas mark 4.

Put the sweetcorn, cornmeal or polenta, eggs and cream into a food processor with half of each of the cheeses. Blitz until you have a textured purée.

To make the filling, mix together the leftover chicken and sauce and some coriander.

To assemble, put half the sweetcorn mixture in a round, ovenproof dish or casserole. Cover with the chicken, then sprinkle over the remaining cheese. Carefully spread over the rest of the sweetcorn. Dot with butter.

Put the lid on or cover with foil. Bake in the oven for around 30 minutes, then remove the lid or foil to allow the top to brown. Serve cut in wedges.

12. PIES, PASTRIES & PUDDINGS

When it comes to encasing chicken in pastry it seems that, for many people, anything goes. I have found recipes for chicken pies which encompass just about every flavour combination found in this book and a lot more besides. However, narrowing down what I wanted to include here wasn't as tricky as I thought it would be.

This is because I've found that there are a lot of things I don't really want to put in a chicken pie. The main food group that I prefer to avoid is starches. So while I will make occasional exceptions (see, for example, the *Caribbean chicken pattie* on page 184), I usually avoid potatoes and pulses and always rice or other grains. For me, they just sit too heavily with pastry. This means I haven't included *kurnik*, a special occasion Russian pie, which is a bit like a chickeny version of coulibiac.

I'm also quite minimalist about vegetables. Too many and you may as well be making a vegetable pie, as the chicken gets pushed out or diluted to an afterthought. Either that or you become repetitious, duplicating pie ingredients in your side dishes. I have never seen the point of putting large chunks of carrots in a pie and in a side dish. I'd much rather just have the latter, preferably glazed in a little butter.

The sauce is very important as it should hold everything together. Pie fillings should not be stick-in-the-throat dry (another reason why starches aren't a good addition, as they soak up liquid), but they shouldn't be very wet to the point of runny either. I've seen 'pies' that are basically non-thickened stews with a pastry cap that have to be served in bowls with a spoon. That isn't a pie. A proper pie needs to hold its ground when cut into. The ideal is something the consistency of a creamy béchamel or velouté which, when released from its crust, will gently roll out. The liquid must not gush out as soon as you cut into it, that is just too messy and makes for a soggy bottom crust. I ruled out a lot of casserole- and stew-type fillings because of this, as not everything lends itself well to thickening.

That does all sound prescriptive, doesn't it? Sorry.

The chicken is of course key, and so is the stock. Most of these pies need a decent chicken stock. Make a rich brown one and reduce it down a little (by around one-third). A general purpose stock will do, but a stock made with bay and garlic will work with all the recipes in this chapter.

Double-crusted chicken pie

My favourite alternative to roast chicken for Sunday lunch. It has everything: lots of pastry, rich creamy gravy, tender chunks of chicken and a few vegetables for good measure. This version has my preferred flavours of leeks, ham and tarragon. If you have leftover gravy, adding it to the sauce here is one of the best things you can do with it. (*Photo overleaf.*)

Serves 6

For the pastry

350g plain flour, plus more to dust
sea salt
100g unsalted butter, chilled and chopped
100g lard, chopped (or just use 200g butter)
chilled water
1 egg, lightly beaten

For the filling

2 large skinless boneless chicken breasts
3 skinless boneless chicken thighs
slice of unsalted butter
4 large leeks, thickly sliced
1 large sprig of tarragon
50ml white wine
150g ham, preferably from a cooked ham hock, chopped
a few plump prunes, halved (optional)

For the sauce

50g unsalted butter
50g plain flour
400ml chicken stock
200ml whole milk
50ml double cream
1 tsp Dijon mustard
leaves from 1 large sprig of tarragon, finely chopped
freshly ground black pepper

First make the pastry. Put the plain flour into a large bowl (or in your food processor if you prefer) and season with salt. Rub in the butter and lard (if using), then drizzle in chilled water, cutting in with a knife if working by hand, until the dough looks like it will come together. Form into a ball and wrap in cling film. Chill until you need it.

To make the filling, cut the chicken breasts and thighs into large pieces. Heat the butter in a large saucepan and add the leeks. Sauté in the butter, covered, for at least six or seven minutes until the leeks are just starting to soften. Then add the chicken and tarragon sprig. Pour over the wine, then put the lid back on and steam/poach very gently for another 10 minutes.

Meanwhile, start making the sauce. Heat the butter in a saucepan and add the flour to make a roux. Stir for a few minutes until the flour has had a chance to lose its raw flavour, then start adding the stock. When you have incorporated all the stock, add the milk, then finally, stir in the cream, mustard and tarragon. Now strain the contents of the saucepan containing the leeks and chicken through a sieve into the béchamel. Season with salt and pepper.

Preheat the oven to 200°C/fan 180°C/400°F/gas mark 6. Put a baking tray in the oven at the same time.

To assemble the pie, take a large round pie dish around 25cm in diameter. Cut the ball of pastry in two, with one slightly larger (between half and one-third) than the other. Take this and roll it out on a floured work surface until it is large enough to line the pie dish, it should be around 3mm thick. Make sure any cracks are patched up and allow the pastry to overhang slightly.

Put the chicken, vegetables and ham and prunes, if using, in the pie and cover with the

sauce. Stir very gently, to turn everything over. Roll the remaining pastry out and use it to cover the pie. Damp the edges down so they will stick together, then trim and crimp. Cut a couple of holes in the top of the pie.

Brush with egg and put on the preheated baking tray. Bake in the oven for 35–40 minutes until the pastry is golden brown.

VARIATIONS: THE SINGLE CRUST; THE COOKIE CUTTER; THE COBBLER; THE CRUMBLE

As I mention above, I err on the side of caution when choosing vegetables for pie; I'll sometimes put in a mire poix of carrot, onion and celery and add mushrooms (see page 182), but I really prefer my vegetables on the side, so generally keep to chicken and leeks. However, I do like to vary the crust. All of the following can be baked in exactly the same way as the double-crusted pie above, except that you don't need to bother with the heated baking tray as this is there primarily to brown the underside of the bottom layer of pastry.

The chicken pot pie There is an argument that a pie with a single layer of pastry – in other words, a chicken pot pie – isn't a pie at all, just a chicken casserole with a cap on. I agree with this, but I think it is occasionally permissible, especially if you are just using up some pastry left over from something else, which does occasionally happen in my household. Put the filling in a rectangular gratin dish or a pie dish. If you use the pie dish you will probably need a pie bird in the centre to prop it up, and it's always best to cut a strip of pastry to line the rim of the dish before you put the top on; it makes it look more substantial. Use either shortcrust or puff pastry. Brush with beaten egg and cook as above.

The cookie cutter pie This is economical, as it can be made with pastry trimmings. I got the idea from my mother, who improvised a dinner party once because she realised she hadn't enough puff pastry to cover her pie dish, so cut up shapes instead. These were brushed with egg, sat snugly on top of the filling and baked just in the same way as a pie. Don't be tempted to bake them separately: I abhor this practice, it's a silly, cheffy deconstruct as bad as the deconstructed sweet crumble which is the same as eating stewed fruit and granola and who wants that for dessert? The point of the pie is that the underside of the pastry will take on some of the flavour and moisture of the filling while the top is crisping up. Sometimes when I make this version, I take out the ham and add a handful of grated cheese to the sauce, along with 2 tbsp chopped capers, 1 tbsp of ouzo or other aniseed-based spirit, and lots of chopped parsley or dill leaves; in other words, I use the flavours I normally use with fish pie and they work just as well with chicken.

The crumble (and gratin) If you are in a hurry and don't want the bother of chilling and rolling pastry, make a crumble instead. Rub unsalted butter into flour, add any herbs you fancy and even a few rolled oats if you like (I don't, often, but like using oatmeal or spelt flour). Spoon on to the filling and bake as above until golden brown. If you are feeling very economical you can use up stale bread here too and make a gratin: use around 150g stale breadcrumbs, mix in herbs and perhaps some parmesan, spoon on to the filling and dot with unsalted butter. This is one of those times when you can add any finely ground gribenes or crisp chicken skin you have.

The cobbler Finally, if you want a complete change from pastry, you don't have to use any at all, you can make a cobbler, which has a topping of American 'biscuits' which are similar to a UK scone. For this, take 200g self-raising flour and mix it with 1 tsp of baking powder and ½ tsp of salt. Mix in 1 large beaten egg and 75ml buttermilk, the consistency should be firm but sticky. Dollop large spoonfuls of this on top of your chicken filling and bake as above. You can grate cheese on top if you like. I am not sure why, but I like to add chopped, cooked butternut squash or pumpkin (around 150g) and dried sage to the filling when I make cobbler. In my mind, they go together. Incidentally, these are good baked in individual ramekins as they're easier to store in the fridge or freezer for light lunches. I love how they rise up like soufflés.

Chicken and mushroom pies

This is a classic chip shop pie of the sort my husband will buy, I will get huffy about and then not be able to resist, mainly because of the layers of puff pastry which change from brittle, crisp and even slightly burnt, to soft, gravy-soaked under-layers which you can peel away in strips.

I've made these in individual servings so they are very freezer-friendly. You can freeze them raw or cooked and they can be cooked from frozen, it will just impact on how long they take to cook afterwards (50 minutes).

Makes 8

2 x 320g packets ready-rolled puff pastry
50g plain flour, plus more to dust
50g unsalted butter, plus 1 tbsp
750g chicken breast and thigh meat, chopped
1 large onion, finely chopped
2 garlic cloves, finely chopped
1 tsp thyme leaves
300g button mushrooms, sliced
100g Portobello or portobellini mushrooms, very finely chopped
400ml well-flavoured chicken stock
200ml whole milk
1 egg, lightly beaten

Preheat the oven to 200°C/fan 180°C/400°F/gas mark 6. Put a baking tray large enough to hold eight individual pies in the oven.

First line the pie dishes. Take one pack of the puff pastry and roll it out on a floured work surface so it's thinner. Use this to line eight small foil pie dishes; I use oval-shaped ones around 15cm long. Make sure the pastry overhangs a little.

To make the filling, heat the 1 tbsp of butter in a saucepan and add the chicken. Cook until lightly coloured all over, then remove to a bowl. Add the onion. Sauté for a few minutes, then add the garlic, thyme and mushrooms. Cook until the mixture is dry; you will find that the mushrooms give out a lot of liquid, so keep going until it's all gone. Transfer this mixture to a bowl.

Add the 50g of butter to the same saucepan. When it has melted, add the flour to make a roux and stir for a couple of minutes to cook the flour. Gradually add the stock and then all the milk until you have a béchamel sauce.

Drain any liquid from the chicken bowl into the béchamel and cook it in briefly. Add the chicken, onion and mushrooms to the sauce and stir to combine. Cool for a few minutes then spoon into the lined pie dishes; you should be able to fill these to the brim, with a very slight dome.

Roll out the remaining puff pastry very lightly, to be a bit thicker than the base. Dampen the edges down and cover the pies, crimping the edges together. Cut a couple of slits in the top of each pie and brush with egg. Put the pies on the preheated baking tray and bake for around 30 minutes, until puffed up and golden.

POSHER VERSIONS

With wine Replace 50ml of the chicken stock with wine and add this first, before the stock and milk. Cook out for a little longer, so the wine loses its rawness. Add a couple of tbsp finely chopped tarragon or parsley leaves.

With leek and truffle Replace the onion with finely chopped leek. Make the béchamel with wine as before, but add a teaspoon of white truffle oil in at the end along with the parsley.

With dried porcini Soak 25g dried porcini in hot water. Chop the mushrooms finely and add along with the fresh. Use the mushroom-soaking liquor to replace some of the chicken stock. Stir in 1 tbsp marsala at the end as well as a couple of tbsp chopped parsley leaves.

A picnic pie

I was in two minds about whether to make a hot water crust pastry for this pie, but I really prefer the flavour of shortcrust, so stuck with an enriched version of that.

I sometimes like to add a layer of caramelised onions to these pies so, if you would like to include them, follow the instructions for caramelising onions (see page 190), using one-third of the quantity.

Serves 6–8

For the pastry
500g plain flour, plus more to dust
150g unsalted butter, chilled and chopped
100g lard, chilled
2 egg yolks
chilled water
1 egg, lightly beaten

For the filling
750g boneless skinless chicken breast and thigh
100g apples or quince, peeled and finely grated
2 tsp dried sage
½ tsp ground allspice
500g sausagemeat
100g thick-cut ham, cut into large chunks

Preheat the oven to 200°C/fan 180°C/400°F/gas mark 6. Heat a baking tray in the oven.

Make the shortcrust pastry (see page 179), adding the egg yolks before you start cutting in iced water. Chill until needed, then use two-thirds of it to line a 20cm springform cake tin, making sure it overhangs the edges, reserving one-third of it for the crust.

Slice the chicken thinly on the diagonal, to give a greater surface area. Add the fruit, sage and allspice to the sausagemeat and mix. Spread half the sausagemeat over the pie crust, making sure it is pushed down firmly around the edges, then top with all the chicken and ham. Top with the remaining sausagemeat. Cover with the reserved pastry and crimp the edges of the vertical sides of the pie over the horizontal. Make a couple of slits in the top for escaping steam. Brush the top of the pie with egg.

Put in the oven on the preheated baking tray and bake for 50 minutes. Check the internal temperature has reached 75°C (167°F), or that an inserted skewer is very hot to touch. Leave to stand in the tin for at least 10 minutes. Carefully remove the sides of the tin and leave to cool.

CARIBBEAN CHICKEN PATTIES

These are the lurid yellow pastries you find all over the Caribbean, especially in Jamaica. There are few things better than to put in these than some leftover *Caribbean chicken curry* (see pages 141–142), supplemented with some cooked, finely chopped regular potato or white sweet potato and some peas. But if you don't have any of this and want to make something much quicker from scratch, follow the recipe below instead. Annatto seeds are used for colour throughout the Caribbean – if you can't find them, use turmeric instead.

Makes 10–12

For the filling
1 large regular potato, or sweet white potato (not orange!), finely chopped
250g minced chicken
sea salt and freshly ground black pepper
50g garden peas or petits pois
1 tbsp vegetable oil
4 spring onions, sliced into thin rounds
2 garlic cloves, finely chopped
3cm piece of root ginger, finely chopped
1 tsp thyme leaves
½ tsp allspice berries, finely ground
2 cloves, finely ground
1 tsp mild curry powder
50ml coconut cream (optional)

For the pastry
200g plain flour, plus more to dust
½ tsp turmeric or ½ tsp ground annatto seeds
sea salt
100g lard or schmaltz or unsalted butter, chilled and chopped

Bring a saucepan of water to the boil, add the potato and boil for three minutes, then drain. Set aside to cool.

Now make the pastry. Mix the flour with the turmeric, if using, and season with salt. If you are using the annatto, bash it about a bit and soak it in a little chilled water. Add the fat to the flour and rub it in until you have a mixture resembling breadcrumbs. Add chilled water (coloured or not with annatto), 1 tbsp at a time, cutting in with a knife, until you have a dough that will hold together. Knead very lightly into a ball, wrap in cling film and chill.

To make the filling, put the chicken in a large bowl and season with salt and pepper. Add the blanched potato and peas. Heat the vegetable oil in a frying pan and fry the spring onions, garlic and ginger for a few minutes and add this to the chicken. Sprinkle over the thyme and spices, add the coconut cream if using, then mix thoroughly.

Preheat the oven to 200°C/fan 180°C/400°F/gas mark 6.

Roll the pastry out thinly on a floured surface and cut into 15cm rounds. Place 2 tbsp filling in one half of each round, then fold over, wet the edges and crimp together. Press round the curved edges with the tines of a fork.

Place on a baking tray and bake in the oven for around 25 minutes, until the pastry is browning and the filling is piping hot.

VARIATION: EMPANADAS, OLD AND NEW WORLD

For these, I use the same dough as above, without the turmeric, but with the addition of some sweet smoked paprika. They should be made smaller, 10–12cm diameter.

For an Iberian version, I fill them with chicken, onion and chorizo. Finely chop a large cooking chorizo (you decide whether you want to use *picante* or *dulce*) and dry-fry it until the fat runs. Drain off most of the fat and set the chorizo aside, then add a finely chopped onion and cook it until it is sweet, soft and translucent. Add garlic, thyme and a little more sweet smoked paprika, then mix with either 250g minced chicken or the same amount of finely chopped cooked chicken. Stir in lots of chopped parsley leaves and season well.

For a more South American version, I'll use smoked or unsmoked bacon instead of chorizo, add cumin as well as sweet smoked paprika and stir in lots of chopped coriander.

Fill either in the same way as the Jamaican patties and bake for around 20 minutes. Fruit – especially dried fruit – is often added to these, but I'm not keen, so I don't.

Savoury tart of wood-smoked chicken, Jerusalem artichokes and chard

This uses a nutty flavoured spelt flour in the pastry as I think it really complements the other components of this tart. However, regular plain flour works just as well if you prefer.

There are all kinds of things I like to put in this kind of tart, really depending on the time of year. Smoked chicken is great with just about anything that works well with smoky bacon; I also really love it with roasted cauliflower and peas, or mushrooms and any kind of green, especially chard, sprouting broccoli or cavolo nero.

Serves 6–8

For the pastry

250g spelt flour
sea salt
150g unsalted butter, chilled and chopped
1 egg yolk
chilled water

For the filling

25g unsalted butter
1 leek, finely chopped
1 sprig of thyme
300g Jerusalem artichokes, peeled and sliced
200g chard leaves, shredded (save the stems for something else)
200g smoked chicken, roughly pulled
sea salt and freshly ground black pepper
½ tsp finely grated unwaxed lemon zest
4 eggs, lightly beaten
300ml double cream (or a mixture of double cream and whole milk)
freshly grated nutmeg

Make the pastry by whisking the flour in a bowl with a large pinch of salt to remove any lumps. Add the butter and rub it into the flour until it resembles fine breadcrumbs. Add the yolk, cutting it in with a knife and drizzle in chilled water, mixing constantly until you have a firm pastry. Wrap in cling film and chill for 30 minutes, then roll it out to line a 28cm flan dish (I use quite a deep ceramic dish). Allow some overhang. Prick the pastry all over with a fork and put in the freezer for 20 minutes.

At the same time, preheat the oven to 200°C/fan 180°C/400°F/gas mark 6 and put a large baking tray in there to heat.

Line the pastry case with baking parchment and cover with baking beans. Put on the baking tray and bake in the oven

for 15 minutes, then remove the baking beans and parchment and bake for a further five minutes.

Meanwhile, to make the filling, melt the butter in a saucepan and sauté the leek with the sprig of thyme until very soft and translucent. Put the artichokes in a saucepan and cover with water. Simmer until tender – around 15 minutes – adding the chard for the last couple of minutes. Drain thoroughly.

Spread the leeks, Jerusalem artichokes and chard over the base of the pastry case. Add the chicken, then season with salt and pepper and sprinkle over the lemon zest. Mix the eggs and cream together then pour this over the lot. Add a very fine grating of nutmeg.

Bake in the oven on the preheated baking tray for 30–35 minutes until the tart has just set; you want it to have a slight wobble in the centre. Remove and trim the edges of the pastry if necessary. Serve slightly warmer than room temperature, with a green salad containing lots of bitter greens, such as frisee, and perhaps some slices of green apple.

Chicken and apricot tart

You don't have to use apricots here, the recipe I based this on used plums, while peaches would also be good if they are sweet and have a good flavour. In fact, using canned peaches would be no bad thing, as long as you drain and dry them thoroughly, it would make this tart a useful assemblage from leftovers and storecupboard ingredients.

Serves 4–6

320g sheet of ready-rolled puff pastry
plain flour, to dust
1 tbsp olive oil
1 onion, finely chopped
6 fresh apricots, 4 finely chopped, 2 sliced into wedges
sea salt and freshly ground black pepper
¼ tsp ground cinnamon
¼ tsp ground allspice
pinch of ground cloves
freshly grated nutmeg
300g cooked chicken, pulled into rough chunks
leaves from a few small sprigs of thyme or lemon thyme
up to 1 tsp soft light brown sugar (optional)
a few slices of taleggio (optional)
1 egg, lightly beaten

Preheat the oven to 200°C/fan 180°C/400°F/ gas mark 6.

Take the pastry and roll it out on a floured surface, then transfer to a baking sheet. Score a 2cm border all the way around with a sharp knife, making sure you don't cut right the way through the pastry.

Heat the olive oil in a frying pan and add the onion. Fry until very soft, translucent and starting to caramelise around the edges. Add the chopped apricots and cook for a further couple of minutes until they start releasing their juices. Season with salt and pepper and sprinkle in the spices. Remove from the heat and stir in the chicken. Spread this mixture over the puff pastry, making sure you don't cover the border. Sprinkle on the thyme leaves, then arrange the apricot wedges evenly over the top. Sprinkle the sugar, if using, over the top of the apricots.

If you want to use the cheese, dot a few squares of it around, too. Brush the pastry border with egg.

Bake in the preheated oven for 30–35 minutes until the apricot wedges have caramelised and the sides of the tart have puffed up and turned a deep golden brown.

Bestilla

This was one of those things that I have eaten countless times and was loathe to make, as I thought it would be too much of a fiddle, with so many ingredients to balance – not to mention the filo assemblage to attempt. I shouldn't have worried as it turned out to be much more straightforward than I had imagined.

This pie is often made with pigeon. You could add a couple of chicken livers to this recipe if you prefer to emulate the slightly gamier flavour.

Serves 6–8
1 tbsp olive oil
4 fat skinless boneless chicken thighs (600–700g)
1 large onion, finely chopped
5cm piece of root ginger, grated
2 garlic cloves, finely chopped
½ tsp ground cinnamon, plus ¼ tsp (optional)
½ tsp turmeric
1 tsp cardamom pods, seeds only, finely ground
¼ tsp freshly grated nutmeg
pinch of saffron strands
500ml chicken stock or water
sea salt and freshly ground black pepper
4 eggs, lightly beaten
125g ground almonds or pistachios
50g finely chopped dried apricots or dates
1 tbsp orange blossom water
1 tsp finely grated orange zest
1 tsp finely grated unwaxed lemon zest, plus juice of ½ lemon
handful of parsley leaves, finely chopped
handful of coriander, finely chopped
320g packet of filo pastry (around 6 rectangular slices)
25g unsalted butter, melted
1 tbsp icing sugar (optional)

Heat the oil in a large, shallow frying pan or casserole (you will need one with a lid). Fry the chicken on both sides until well browned, then remove. Add the onion, ginger and garlic and sauté over a gentle heat until the onion is translucent. Sprinkle over the spices and cook for another minute. Pour over the stock or water and allow to bubble, scraping up any brown bits which have stuck to the bottom of the pan. Return the chicken and season with salt and pepper. Heat to a gentle simmer, cover and cook for around 30 minutes, until the chicken is tender.

Remove the chicken from the pan and set aside. Increase the heat under the pan and boil until reduced by half. When the chicken is cool enough to handle, remove the skin and cut into small pieces, allowing some of it to shred.

When the cooking liquid is well reduced, reduce the heat. Stir in the eggs and mix until you have something that resembles a richly coloured, creamy scrambled eggs. Don't overcook at this stage as you don't want them to completely curdle. Sprinkle in the ground almonds – this will help stop the eggs from curdling – and combine thoroughly.

Sprinkle in the apricots or dates and add the orange blossom water, the zests and lemon juice, the herbs and, finally, the shredded chicken. Remove from the heat and allow to cool. At this stage, you can chill the mixture until you are ready to make the pie.

Preheat the oven to 200°C/fan 180°C/400°F/gas mark 6. Place a baking tray inside to warm up.

Take a large 28cm flan dish (mine is ceramic). Take the first sheet of filo pastry and brush it with butter. Lie it across the dish so the centre of the pastry sheet is in the centre of the dish. Tuck the pastry into the edges of the dish and let the rest overhang. Repeat, this time arranging the sheet at right angles to the first. Arrange the next two sheets on the diagonals to this first pastry cross, each time making sure you push the pastry to the edge of the dish. Fill the pastry with the filling, then drape over the overhanging pastry, in reverse order (start with the last sheet you laid in the dish and finish with the first). You should find the filling is completely covered. Finally, take the remaining pieces of filo and cut into squares to fit the dish, trim the corners or tuck them down the sides. Brush with more butter.

Bake in the oven on the preheated baking tray for 20–25 minutes until golden brown. Sprinkle with a little icing sugar and cinnamon, if you like.

Chicken and onion suet pudding

This layered suet pudding is quite labour-intensive, but worth it, I think. Just in case you fancy a chicken suet pudding without spending ages caramelising onions, I've added a quicker option at the end.

Serves 4–6
For the filling
25g unsalted butter
4 large onions, finely sliced (around 600g)
1 sprig of thyme
2 bay leaves
2 star anise
1 tsp caster sugar
1 garlic clove, finely chopped
sea salt and freshly ground black pepper
4–5 skinless boneless chicken thighs, flattened

For the pastry
200g self-raising flour, plus more to dust
1 tsp thyme leaves (optional)
25g unsalted butter, chilled and chopped, plus more for the pudding basin
75g suet
chilled water

For the gravy
300ml Noilly Prat or white wine
300ml well-flavoured chicken stock
50ml double cream

Start the filling first. Melt the butter in a wide, lidded frying pan or casserole. Add the onions, herbs and star anise. Stir until completely coated in the butter, then reduce the heat to low and cover. Cook gently for 20 minutes, turning every so often, until the onions are soft. Remove the lid and increase the heat. Sprinkle in the sugar and cook for a further 10–15 minutes, stirring every couple of minutes, until the onions are sticky and a rich caramel colour. Add the garlic and season with salt and pepper.

Prepare the chicken – slice the thighs as thinly as you can so you have a large surface area – the best way to do this is to slice them diagonally into thin medallions.

To make the pastry, put the flour in a bowl and add a generous pinch of salt and the thyme, if using. Rub in the butter until the mixture looks like very fine breadcrumbs then stir in the suet. Gradually add up to 100ml of chilled water, cutting it in with a

knife, until you have a soft, pliable dough. Wrap in cling film and chill until you are ready to use.

Roll the pastry out on a floured surface into a round, then cut a quarter segment out of it. Generously butter a one-litre pudding basin and use the larger piece of pastry to line it, overlapping the two straight edges and making sure they are seamlessly pressed together. Make sure there aren't any holes anywhere and that the edges overlap the basin.

Add the filling: put one-third of the onions in the base of the pudding (leave behind the herbs and star anise), then add a layer of chicken and season with salt and pepper. Continue until you have used up all the onion and chicken. Don't wash up the onion frying pan; you'll need it later. Shape the remaining piece of pastry into a round, brush around the edge with water and place this on top, pressing the edges together. If your basin isn't lidded, cover with foil, making a pleat in the centre to allow for rising.

To cook the pudding, place in a steamer basket over a saucepan or, failing that, fold up a tea towel inside a large saucepan and place the basin on that. Steam for 1½–2 hours. To do this in a pressure cooker, use the upturned steamer basket or a tea towel. Steam for 15 minutes, then at high pressure for a further 30 minutes. Allow the pressure to drop naturally.

To make the gravy, use the same pan you fried the onions in. Leave in the herbs and star anise and pour over the vermouth. Bring to the boil and stir, scraping the base of the pan until it is clean to help give the gravy a good rich flavour. Reduce the vermouth by half, then add the stock. Reduce the liquid by half again, then add the cream. Simmer until the gravy has thickened slightly, then strain into a jug or gravy boat.
Release the pudding from its basin by running a palette knife around the edge, then turn it out on to a serving plate. Serve with plenty of gravy. This is good with mashed potato and spring greens.

VARIATION: A FASTER WAY
You can make a much quicker suet pudding without having to pre-cook any of the ingredients. Take 300g chopped chicken, 2 sliced leeks and 100g button mushrooms. Put them in a large bowl and dust with 1 tbsp seasoned plain flour. You can leave the flour plain, or add dried herbs, 1 tsp sweet smoked paprika, English mustard powder, or – continuing the slightly sweet Chinese flavours – Chinese 5-spice which works remarkably well with leeks. Toss everything in the flour, then pile into the suet pastry-lined basin and proceed as above.

For this one, you don't have to follow the same gravy recipe, instead use some leftover gravy (follow the recipe with *My best roast chicken*, see page 59) or try it with *Caper sauce* (see pages 46–47).

13. CHICKEN SALADS

I'm sure I'm not the only one who came to the delights of salad well into adulthood. I grew up in a time way before all the ingredients we take for granted today became so readily available. No rocket, no variety in salad leaves (it was floppy green lettuce or Iceberg, that was it) and beetroot was always pickled. Salads at school or in restaurants tended to be either creamy, heavy affairs: egg mayonnaise, or Waldorf, or a revolting version of Salade Olivier made with reconstituted vegetables that makes me shudder thinking about it now, or simply standard salad ingredients doused in salad cream and too often an afterthought or a garnish. I fared much better at home, because at least then the ingredients were home-grown and the eggs freshly laid.

Now, I find a salad the most satisfying of dishes to put together. Partly because I love trying out different combinations and achieving that fine balancing act between main ingredients and dressing, but also because they just look so beautiful. I experiment a lot and don't always win (I couldn't eat dill for months after an unfortunate experiment with tahini dressing that turned my stomach) but, when I do, the results are superb.

Of course, when it comes to chicken and salad, I don't want the chicken stuck on top as an afterthought, just because it is there and available, a bit of necessary-but-unappreciated protein. There are few things as unimaginative and soul-destroying as a load of limp salad topped with some anaemic and dried-out-looking chicken strips; this belongs to the people who see salad as the worthy option, more to be endured than enjoyed. I have no truck with that. The connection between the chicken and the other ingredients must be thought through and the chicken must be integral to the salad, otherwise there is no point to it being there.

All recipes serve four, though the chicken oyster salad will do so only as a starter.

Chicken tarragon salad, two ways

This has two dressings, one a classic creamy version and the other more like a salsa verde. You can make either, or use both, as I think they really work well together.

The chicken breasts are barbecued or grilled here and I do like to give them a citrus wash first. But you can of course skip this step and either just grill some chicken or use some leftovers. This is very good to eat with roasted new potatoes.

For the salad
2 chicken breasts, butterflied and flattened (see page 11)
lime or lemon juice, to citrus wash (optional)
1 tbsp olive oil
100g runner beans, cooked until tender
sea salt and freshly ground black pepper
100g bag of watercress, coarse stalks removed
a few flaked almonds or pine nuts, lightly toasted

For the creamy tarragon dressing
2 tbsp sour cream
1 tbsp olive oil
1 tsp lime juice
1 tsp white wine vinegar
pinch of caster sugar
2 tbsp finely chopped tarragon leaves
1 tbsp warm water, if necessary, to thin

For the salsa verde tarragon dressing
25g tarragon leaves (and the softer stems), finely chopped
25g parsley, finely chopped
finely grated zest and juice of 1 lime
5 tbsp olive oil

If you are citrus washing your chicken, follow the instructions on page 23. Heat a griddle until smoking. Rub the chicken with the olive oil, then grill; it should only need two minutes on each side. Leave to rest for a few minutes, then slice into strips.

Meanwhile, blanch the runner beans in boiling salted water for three to four minutes, or until tender.

Whisk together the dressing ingredients. Assemble all the salad ingredients in a bowl or serving platter and add the chicken pieces. Drizzle over the salad dressing(s) – if using both, add the creamy version first.

Chicken with artichokes and a saffron dressing

This is ridiculously simple, once you have sorted out the chicken. Poach it (see page 46), then drain and put on a hot griddle to get some char marks and add smokiness. Slice thinly on the diagonal. (*Photo opposite.*)

For the salad
100g bag of lamb's lettuce
280g jar of artichoke hearts in olive oil, drained and rinsed to get rid of excess oil (or fresh artichoke hearts, if you want to exert yourself), plus 1 tbsp oil from the jar
finely grated zest of 1 unwaxed lemon
2 freshly poached chicken breasts, griddled and sliced
sea salt and freshly ground black pepper

For the saffron dressing
large pinch of saffron strands, soaked in a little warm water for 30 minutes
100ml Greek-style natural yogurt
juice of ½ lemon
pinch of caster sugar

Arrange the salad leaves and artichokes on a plate and sprinkle over the lemon zest. Add the chicken breast and season with salt and pepper. Drizzle over the olive oil.

Whisk the saffron into the yogurt and add the lemon juice and sugar. Add hot water until you have a smooth dressing and drizzle this over the salad.

Chicken, avocado and Little Gem salad

This is a standard salad, much beloved in my house for the buttery avocado. It's pepped up with a smoky paprika dressing. Blue cheese is something I occasionally add as it is good with all the other ingredients, but it is entirely up to you whether to include it.

As with the chicken tarragon salad, sautéed potatoes are really good here, as are traditional croutons.

For the marinade (optional)
1 tbsp sea salt
finely grated zest and juice of 1 lime
1 tbsp olive oil
1 tsp sweet smoked paprika
1 tsp dried thyme

For the salad
2 chicken breasts, butterflied (see page 11)
1 large avocado, chopped
4 Little Gems, cut into wedges lengthways
75g blue cheese (optional)
a few basil leaves, to serve (optional)

For the dressing
1 tbsp olive oil
1 garlic clove, finely chopped
2 ripe tomatoes, very finely chopped and drained
1 tsp balsamic vinegar
squeeze of lime juice
½ tsp sweet smoked paprika
sea salt and freshly ground black pepper

If marinating the chicken, mix all the ingredients for the marinade together and rub it over the chicken. Leave for one hour or so in the fridge. When you are ready to cook, heat a griddle and cook the chicken, it should not take more than a couple of minutes on each side.

Arrange the avocado, Little Gems and blue cheese, if using, in a salad bowl or serving platter. To make the dressing, heat the olive oil, then cook the garlic for a scant minute. Add the tomatoes and, after a minute, remove from the heat; the idea isn't to cook the tomatoes, just to help them release their juices. Add the other dressing ingredients and season with salt and pepper.

Cut or tear up the chicken and add to the salad bowl. Drizzle over the warm dressing and sprinkle with basil leaves, if you want.

Chicken oysters with griddled chicory and mustard dressing

This is one to do if you can bear to save the oysters from a roast or poached chicken just to be able to make a salad. If you can't, then use some leftover cooked chicken instead.

For the salad
2–3 heads of red chicory, quartered lengthways
12 cooked chicken oysters
enough chicken stock to cover
couple of handfuls of lamb's lettuce
a few chives, finely chopped

a few salted capers, rinsed and drained
a few micro basil leaves, or small basil leaves

For the dressing
1 tbsp Dijon mustard
1 tbsp olive oil
1 tsp honey
½ tsp freshly ground black pepper
2 tsp balsamic, fig or sherry vinegar (a fairly sweet one)
dash of Tabasco
sea salt

Immerse the chicory in water briefly and shake off any excess. Heat a griddle until smoking, then put in the chicory, cut-sides down, and cook until it has char lines across it and has started to wilt. Remove from the griddle and set aside.

Put the chicken oysters in a small pan and cover with stock. Place over a low heat until the chicken oysters are just heated through and very tender.

To make the dressing, whisk all the ingredients together with some salt and pepper, then add some of the chicken stock from the pan until you have a smooth dressing, just thick enough to cling to the salad ingredients.

Arrange the lamb's lettuce on a serving plate, then add the chicory. Heat the griddle until smoking once more. Strain the oysters. Dip them very briefly in the dressing and put on the griddle, just for a few moments on each side, to add a little crispness and shine. Arrange these on top of the salad leaves, and then sprinkle over the chives and capers.

Drizzle over more of the dressing and serve, sprinkled with the basil leaves.

Chicken, peach and freekeh salad with a citrus and pomegranate molasses dressing

Or 'freekin' chicken' as my husband calls it. I don't seem to be able to get enough of freekeh. It is my favourite grain, thanks to its smoky, nutty flavour and dense, chewy texture. And unlike brown rice and barley and various other grains – which make me feel as though what I'm eating is too worthy to be delicious – every mouthful is a joy.

For the freekeh
150g freekeh
25g unsalted butter
1 onion, finely chopped
2 garlic cloves, finely chopped
½ tsp ground allspice
2 tbsp finely chopped parsley stems
300ml chicken stock
sea salt and freshly ground black pepper

For the rest
1 tbsp olive oil
500g skinless boneless chicken thighs, cut into bite-sized pieces
juice of 1 lemon
juice of 1 orange
3 tbsp pomegranate molasses
watercress or other robust salad greens, any coarse stalks removed
large handfuls of mint and parsley leaves
1 large ripe peach (or 2–3 of the flat sort), peeled and cut into chunks
a few fresh or dried rose petals

Put the freekeh in a large bowl and cover generously with water. Leave for five minutes, then drain it well. Heat the butter in a heavy-

based saucepan. Add the onion and garlic and sauté over a low heat for around five minutes, until softened. Add the allspice and parsley stems. Add the drained freekeh and stir for a couple of minutes until well coated with the buttery onions. Pour in the stock and season with salt and pepper. Bring to the boil, reduce the heat and cover. Simmer very gently until all the liquid is absorbed. Remove from the heat and leave to steam with the lid on for a few minutes.

Meanwhile, cook the chicken. Heat the olive oil in a large frying pan. Add the chicken and brown quickly on all sides. Mix together the lemon juice, orange juice and pomegranate molasses and pour half of this mixture over the chicken. Continue to cook the chicken, stirring frequently, until it has taken on a sheen from the molasses and is cooked through. If it crisps up round the edges, all to the good.

Arrange the watercress on a large serving platter and cover with the freekeh, forking it up slightly. Add half the chicken, herbs and peach and gently fold into the freekeh. Scatter the remaining ingredients on top with the rose petals and pour over the rest of the pomegranate molasses dressing. This is best served at room temperature.

Caribbean chicken, christophene and mango salad

Christophene is like a cross between a squash and a crisp melon. It's pear shaped, very refreshing and can be eaten raw or cooked. If you can't find it, use unripe melon or cucumber instead.

Seasoning peppers are almost impossible to get hold of here: they're a very mild, fragrant pepper similar in appearance and flavour to scotch bonnets but without the searing heat. I'm hoping that one day they will be as widely available here as they are in the Caribbean.

For the salad

1 christophene, deseeded and coarsely grated
1 carrot, coarsely grated
sea salt and freshly ground black pepper
3cm piece of root ginger, grated, juices saved (see page 161)
200g cooked chicken, finely chopped
200g bag of salad leaves
1 small, fairly firm but ripe mango, peeled and sliced
1 red pepper, sliced
4 spring onions, shredded
2 celery sticks, finely chopped
1 seasoning pepper, finely chopped, or ¼ green pepper plus ¼ scotch bonnet, finely chopped
a little olive oil
a little lime juice

For the dressing

2 tbsp olive oil
2 tbsp natural yogurt
1 tsp cider vinegar
1 garlic clove, crushed
dash of Pickapeppa or Worcestershire sauce
½ tsp Dijon mustard
½ tsp hot sauce (make sure it's a scotch bonnet one)
juice of ½ lime

Put the christophene and carrot in a bowl. Season with salt and black pepper, then squeeze over the grated ginger (throw away the ginger fibres). Add a splash of water and toss. Leave until you have prepared the rest of the ingredients, then drain and wring out slightly.

Spread the salad leaves over a large platter, then sprinkle over the carrot and christophene. Arrange the chicken and the other salad ingredients on top. Drizzle over some oil and squeeze over some lime. Season with salt and pepper.

Whisk together the dressing ingredients, adding a little water towards the end if it's too thick. Drizzle over the salad and serve.

Wood-smoked chicken with Puy lentils, fennel and a blackberry vinaigrette

The fennel here works to cut through all the earthier flavours, but sometimes I want to stick with the autumnal feel of this salad. Then I will add some roasted pumpkin or onion squash to the lentils in place of the fennel. I would also add some toasted pumpkin seeds. You need ripe, very fragrant blackberries for this. (*Photo opposite.*)

For the dressing
50g blackberries
2 tbsp apple juice
1 tbsp blackberry vinegar or 1 tbsp crème de mûre mixed with 1 tsp cider vinegar
½ tsp Dijon mustard (optional)
4 tbsp olive oil or a nut oil (hazelnut is good, if you have it)

For the salad
200g cooked Puy lentils, still quite al dente
1 fennel bulb, shredded
2 cooked beetroot, cut into wedges
couple of large handfuls of rocket or spinach
leaves from a few sprigs of thyme
a few blackberries (to garnish)
2 smoked chicken breasts (see pages 24–26)

To make the dressing, heat the blackberries very gently in a small saucepan with the apple juice; this is not to really cook them, just to release their wonderful aroma and make their juices bleed out. Remove from the heat and add the blackberry vinegar or crème de mûre and cider vinegar, the mustard, if using, then whisk in the olive oil. Add a little more liquid if you think it needs to be thinner.

Mix the lentils, fennel, beetroot, leaves and thyme together, then slice the chicken breasts and add those, too. Sprinkle over some of the dressing and top with the blackberries. Serve the remaining dressing on the side.

Chicken with blood oranges and cauliflower 'couscous'

Cauliflower 'couscous' is one of those things much loved by anyone on a low-carb diet. I am definitely not one of those, but I do love cauliflower's sweet nuttiness and think it is wonderful here as a foil for the gently spiced chicken. You do not have to cook the cauliflower if you don't want to, but I think a little softening and browning helps it along no end.

You can add any salad vegetables to this; I've kept it simple with just some herbs and watercress leaves.

For the salad
4 tbsp natural yogurt
juice of 1 orange
pinch of saffron strands

¼ tsp ground cinnamon
¼ tsp ground cumin
¼ tsp cayenne pepper
¼ tsp turmeric
¼ tsp ground ginger
sea salt and freshly ground black pepper
4 bone-in skin-on chicken thighs
a little olive oil
splash of chicken stock or water
2 oranges, peeled and segmented, reserving any juice
dash of sherry vinegar
handful of watercress, coarse stalks removed
chopped parsley and mint leaves

For the cauliflower couscous
1 cauliflower, broken into florets
1 tbsp olive oil
1 tsp fennel seeds
1 tsp nigella seeds
finely grated zest of 1 orange (from one of the oranges you are using for the salad)

Mix together the yogurt, orange juice and spices. Season and pour over the chicken thighs. Leave to marinate for at least a couple of hours, or overnight.

When you are ready to cook, heat some olive oil in a frying pan. Scrape off as much of the marinade from the chicken as possible, add the chicken to the frying pan and brown well on both sides. Add a splash of stock or water and braise the chicken, partially covered, for around 20 minutes, topping up the liquid when necessary.

Remove the chicken from the frying pan, cut out the bone and cut the meat into bite-sized pieces. (Or you could serve the thighs whole.) Deglaze the pan with any orange juice you have from segmenting the oranges and a little sherry vinegar.

To make the couscous, put the cauliflower in a food processor. Blitz until it is the texture of large breadcrumbs. (You may have to do this in more than one batch.)

Heat the 1 tbsp olive oil in a large, non-stick frying pan. Add the fennel and nigella seeds and roast for one minute, then coat the base of the pan with water (around 100ml). Evenly spread the cauliflower crumbs over the frying pan and season with some salt and pepper. Sprinkle over the orange zest. Cook over a medium heat for around five minutes, stirring regularly, until the water has evaporated and the cauliflower is quite dry. Remove from the heat. You should find that the cauliflower will 'fluff up' in a similar way to couscous when you fork it over.

To assemble, arrange the salad greens on a plate. Spoon over the couscous then arrange the chicken and oranges over that. Drizzle over the glaze from the frying pan and sprinkle with the herbs.

Chicken succotash

This is Native American succotash, adapted slightly to include squash or pumpkin, thus combining ingredients from their traditional 'three sisters' method of growing corn, beans and squash together. This year my son was desperate to grow 'bean stalks' and I thought this grouping was the most dramatic for children, as the beans and corn grow very tall, the vegetation is lush and the squash or pumpkins can be prolific and grow to huge sizes. This salad came after several meals of gorging on buttery corn on the cob.

The herb of choice with a regular succotash seems to be basil, but you don't have to stick to this. Savory or thyme is lovely if added at the sauté stage, and I like using coriander at the end in place of the basil.

4 boneless skin-on chicken thighs, or 200g cooked chicken meat
1 tsp hickory smoked salt (or any other smoked salt)
1 tsp dried oregano
1 tbsp olive oil (optional)
knob of unsalted butter (optional)
1 large onion, finely chopped
200g pumpkin or squash, chopped
300g courgette (1 large), chopped
2 garlic cloves, finely chopped
2 sweetcorn cobs
200g broad beans, fresh or frozen
200g runner beans, cut into diamonds
250g cooked black-eyed peas (tinned is fine, or any other type of bean)
sea salt and freshly ground black pepper
large handful of basil or coriander leaves

If you are using chicken thighs, preheat the oven to 220°C/fan 200°C/425°F/gas mark 7. Put the chicken, skin-side down, in a large, shallow, ovenproof pan and cook over a high heat for around 10 minutes until well browned. Turn over, sprinkle with the smoked salt and dried herbs, then transfer to the oven. Cook for a further 15–20 minutes until cooked through. Remove from the oven and transfer to a plate. Keep warm. If there is a lot of rendered chicken fat in the pan, you should strain some of this off, especially if you think you are likely to have leftovers as you don't want it unpleasantly greasy from the fridge.

If you are using cooked chicken, add olive oil and butter to the pan. When the butter is foaming, add the onion, pumpkin or squash, courgette and garlic. Stir over a high heat for a couple of minutes, then cover and leave to cook for five minutes, by which point the vegetables should be cooked through, but not tender to the point of breaking up. Meanwhile, prepare the corn. You have a choice here. You can either heat a griddle pan or barbecue and char the corn on all sides, until blackened in patches, then cut the kernels from the cob. Or you can cut the kernels from the cob first, then dry-fry them in a frying pan until they take on some colour. I find the latter much quicker and easier, so will usually do this.

Bring a pan of water to the boil, add the broad beans and runner beans and blanch for two minutes. Drain.

Add the corn, black-eyed peas, broad beans and flat beans to the pumpkin pan. Cut the chicken into thin slices, skin and all, and add this to the pan, too. Season with salt and pepper, then stir to combine. Heat until just warmed through, then serve with lots of herbs.

Leftovers This is great the next day, if you let it return to room temperature and perhaps freshen it up with a drizzle of olive oil and a squeeze of lime juice. Alternatively, put the lot back in a saucepan, add a splash of water and stock and heat through. Stir through a large handful of grated cheese – cheddar is fine – and stir until melted. Serve hot.

Ginger-scented chicken with cucumber, basil and cherries

This recipe came about when I was casting my eye around the kitchen, wondering what I could put with some eftover ginger-scented chicken just when I happened to have a large box of cherries to hand. I was surprised how well it worked: cool cucumbers, fragrant,

peppery basil and sweet cherries combine beautifully together. A caveat, though: the cherries have to have a good flavour or there's really no point.

I tried this recipe two ways and everyone loved both, so here they are. The first is sweet, summery and delicate; the second a bit more robust. (*Photo opposite.*)

For the salad
200g leftover Ginger-scented chicken *(see pages 54–56)*
ladleful of chicken stock
couple of handfuls of lamb's lettuce or oak leaf lettuce
1 large cucumber, peeled, deseeded and cut into thin crescents
3 spring onions, halved and shredded lengthways
handful of basil leaves
100g cherries, pitted and halved

For the dressing (1)
1 tbsp olive oil
1 tbsp lime juice
pinch of caster sugar
sea salt and freshly ground black pepper

For the dressing (2)
1 tbsp soy sauce
1 tsp mirin
1 tsp honey
1 garlic clove, crushed or grated
a few drops of sesame oil
sesame seeds, to serve

Cut or tear the chicken into bite-sized pieces. Put it in a small pan and pour over the stock. Reheat gently and set aside until you are ready to assemble.

Pile the salad leaves on to a serving plate and cover with the cucumber. Drain the chicken from the broth and arrange this over the salad ingredients if using the first dressing, or set aside if using the second. Sprinkle the spring onions, basil leaves and cherries over the salad.

For the first dressing, mix together the dressing ingredients, then season with salt and pepper. Drizzle over the salad.

For the second dressing, add the soy sauce, mirin, honey and garlic to the stock in the pan. Heat until well-reduced and syrupy, then return the chicken and coat it thoroughly in the sauce. Proceed as before, but drizzle some of the remaining sauce over the salad, along with a few drops of sesame oil and seeds.

Salad of confit chicken, endive and pears

Confit chicken is very rich and savoury, so needs something to cut through it. Crisp endive, sweet pear and a mustardy dressing manage this admirably. If you can handle more richness, you could also crumble over a bit of blue cheese as well. (*Photo opposite.*)

For the salad
1 'Confit' chicken leg *(see pages 23–24)*
4 heads of white or red endive, shredded
2 pears, peeled, sliced into thin slivers
a few tiny sprigs of thyme
a few toasted hazelnuts, lightly crushed

For the dressing
2 tbsp olive or hazelnut oil
juice of ½ lemon
½ garlic clove, crushed
1 tsp Dijon mustard
1 tsp honey
sea salt and freshly ground black pepper

Put the chicken in a frying pan and fry until heated through and crisp on all sides. Remove and shred with a couple of forks.

Arrange the endive over a serving plate, then add the chicken and pears.

Whisk together the dressing ingredients and season with salt and pepper (do this sparingly, as the confit chicken will be salty).

Drizzle the dressing over the salad, then sprinkle over a few thyme leaves and the crushed hazelnuts.

A COUPLE OF SALADS INSPIRED BY THE FAR EAST

Bang bang chicken

You can make a much quicker version of this by using cooked chicken in place of the marinated and poached chicken I use here. *Ginger-scented chicken* (see pages 54–56) would be especially good to use.

For the chicken
2 boneless skinless chicken breasts, or 4 thighs
2 tsp Chinese 5-spice powder
2 tbsp soy sauce
1 tbsp vegetable oil
5cm piece of root ginger, sliced
2 garlic cloves, sliced
a little sesame oil

For the peanut sauce
1 tbsp peanut or vegetable oil
1 shallot, finely chopped
2 red chillies, chopped
2 garlic cloves, crushed
2cm piece of root ginger, grated
200ml chicken stock
100ml coconut milk
1 tbsp rice vinegar
1 tsp sesame oil
1 tsp palm sugar (or soft light brown sugar)
1 tbsp kecap manis
1 tbsp lime juice
100g unsalted peanuts, ground with some texture

For the salad
1 large lettuce (Cos or similar), shredded
1 large carrot, cut into matchsticks
½ cucumber, cut into matchsticks
½ white cabbage, very finely shredded
½ red pepper, thinly sliced
4 spring onions, shredded
1 tbsp sesame seeds
large handful of coriander leaves

To cook the chicken, cut into thin slices. Whisk the Chinese 5-spice into the soy sauce. Add the chicken, make sure it gets completely coated and leave for a few minutes. Heat the vegetable oil in a large wok or frying pan and add the ginger and garlic. Fry for a minute, then add the chicken and fry for two or three minutes until cooked through. Drizzle with a little sesame oil, then remove from the pan and allow to cool slightly.

To make the peanut sauce, heat the peanut or vegetable oil in a frying pan and add the shallot, chillies, garlic and ginger. Fry until just turning golden brown, then add all the other ingredients and simmer for a few minutes.

Arrange the lettuce, carrot, cucumber, cabbage and pepper over a large serving platter. Add the chicken, then drizzle over some of the peanut sauce. Sprinkle over the spring onions, sesame seeds and coriander leaves. Serve immediately.

A hot and sour salad

This is inspired by all those very fragrant salads from the Far East (*photo opposite*). It's quite generic and so easily varied. I will use whatever crunchy vegetables I have around: courgettes might take the place of the cucumber, I'll use mooli in place of radishes, if I have one (this isn't often, admittedly), and if I find one at a reasonable price, I might include green or semi-ripe papaya or mango.

I use shredded chicken here, but it would also be good with griddled chicken, as the smoky flavour will add more depth to the dish. If this is what you would prefer to use, follow the instructions for griddling in the *Chicken tarragon salad* (see page 194).

For the salad
2 poached chicken breasts (see page 46), shredded, or 1 quantity Ginger-scented chicken (see pages 54–56)
ladleful of chicken stock (optional)
1 heart of Romaine lettuce (or 3 Little Gems), shredded
½ cucumber, cut into ribbons
4 spring onions, shredded
1 carrot, grated
bunch of radishes, cut into thin rounds
large handfuls of mint and coriander leaves

For the dressing
2 tbsp fish sauce
2 tbsp lime juice
½ tsp palm sugar or caster sugar, to taste
2 garlic cloves, finely chopped
small piece of root ginger, finely chopped
2 red chillies, finely chopped

If you are using the shredded chicken, heat it through in a little stock, just to soften it up a little.

Arrange all the salad ingredients on a platter, then sprinkle over the chicken.

Whisk together the fish sauce, lime juice and sugar until the sugar is dissolved, then add the garlic, ginger and chillies. Pour this over the salad and leave to stand for a couple of minutes. Serve while still warm.

14. CHICKEN ON THE GRILL

One of Elizabeth David's many pronouncements concerns the dressing of grilled chicken. She felt that it shouldn't be necessary and will only interfere with the flavour of the chicken. In some respects I agree, well-seasoned chicken is wonderful with just the smoky flavours of the charcoal and a squeeze of lemon juice. But I do think it can be equally lovely when more elaborately adorned.

There is a huge amount of information available about grilling or barbecuing chicken, and it's quite easy to get bogged down with every stage of the operation. Should you brine, marinate, salt or just rub, or a combination of the lot? Is it ever a good idea to pre-cook by poaching or baking, or is that a cheat? Does chicken always need basting? Should it be glazed? And what about sauces, relishes, dips? It can get very complicated very quickly. In an attempt to keep it straightforward, you will find here some instructions on the best way to grill the various cuts of chicken. That way you can use whichever cut you like with the recipes and treat my suggestions as just that, suggestions.

You can of course cook everything in this chapter in the oven, or on a griddle pan (just make sure you have your extractor fan on!) so I provide instructions for that, too.

All recipes serve six people, unless otherwise stated.

SOME GENERAL TIPS ON BARBECUING CHICKEN Trim the chicken of any large pieces of fat or extraneous skin; you can use these elsewhere, you don't have to throw them away. Removing them will help prevent flare-ups, which are usually caused by fat dripping on to the hot coals.

Air-dry the chicken in the fridge first, regardless of marinade. I will always apply marinade, then, instead of letting the chicken sit in it, I lay it out on a rack and allow to dry. That way the salt will do its work at the same time as the marinade flavours the outer layer of skin. It will also mean you don't have wet marinade dripping off the chicken on to the coals. Any leftover marinade can be used for basting during the cooking process. Make sure your meat is at room temperature before you start grilling, though.

Use wood. The smoke will add aroma and some flavour to the chicken. You can use chips, kindling or sawdust, but whatever you choose, it must be soaked first. I use cherry wood twigs from my garden, or put sawdust in those little smoking boxes you can buy that release the smoke at a steadier rate than putting the wood directly on to the coals. It is up to you what kind of wood you use. I use orchard fruits, oak or hickory. I avoid pine as it is too resinous and spits, and mesquite, as it is too strongly flavoured for chicken.

Use herbs and spices. I love lying chicken on a bed of bay leaves, or using rosemary or lemon grass stalks as skewers, or wrapping pieces of chicken in lime or pandan leaves. These all imbue the meat with aroma and flavour. You can also add any woody herbs or spices to the coals, or to your smoke box. Soak them first, as with wood, and, if putting directly on the coals, spritz them with water or any other liquid so they don't burn and turn the smoke acrid. Try juniper with Mediterranean flavours, or allspice when making anything from the Americas, particularly jerk.

Spritz. Keep a spray bottle of liquid to hand when barbecuing to create steam and help keep any wood, aromatics, and even the chicken from burning too quickly. Just water is fine, but you can use other things too: beer works well with jerk, while watered-down wine or lemon juice is good with anything Mediterranean.

Indirect and direct cooking

The larger cuts of chicken do much better cooked first over indirect heat, and even wings can benefit from being cooked slowly this way before a final browning over direct heat. This means that you need to get your barbecue to a fairly moderate heat, around 160°C/325°F. If you don't have a temperature-controlled barbecue, pile the charcoal into the middle of the barbecue and, as soon as the pieces all turn white, push them to the sides. You can then start cooking, often with the lid on. The other thing to remember is to put a drip tray (an aluminium foil one should do), one-third filled with liquid, in the centre of the barbecue. This will catch juices and give you a light gravy at the same time, and also create steam in the barbecue which will help with the cooking. Remove the lid and put the chicken over direct heat for the last few minutes if you want more charring.

Direct cooking is reserved for crisping everything up, charring and – in the case of skewers – cooking things completely, very fast. You still balance everything on a rack, but directly over the hot coals and the temperature in this hot spot can exceed 250°C/482°F easily. So the potential to burn is high and the chicken will need careful watching and turning.

The whole chicken

There are two, perhaps three, ways to deal with this. The first, if you have a barbecue deep enough, is to cook it vertically. This is the infamous 'beer can chicken', for which you can substitute anything else, including cider and even cola; or just a vertical roast, which is what I prefer to do. The idea is that you pour out half the contents of a tall can, put the chicken over it, then balance it on a low rack over a drip tray for as long as it takes. Make sure the barbecue has reached around 160°C/325°F, push the coals to the sides to help the heat radiate around the chicken, then balance the chicken on the rack. Cook for 75–90 minutes, depending on size.

For instructions on how to do this in the oven, with a vertical roaster, see page 62. The rub I use there is also the one I prefer to use here. But for the barbecued version, it's good to get the temperature up for the last 20 minutes and glaze the chicken with a mixture of maple syrup and bourbon, which works beautifully with the fennel, smoked paprika and charred skin.

A brick-flattened spatchcocked chicken

Heat the barbecue to medium. Use a salted and air-dried chicken (see pages 22–23), already rubbed with a spice rub (see pages 222–223). Rub with groundnut or vegetable oil, then put the chicken skin-side down on the hot grate, then top with a baking tray weighted down with a couple of foil-wrapped bricks. Grill for around 15 minutes, then turn. Baste the skin lightly if you like, then put flesh-side down, again covered with the tray and bricks, for another eight to 10 minutes. Finally, flip again and dispense with the bricks. Continue to cook, basting, for another five to 10 minutes, turning regularly, until the skin is well charred and the internal part of the thickest piece of meat (thigh or breast) is completely cooked.

You don't have to use the bricks here, you can thread the spatchcocked chicken on a couple of skewers to hold it flat, then just press it down with your spatula as it cooks. It will take slightly longer, unless you cook it with the barbecue lid on for the first 15 minutes. (For the oven version of this method, see pages 61–63.)

Chicken legs, or drumsticks, or bone-in chicken breasts

Usually anything on the bone I prefer to eat with the stickier marinades and glazes. I find them the hardest to get right on the grill, because stickiness = sugar/honey/maple/pomegranate molasses = burning. So, indirect heat is vital. And I'm afraid there have been times when I've baked the chicken in a moderate oven, covered in foil, for 30 minutes before moving it to the barbecue. I always feel slightly cowardly when I do this, though if you just have a regular-sized kettle drum, like me, and you're feeding a lot of people, it's the only way to go.

Make sure, no matter what marinade or rub you are using, you cut slashes through to the flesh. This will help with the cooking. I do sometimes loosen the meat around the bone slightly, too. Cook over indirect heat, turning regularly, covered with the lid of the barbecue, for at least half the time; it should take 30–45 minutes, depending on the thickness of the meat. It is up to you whether you keep the skin on or not. I do for some things, such as jerk, and not for others, such as tandoori chicken.

To bake instead, cook at 180°C/fan 160°C/350°F/gas mark 4 for 30 minutes, then increase the heat to 220°C/fan 200°C/425°F/gas mark 7 to brown for a further 10. This will ensure the chicken is cooked through and stop any glaze from burning.

Breasts, butterflied or in strips for skewers

There are a few ways to cook breasts on the barbecue, but I will never, ever do them

whole, not even with a stuffing which is supposed to keep the meat moist. Butterflying them takes seconds (see page 11) and the results are so much better and quicker. I will also cut them into strips and thread on to skewers, or chop them up for kebabs (along with thigh meat), or wrap in leaves.

To cook a marinated, butterflied chicken breast couldn't be easier. I don't usually bother pounding these, just cook over direct heat for three minutes on each side, then repeat. That should be enough, but check it's cooked through just in case. Cook skewers of chicken strips in the same way, but check just before you turn them for the third time, as they'll probably be done by then. Kebabs should also be cooked over direct heat, for around 10 minutes, turning regularly.

To cook in the kitchen, heat a griddle until smoking, then cook as above. It should take the same amount of time.

Wings

The wings are one of the few cuts I occasionally marinate in a smoked ham stock (see page 26), but I prefer to salt and rub them instead and always air-dry them (see pages 22–23). There are various ways to grill them. I like wings to be quite sticky, so I cook them over gentle indirect heat for around 45 minutes before browning them up over direct heat. But they can be cooked much quicker: 20–25 minutes of regular turning over a medium direct heat should do it, but make sure they are cooked through and let them stand for a few minutes afterwards.

To oven-bake them, preheat the oven to 190°C/fan 170°C/375°F/gas mark 5. Cook on a rack over a roasting tin for 30 minutes, then increase the oven temperature to 220°C/fan 200°C/425°F/gas mark 7, drain off any liquid and cook for a further 25–30 minutes, basting as necessary.

A good multipurpose barbecue sauce

I like barbecue sauces that are slightly smoky, sweet and hot. This one is based on one in Thane Prince's *Perfect Preserves*. I like it because it isn't made with ketchup and isn't too tomatoey, which I find most are (yes there's 100g of tomato purée here, but that's still much less than many I've tried). This will keep indefinitely and it can be used as a condiment, mixed with oil and vinegar or lemon juice to serve as a marinade and, finally, as a glaze.

Makes around 750ml

10cm piece of root ginger, peeled and roughly chopped
1 bulb of garlic, cloves peeled and roughly chopped
4 medium-hot red chillies (or 1–2 scotch bonnets) chopped
150ml cider vinegar
250ml apple or pineapple juice
175g light muscovado sugar
200ml Worcestershire sauce or tamarind water
200ml dark soy sauce
100g tomato purée
1 tsp sweet smoked paprika
1 tsp English mustard powder
1 bay leaf
1 tsp sea salt

Blitz together the ginger, garlic and chillies with some of the cider vinegar, trying to get the mixture as smooth as possible. Scrape this into a large saucepan and add all the other ingredients. Heat gently, stirring or whisking constantly, until all the sugar has dissolved, then increase the heat to medium and simmer for around 15 minutes, until the sauce has thickened.

Push through a sieve if you like, to make sure it is completely smooth, then decant into sterilised bottles (see page 24). This will keep for at least two months in the fridge.

SOME MARINADES

The basic

Just about every country around the Med and the Middle East has a grilled chicken recipe using lemon juice and olive oil. I am often happy to keep it simple, with just some salt and pepper. Here is the basic marinade and method:

juice of 2 lemons (and finely grated unwaxed zest, too, if you want)
50ml olive oil
1 tsp sea salt
1 tsp freshly ground black pepper

This is enough to rub into the equivalent of one chicken, or four butterflied chicken breasts, or chopped chicken from two breasts and four thighs. Marinate the chicken for two to three hours, or overnight. (I wouldn't marinate butterflied breasts overnight, just for a couple of hours or it will adversely affect the texture; every other cut will be fine.) Make sure you drain the chicken well before grilling, as the oil can cause flare-ups. Cook according to the instructions at the start of the chapter (see page 210–211).

VARIATION: POLLO ALLA DIAVOLO
This is for the (many) people in my life who can't eat anything without covering it in black pepper, and gives intense flavour for very little effort. Simply increase the amount of black peppercorns to 2 tbsp. I think this works best with a spatchcocked chicken, but you could use it with kebabs instead.

VARIATION: CHICKEN SHAWARMA
The traditional chicken kebab. I use a mixture of chopped chicken breasts and thighs and don't bother adding anything else to the skewers, although my husband says I should pre-roast onions and add those, too. Add as few or as many spices as you like. You can be very minimalist and just add teaspoons of cinnamon, nutmeg or cumin, or you can go for a more complex flavour. If I am taking this route I will probably use the following, but use a ready-made ras el hanout if you prefer.

4 garlic cloves, crushed
2 tsp ground cumin
1 tsp sweet smoked paprika
½ tsp ground ginger
¼ tsp ground cinnamon
¼ tsp ground cardamom
¼ tsp turmeric

Add the ingredients above to chicken, lemon juice, olive oil and marinate and cook as described, remembering to soak the skewers if they are made from bamboo. I like to sprinkle on sumac towards the end. Serve with salad, or sandwich with *Zhug* and/or *Tahini sauce* (see pages 224 and 234–235). Or try the following sweeter sauce:

300ml Greek-style natural yogurt
3 tbsp pomegranate molasses

squeeze of lemon juice
sea salt and freshly ground black pepper
sprinkle of sumac

Stir everything except the sumac together, sprinkle the sumac on top and, when serving with the kebabs, have lots of chopped coriander to hand.

VARIATION: CHICKEN SOUVLAKI

This is to Greece what the shawarma is to the Middle East, the main difference is that the oil and lemon juice marinade is flavoured with herbs instead of spices. To the oil and lemon juice marinade add:

4 garlic cloves, crushed
1 tbsp dried oregano
OR
2 tsp dried oregano
1 tsp dried thyme
1 tsp dried rosemary
½ tsp dried sage
2 tbsp red wine vinegar

Cook as before. Again, I don't usually add vegetables to this kebab as I prefer to keep their flavours away from the chicken. Instead, I will serve the kebabs with a simple tomato salad and whisk together the following ingredients for tzakziki:

300ml Greek-style natural yogurt
½ cucumber, peeled, deseeded, grated and wrung out in a tea towel to remove excess moisture
2 tsp dried mint
1 garlic clove, crushed
1 tsp white wine vinegar
pinch of caster sugar
sea salt and freshly ground black pepper

VARIATION: MY MOTHER'S BAY LEAF CHICKEN

It was my mother who taught me about grilling over bay leaves. She lives in Greece and has huge trees of them to sacrifice to the fire. I don't have so many fresh, so instead usually use dried; you can buy large bags of them very cheaply. Soak them well and put them either on the coals or on the grate under the chicken. I use the same marinade for this as I do for the souvlaki.

Use large bay leaves to half-wrap diced chicken before threading the pieces on to skewers. It can look quite impressive. Besides using bay you can use any edible, well-flavoured leaf.

CARIBBEAN VARIATION

In the Caribbean I used large cinnamon, avocado, lime or orange leaves. I would use a lemon juice and olive oil (see page 215) marinade, but replace the lemon juice with either lime juice, or a mixture of lime, orange or tangerine juice. I would also add 3cm piece of root ginger, grated. I don't want to add spices to the marinade here (you could add allspice, cumin or coriander if you like); instead, I would rather hint at their aroma by soaking the seeds and adding them to the smoke box or the coals.

FAR-EASTERN VARIATION

Pandan leaves can also be used. Marinate chicken pieces in olive oil, lime juice, 1 tbsp fish sauce, grated garlic and root ginger, lime zest and, if you have it, some lemon grass. Wrap the marinated chicken pieces with pandan leaves, following the instructions for the *Steamed chicken meatballs* (see pages 166–167). This is good with the same dipping sauce as I use with the Steamed chicken meatballs.

An Indian-inspired green kebab

Again, I use exactly the same base as for the lemon juice and olive oil marinade (see page 215), but I add 100ml natural yogurt, 3cm piece of root ginger, grated, the same amount of black pepper (2 tbsp) as for the diavolo, then 1 tbsp of my favourite Garam masala (see page 136) and ½ tsp turmeric. It's common to add coriander leaves to this. I don't; I add 3 tbsp very finely chopped coriander stems instead. Then I will make a chutney with the coriander leaves to serve alongside (see below). I also don't like making this really spicy. I think this is a marinade that also works very well with butterflied chicken breasts, as yogurt is especially good at tenderising breast pieces.

CORIANDER CHUTNEY

Take the leaves from 1 large bunch of coriander and 1 small bunch of mint. Blitz in a food processor with 2 green chillies, 3 garlic cloves, 1 tsp ground cumin, 1 tsp caster sugar, the juice of 1 lime (or juice of ½ lemon), salt and freshly ground black pepper. Add a little water if it is proving difficult to mix, but be sparing. If you prefer, you could add 2–3 tbsp freshly grated coconut in place of the sugar. This is best left to stand for a while before using, so the flavours really meld.

OTHER MARINADES

Jerk chicken

It's almost impossible to get away from the smell of wood smoke in the Caribbean, not that you would want to. The aroma is always tantalisingly complex: breadfruit, charred whole in their skins, give off a very particular, heady scent; jerk and other types of grilled chicken are always accompanied by fragrant allspice branches, or cooked with dried bay. In Dominica in particular, the local variety of bay is one of their largest crops (it makes very pure, aviation-standard oil) so is always plentiful for the barbecue. As it is virtually impossible to get allspice wood in the UK, I recommend adding soaked allspice berries to your coals when you start to cook, and buying a large bag of dried bay leaves (cheap in most Asian supermarkets) to lay the chicken pieces on.

Jerk is spicy, or at least it is as spicy as you want it. For this reason, I like a high meat-to-skin ratio so there is not too much searingly spicy surface area on the end result; I prefer to use thighs, or breast on the bone, cut in half so you have two thick pieces.

12 chicken pieces (see recipe introduction)
juice of 2 limes
1 tsp sea salt

For the marinade
2–4 scotch bonnets, depending how hot you want it, seeds left in
6 spring onions, chopped
6 garlic cloves, chopped
4cm piece of root ginger, chopped
2 tbsp thyme leaves
2 tbsp red wine vinegar
2 tbsp vegetable oil
2 tbsp soft dark brown sugar
2 tbsp allspice berries, crushed or ground (or 1 tbsp ground allspice)
½ tsp ground cinnamon
½ tsp freshly grated nutmeg
1 tsp freshly ground black pepper
1 tsp sea salt

To grill (optional)
2 tbsp allspice berries
large handful of dried bay leaves
spray bottle filled with water or beer

Leave the skin on the chicken, cut slashes into the skin where you can and put into a bowl. Pour over the lime juice, sprinkle with the salt and rub in.

Put all the marinade ingredients in a food processor or blender and blitz until fairly smooth.

Put the chicken in a large bowl and pour over the marinade. Massage it into the chicken (you would be well advised to wear disposable gloves for this). Cover and leave in the fridge for at least 12 hours, preferably overnight. Drain thoroughly on a rack while you get the barbecue going.

If using, soak the allspice berries and the bay leaves separately. Add the allspice berries to the coals 1 tsp at a time throughout the cooking process, while spritzing the wood, aromatics and chicken. Lay the bay leaves over the grate and put the chicken pieces on top. Follow the instructions for grilling chicken pieces (see page 212).

Tandoori chicken
(or chicken tikka, if serving off the bone)

There is absolutely no shame in using a ready-made paste for this, as some of them are very good. If using the recipe below, it seems traditional to add red colouring when cooking tandoori and leave it out when cooking tikka. I have no idea why. Use skinned chicken for this, unless using wings, and make sure the grate is lightly oiled.

For the spice mix
1 tbsp cumin seeds
1 tbsp coriander seeds
10 green cardamom pods
2 cloves
½ tsp black peppercorns
½ tsp fenugreek seeds
½ tsp fennel seeds
1 tbsp Kashmiri chilli powder
1 tsp turmeric
½ tsp ground cinnamon
½ tsp sweet smoked paprika
4 garlic cloves, crushed
5cm piece of root ginger, grated
2 tbsp lemon juice
150ml natural yogurt
1 tsp sea salt
a few drops of red colouring (optional)
12 chicken pieces, preferably drumsticks

Toast all the whole spices until aromatic, then cool and grind to a fine powder. Mix with the ready ground spices, then put in a bowl with the garlic, ginger, lemon juice, yogurt and salt. Add the food colouring, if using, then mix thoroughly. Cut slashes all over the chicken and rub in the marinade. Leave to marinate for at least a couple of hours, preferably overnight.

Drain off any excess marinade and grill as described (see page 212), depending on what kind of cut you are using. Serve with *Raita* (see page 224), lemon wedges and a few leaves of coriander.

Peri peri chicken

My preferred versions of this fiery hot sauce are the marinades by African Volcano; these are developed by South African chef Grant Hawthorne and are far above anything else you can buy. Here's a recipe inspired by Grant's. He will usually use split chicken wings for this. As this is so hot, I use similar cuts to jerk chicken (see pages 218–220).

3 tbsp vegetable or olive oil
1 onion, finely chopped
4 garlic cloves, finely chopped
2 scotch bonnets, or other chillies, finely chopped, deseeded if you like
1 tsp sweet smoked paprika
1 tsp dried oregano
2 tomatoes, peeled and finely chopped
1 tbsp red wine vinegar
75ml red wine
2 tsp brown sugar
sea salt and freshly ground black pepper
dash of Worcestershire sauce
squeeze of lemon juice
12 skin-on bone-in chicken pieces

Heat the oil in a frying pan or casserole, then sauté the onion until very soft. Add the garlic and chillies and cook for a couple more minutes, then add the paprika, oregano, tomatoes, red wine vinegar, red wine and brown sugar. Season with salt and pepper, then simmer for 10 minutes, until everything has a chance to meld together. Taste and add dashes of Worcestershire sauce and lemon juice to round out the flavour if you like. Blend until smooth. Use this both as a marinade, diluted with a little oil, and to baste during the cooking process.

VARIATION
You can turn this into a smoky South American affair by replacing the scotch bonnets with rehydrated chipotles, or chipotle paste, and adding 1 tsp ground cumin and the juice of a lime.

VARIATION
This will store well in the fridge, so you can also use it diluted: try mixing a couple of tbsp of it with 1 tbsp vegetable oil, the zest and juice of 1 lime, 1 tbsp dark rum, 2 tbsp soy sauce, some grated root ginger and 2 crushed garlic cloves. This is particularly good when used in conjunction with the butter glaze (see page 223).

A soy-based marinade

Blend together the following: 50ml dark soy sauce, 50ml rice wine vinegar, 2 tbsp soft brown sugar, 2 crushed garlic cloves, 2cm grated root ginger, 1 tsp Chinese 5-spice and 1 tbsp sesame oil. You can use this as a glaze as well, but it works better if you replace the sugar with honey if doing so. Add chilli powder if you like.

Chicken satay

The perfect strip of meat to use for proper chicken satay is the mini fillet (or 'tenders' as they are sometimes known) that is found on the flesh side of chicken breast. So you can use these as a guide for the rest of the strips you cut here.

You always need more of these than you think, as they get eaten so quickly. So it's worth marinating more than four chicken breasts and you can freeze leftovers.

For the chicken and marinade
4 chicken breasts
2 tbsp peanut oil
1 shallot, finely chopped
3 garlic cloves, finely chopped
2cm piece of root ginger, finely chopped

1 tsp ground coriander
1 tsp ground cumin
½ tsp turmeric
1 tsp sea salt
2 tbsp soy sauce
1 tbsp palm sugar
1 tbsp tamarind paste
100ml coconut milk
a little chicken stock or water, if needed

For the sauce
1 quantity Peanut sauce (see page 207)
50ml coconut milk
1 tbsp kecap manis
juice of ½ lime

Peel off the mini fillet from the chicken breasts, then cut the breasts into thin strips of a similar size and shape.

For the marinade, heat the oil in a frying pan and add the shallot. Fry over a high heat until golden brown. Remove from the heat and stir in all the remaining ingredients. If the mixture seems too thick, add a little water or chicken stock. Add the strips of chicken and stir to combine. Cover and leave in the fridge for at least eight hours, or overnight. Remove from the marinade, leave to dry out a little on a rack, then thread on to soaked skewers in such a way that you end up with a concertina effect. Grill as described on pages 212–214.

Make the peanut sauce, then add the coconut milk, kecap manis and lime juice and stir until combined.

SOME RUBS

You can use these with any cuts of chicken, but I prefer to use either butterflied chickens, wings or spatchcocked chicken. My default rub is with smoked paprika and fennel (see below). With this or any rub, simply rub on the chicken and air-dry overnight.

Alternatively, salt and air-dry overnight (see pages 22–23), then mix the rub with a little oil and rub it over 30 minutes before grilling. Here are few other combinations for rubs, with serving suggestions.

You can of course use any spice mixes of your own, or some of the others dotted throughout this book, as a rub. Just make sure you add salt before using them and always coat the chicken with a little oil before cooking. Again, each recipe makes enough glaze for 12 pieces, or 24 wings.

SMOKED PAPRIKA AND FENNEL
Mix together 2 tbsp sea salt, 2 tbsp fennel seeds, 1 tsp sweet smoked paprika and a few black peppercorns. Blitz. To make this spicy, add 1 tsp hot smoked paprika or ground chipotle as well. To make it smokier, replace the sea salt with smoked salt; I like hickory. To make it sweeter, add 2 tbsp brown sugar. Other optional extras include 1 tsp garlic powder. Use the rub as is, or in conjunction with *A good multipurpose barbecue sauce* (see pages 214–215).

BLACKENED CHICKEN Use the *Cajun spice mix* (see page 43), but add 1 tsp dried basil. If you want to leave this out, do so; I doubt you'll find any other use for dried basil, but it does make just enough of a difference to make it worthwhile. Serve with either *A quick peach relish* or *Peach ketchup* (see pages 225 and 226).

HERB AND CITRUS RUB Preheat your oven to its lowest setting. Finely zest 2 limes or unwaxed lemons, then spread out on a lined baking tray with any woody herbs of your choice: thyme or rosemary are best. Dry out in the oven for 30 minutes. Add a few black peppercorns or any other whole spices for the last five minutes. Cool, then blitz to a powder with 1 tbsp sea salt.

ZA'ATAR This is best used in conjunction with an oil and lemon juice marinade; either add it to the lemon juice, olive oil version (see page 215), or rub this on first. You can also use it to make crisp, dry wings. Just use with salt, air-dry (see pages 22–23) and rub with oil before grilling. Toast 3 tbsp white sesame seeds and blitz with 2 tbsp dried thyme, 1 tbsp sumac, 1 tbsp ground cumin and 2 tsp sea salt.

SOME GLAZES

Each recipe makes enough glaze for 12 pieces, or 24 wings.

A couple of these – the first two in particular – are multipurpose and can be used as a marinade as well as a glaze, but I prefer to use them in conjunction with rubs (see above) or marinades. Start applying the glazes lightly towards the end of cooking time when over direct heat, then brush on a little more and leave to rest over indirect heat, or a shelf above the rack, for a few minutes more.

MAPLE-BOURBON GLAZE Put 100ml maple syrup, 100ml bourbon (or dark rum), 1 tbsp soft light brown sugar and 2 crushed garlic cloves in a saucepan. Simmer until the sugar has dissolved, stirring. Remove from the heat and decant to a bowl. Use as a marinade, glaze, or both.

COLA GLAZE Ultra-trashy this, but I like it occasionally. I only realised fairly recently what a popular cooking ingredient cola is in China and how it is used in all kinds of Chinese fusion dishes such as this one, based on a marinade popular amongst Chinese immigrants in Peru. Put the juice of 2 limes, 250ml cola, 50ml cider vinegar, 50g soft light brown sugar, 1 tbsp hot sauce and 4 crushed garlic cloves in a saucepan and stir over a low heat until dissolved. Use as described above.

POMEGRANATE MOLASSES GLAZE I normally use this in conjunction with either an oil and lemon juice marinade (see page 215) or a citrus or other spice rub (see opposite) and keep the glaze itself very simple. Just whisk together around 75ml pomegranate molasses, 2 crushed garlic cloves, 1 tsp ground cumin and 1 tsp sumac. Baste the chicken sparingly with this towards the end of the cooking time.

BUTTER GLAZE This is one I've been using for years with the rum marinade on page 221. It works with anything very hot or savoury. Melt 50g unsalted butter in a pan then whisk in 3 tbsp tomato ketchup or *Peach ketchup* (see pages 225–226) with 1 tsp red wine vinegar or 3 tbsp *Good barbecue sauce* (see pages 214–215). Use towards the end of the cooking time.

Shami chicken kebabs

To make these more authentic, by which I mean softer, you could replace the breadcrumbs with cooked and mashed chana dal. You would need to make sure they are very well drained before you mash them, as they can make the mixture harder to work with, but it is well worth persevering with.

1 tbsp vegetable oil
½ small onion, very finely chopped
2 garlic cloves, finely chopped
3cm piece of root ginger, peeled and chopped
2 green chillies, finely chopped
juice of 1 lemon
2 tbsp very finely chopped coriander stems
750g minced chicken thighs
75g breadcrumbs
2 tbsp natural yogurt
1 egg, lightly beaten
1 tbsp mild curry powder, or the spice mix from Coriander chicken *(see pages 136–138)*
sea salt and freshly ground black pepper

Heat the oil in a frying pan and sauté the onion until very soft. Add the garlic, ginger and chillies, then cook for a further minute. Allow to cool, then purée with the lemon juice and coriander stalks. Add this to the minced chicken with all the other ingredients. Season well.

Mould on to soaked bamboo skewers. Arrange over a well-oiled and heated grate. Grill over direct heat for 10–15 minutes, turning a couple of times. Serve with a simple raita: just mix a couple of tsp dried mint into around 300ml natural yogurt.

TO FINISH

There are some sauces above which are excellent with specific marinades; here you will find others I like with a fairly plain grilled chicken. I don't always bother; sometimes I will just drizzle pomegranate molasses or kecap manis over the meat, or squeeze over some citrus juice. I am also slightly addicted to using *Multi-purpose barbecue sauce* on everything. Each of these recipes will serves at least six or eight people, perhaps a crowd, as you don't need much.

Zhug

A popular Middle Eastern condiment, originally from the Yemen. I often have a jar of it sitting in the fridge, as it's so good with grilled or poached chicken. I love it with any of the lemon- and oil-based marinated dishes above, especially schawarma.

½ tsp caraway seeds
seeds from 1 tsp green cardamom pods
1 tsp cumin seeds
1 tsp coriander seeds
1 tsp peppercorns
large bunch of coriander
leaves from a small bunch of parsley
leaves from a small bunch of mint
2 green chillies, chopped
4 garlic cloves, chopped
juice of 1 lemon
4 tbsp olive oil

Lightly toast the whole spices in a dry frying pan, shaking constantly and removing as soon as they become aromatic. Cool, then grind together. Put in a blender with the remaining ingredients. Blitz until smooth.

Romesco sauce

I use a smoked ham stock (see page 26) when barbecuing pieces or baking wings which I want to infuse with a smoky ham flavour.

After the marinating I will always air-dry it in the fridge (see pages 22–23), to get the skin as crisp as possible. There are two sauces in particular I like serving with these. The first, romesco, was given to me by Catalan expert Rachel McCormack. She says the secret to great romesco is balance: you should be able to taste all the ingredients, with no one thing dominant.

2 medium tomatoes
½ bulb of garlic, cloves separated
12 almonds
12 hazelnuts
3 sprigs of parsley
up to 125ml olive oil
1½ tbsp white wine vinegar, plus more if needed
1 slice of stale country-style bread, toasted and ground into breadcrumbs
sea salt
up to 2 tsp sweet smoked paprika

Preheat the oven to 200°C/fan 180°C/400°F/gas mark 6. Put the tomatoes and garlic in a small roasting tin and place in the oven. Roast for around 25 minutes, or until the garlic flesh is tender. Remove from the oven and when cool enough to handle, peel the cloves. Put in a bowl of a food processor with the tomatoes.

Put the almonds and hazelnuts in a frying pan and dry toast over a low heat for around seven minutes, until evenly toasted. Watch them like a hawk and shake regularly as they will easily burn if left. Add the parsley for the last minute, then remove from the heat and cool. Add to the tomatoes and garlic.

Add the oil and half the vinegar to the mixture, then blend everything until smooth. Add the breadcrumbs and blend again. Season with salt, then sprinkle in some of the paprika and mix to taste; keep adding the spice until you think you have added the right amount. Add more vinegar if you think it needs it, but be sparing, it shouldn't be too vinegary and the amount given above should be the absolute limit. Check for seasoning and add salt.

Romesco is best made at least 20 minutes in advance and left to settle.

Mojo picon sauce

This is the other sauce I like with a sweet/smoky ham-marinated piece of barbecued chicken (see page 26).

1 tbsp olive oil, plus 75ml
1 slice of stale country-style bread
2 garlic cloves, chopped
1 tsp hot smoked paprika
1 tsp sweet smoked paprika
1 tsp cumin seeds
1 tsp fennel seeds
2 tsp sherry vinegar
sea salt and freshly ground black pepper

Heat the 1 tbsp of olive oil in a frying pan and fry the bread until golden on both sides. Tear up and put in a food processor.

Add the garlic, spices and sherry vinegar and season. Purée roughly, then start drizzling in the 75ml of olive oil until it is all combined.

Peach ketchup

One of the things I discovered when writing this book was how much I like chicken with fruit, especially fresh orchard fruits. Peach ketchup is a great alternative to tomato ketchup and can be varied quite considerably. Try using mangoes instead. I like serving this with blackened chicken.

1 tbsp vegetable oil
1 large onion, finely chopped
5 large ripe peaches, skinned, pitted and chopped
3 tbsp maple syrup
2 tbsp dark soft brown sugar
2 tbsp caster sugar
1 tsp sea salt
½ tsp black pepper
¼ tsp ground allspice
60ml cider vinegar
2 tbsp lemon juice

Heat the oil in a frying pan and sauté the onion until very soft and starting to caramelise. Add the peaches and continue to cook over a fairly low heat for a further five minutes. Add all the other ingredients, except the lemon juice.

Simmer for up to one hour, until it has reduced and thickened, and you can carve a path along the base of the pan with a wooden spoon. Make sure you stir very regularly, as it will burn if not carefully attended. Blitz in a blender or food processor, then push through a sieve. Put in a sterilised jar (see page 24) and store in the fridge; it will keep for at least two months.

A quick peach relish

Again, this will also work with mango, even pineapple.

4 ripe peaches, skinned, pitted and chopped
1 red pepper, finely chopped
1 red onion, sliced into very thin crescents
1 red chilli, finely chopped
1cm piece of root ginger, finely chopped
1 tbsp olive oil
juice of ½ orange
juice of 2 limes
1 tsp caster sugar
sea salt and freshly ground black pepper
mint and coriander leaves, finely chopped

Put the peaches, pepper, onion, chilli and ginger in a bowl. Whisk together the olive oil, orange and lime juices with the sugar and season with salt and pepper.

Pour this over the peaches, then mix in lots of herbs.

A Georgian walnut and coriander sauce

This sauce is a great accompaniment to any grilled chicken.

You can add more or less apricot or walnut, depending on how sweet you want it.

I prefer to make this a day in advance, as the flavours of the herbs will both meld together and become more distinct after that time.

25g dried apricots, soaked in boiling water for one hour
25g walnuts
2 garlic cloves, chopped
juice of 1 lemon or 1½ limes
large bunch of coriander, chopped
1 tbsp each of finely chopped parsley, dill, basil and tarragon leaves
pinch of cayenne pepper
pinch of sweet smoked paprika
sea salt and freshly ground black pepper
4 tbsp walnut oil

Drain the apricots, reserving their soaking liquid, and roughly chop. Put the walnuts in a food processor or blender and grind until fairly fine. Add the garlic and continue to process, then add the apricots, lemon or lime juice, herbs and spices. Season with salt and pepper. Blitz until you have a paste that is on the verge of becoming smooth, but you want a very little texture here.

Start drizzling in the oil, it should start to emulsify. Finally, if it is very thick, dilute with a little of the reserved soaking liquor.

Barbecued chicken skin

This is a novel idea. It's something you can do on the side when you have some chicken skin left over – it is apparently done quite often in yakitori restaurants. It's simple and you can use all kinds of vegetables, or none at all.

I'm including here a traditional yakatori marinade/baste, but you can use any of the glazes on previous pages. Just make sure that the skin is bone dry and salted (see pages 21–22). Also, if the fat under the skin is particularly thick in places, it's probably best to scrape some off; too much will cause a flare-up.

For the sauce
100ml tamari or light soy sauce
100ml mirin
50ml sake
2 tsp light soft brown sugar
2 spring onions, sliced
2cm piece of root ginger, grated (optional)

For the skewers
150g chicken skin
bunch of asparagus, cut into 4cm lengths
bunch of spring onions or baby leeks, cut into 4cm lengths
sea salt

To make the sauce, heat all the ingredients together, stirring until the sugar has dissolved. Simmer until reduced by half. It is now ready to use.

Soak your bamboo skewers in water for 30 minutes. Thread pieces of chicken skin on to the skewers, alternating with the asparagus, spring onions or baby leeks. Sprinkle with salt.

Put on the grill and cook for around 10 minutes on indirect heat, turning regularly, then start basting with the sauce. Cook for another five minutes on indirect heat, then move to a hotter part of the grill and cook for a further five minutes or so, still basting, until the skin is crisp and darkened and the vegetables look slightly charred.

VARIATION
Keep the asparagus spears and spring onions whole, and wrap them in chicken skin. Thread on to lemon grass 'skewers' and grill as above, serving with the same sauce.

15. THE CHICKEN SANDWICH

(and other chicken/bread combinations)

During the course of writing this book I've had a lot of chicken leftovers to get through and that has meant I've assembled and eaten a lot of chicken sandwiches. Consequently, this chapter has evolved quite randomly; while there are some classic combinations, there are also quite a few that put I put together purely based on what I had to hand. I haven't included these as some didn't work, such as the chicken with cold walnut sauce and rocket that I thought would be so good. On the other hand, the sandwich I made with a herb butter was so good I had to include it.

Of all those standard sandwich recipes you would normally associate with chicken, I've been picky, and stuck to those where the chicken flavour dominates. I find that with a lot of sandwiches and assemblages (I'm including wraps such as burritos here, too), there is so much else going on that you lose the flavour of the meat. I also avoided some of the sandwiches purely because I don't like the wrapper. So, after a heated discussion with my husband, who is very much of the 'bigger is best' school of thought when it comes to sandwiches, the chicken club sandwich went. I can't think of many things worse: that middle slice of toasted bread is extraneous and, even if you can get the whole thing into your mouth, the chances are that you will still struggle to get it down your throat. If you want those flavours, just make a sandwich with two slices and stuff it with chicken, bacon, avocado and tomato. I also left out *arepas*, a central American flatbread, as I'm not that keen on corn or choclo bread.

The first few sandwiches here are simple, where the chicken has absolutely nowhere to hide so the flavour is paramount. The rest have much more going on flavour wise but, really, everything included is there primarily to complement the chicken.

My best chicken sandwich

Uncomplicated this, but I can say absolutely it's my favourite chicken sandwich. I've probably eaten hundreds of these over the years; many of them in the past few months. I love all the other sandwiches in this book but always go back to this one, despite always having at hand a plethora of condiments and other ingredients I could add.

Take two slices of bread. What kind is up to you, I veer between sourdough and a decent white or granary. Butter them with proper unsalted butter. Arrange some slices of chicken on one of the slices; if you are anything like me, the chicken will be roughly torn rather than neatly sliced, but still. Sprinkle with sea salt and add a grinding of black pepper. Top with some crunchy lettuce: Little Gem and Cos are ideal, then more salt and pepper. Top with the remaining slice of bread. Cut in half if you can be bothered. Eat. A plate is useful, if only to catch any pieces of escaping chicken (this will happen), unless you are eating standing up over the kitchen worktop, in which case, don't bother.

That is the reality of many of my lunches, but I honestly do believe that it can't be beaten.

If your fingers are itching to add more, try to resist. But if it's impossible, try a smear of mustard, perhaps some leftover stuffing or salad dressing (the tarragon versions on page 194 are good here), or even a slice or two of bacon. A sweet, ripe tomato is OK, cucumber is unnecessary. Being a person who doesn't really do dry food and wants sauce or gravy with everything, I am often tempted by salad cream or mayonnaise, thinking they might help things along. In this rare instance, they don't.

Now to the other sandwiches.

The garlic lover's sandwich

This is my husband's idea of the best chicken sandwich, as he thinks mine is a wasted opportunity to add garlic and mayonnaise. It comes courtesy of Helen Graves, author of one of my favourite food blogs, *Food Stories*, and of the book *101 Sandwiches*. To make it, you will need all the oil and at least some of the chicken and garlic from the *Chicken with 40 cloves of garlic* (see page 71).

2 egg yolks
sea salt and freshly ground black pepper
leftover oil, meat and garlic from Chicken with 40 cloves of garlic *(the confit version, see page 71)*
lemon juice
slices of sourdough
unsalted butter
curly endive or other bitter salad leaves

Make a mayonnaise. Put the egg yolks in a bowl and whisk together. Season with salt and pepper. Drizzle in the oil, a few drops at a time, whisking constantly. Once the oil and yolks start to emulsify, add the oil in a steady stream until it is all incorporated and you have a thick mayonnaise. Add a squeeze of lemon juice.

To assemble, pull the reserved chicken into rough pieces and mix with 1 tbsp of the garlic mayonnaise. Spread the bread with butter, then squeeze out the flesh from some of the garlic cloves and spread this on top of the butter. Add the chicken mayonnaise, then some leaves. Top with the other slice of bread.

I quite like cherry tomatoes in this as well, but that isn't at all authentic to Helen's recipe. This is also good with a large dollop of Dijon mustard added to the mayonnaise.

Another garlic lover's sandwich

This is one still uses the confit garlic from the Chicken with 40 cloves of garlic recipe. However, it makes a different dressing, which is sweeter and less pungent.

around 20 cloves of roast/confit garlic, skinned and mashed
4 tbsp mayonnaise
100ml buttermilk
½ tsp caster sugar
few drops of Worcestershire sauce
sea salt and freshly ground black pepper
unsalted butter
your choice of bread
leftover chicken, ideally breaded chicken
lemon juice
hot sauce (optional)
crisp lettuce leaves

Make the dressing by whisking the mashed garlic with the mayonnaise, buttermilk, sugar, Worcestershire sauce and seasoning. Butter your choice of bread, pile in some leftover chicken. Anything breaded is especially good here, so try *Chicken parmigiana, Chicken goujons* or *Classic Southern-fried chicken* (see pages 120, 86 and 149–151).

Squeeze over lemon juice and drizzle over lots of the garlic sauce. Add a few drops of hot sauce as well if you like, and some crisp lettuce for contrast.

SOME OTHER SIMPLE CHICKEN SANDWICHES

The chicken French dip

This is the best sandwich to make when you have leftover chicken and gravy, especially if you have a few people to feed as it's quite a crowd pleaser. In fact, there's an argument for roasting a chicken just so you can make this sandwich, just as people roast a slab of cow for the beefy version.

Take a large baguette and split it lengthways. Press it open slightly and butter both sides. Cover the whole of one side with slices of chicken.

If you have any onion left over from roasting the chicken (doubtful, but still), heat this up with the leftover gravy. Strain it from the gravy and spread it over the chicken.

Season with salt and freshly ground black pepper. Check the seasoning of the gravy and make sure it's heated almost to boiling point.

Close the baguette firmly, pressing down hard, and cut it into chunks. Put the gravy on the table and pass it around so everyone can take it in turns to dunk their pieces of chicken baguette into the gravy. Or give everyone a small pot each, but make sure the pots are quite wide or it could get very messy.

You might also want to try adding a bit of smokiness to the gravy, with hickory smoked salt. Either way, this is very good indeed. And if you want to add anything else, I would stick with either handfuls of rocket or watercress in the baguette. Both are more than capable of standing up to a well-flavoured gravy.

The egg and chicken sandwich

I invented this on a day when I was feeling slightly below par and craving a fried egg sandwich. By happy coincidence I also had a store of fresh chicken gribenes which I'd doused with hickory smoked salt and ground chipotle pepper.

Butter two slices of bread. Take a large knob of unsalted butter and melt it slowly in a frying pan. Add two eggs and fry very gently until the whites are just set and the yolks are still runny. Take a handful of gribenes or scratchings and throw them in a blender. Blitz. They may be slightly oily and try to clump together, but this doesn't really matter. Taste. You may want to add more hickory salt and chipotle powder. Put the eggs on one of the buttered slices and sprinkle over the ground-up gribenes. Top with the other slice of bread and cut in half if you like. This will also be messy, but well worth it.

Note If you don't have a store of gribenes, this is definitely worth frying or roasting some chicken skin for (see page 22).

Pulled chicken sandwich

If you want to, follow the smoked chicken recipe (see page 26) and shred that; with some barbecue sauce it will work brilliantly. But this is how you make pulled chicken if you don't want to light the barbecue. It's not much quicker, but you can also pressure cook it; the instructions are at the end of the recipe.

This recipe needs a certain amount of fat, so I normally use chicken thighs, skinned but not trimmed of excess fat, and left on the bone. I'll also add just one chicken breast as it shreds so well and helps with the whole pulled texture.

You may think it's crazy to cook chicken just for sandwiches, but this one is worth it, and anyway you can store the chicken in sandwich-sized portions in the freezer.

You are spoilt for choice about getting smoky flavour in here. If you have made smoked schmaltz (see page 21) that will get things going a bit. Then chipotle and smoked paprika will also help. Finally, I season with smoked hickory salt. This makes enough for 6–8 sandwiches.

For the chicken
1 tbsp vegetable oil or smoked schmaltz
750g skinless bone-in chicken thighs
1 large skinless chicken breast
200g canned tomatoes
150ml light beer, lager or water
sea salt (optional)
½ tsp hickory salt

For the paste
1 medium onion, roughly chopped
4 garlic cloves, chopped
1 dried chipotle, or 1 tsp ground chipotle (optional, this doesn't have to be a hot sauce)
2 tbsp soft light brown sugar
2 tbsp cider vinegar
1 tsp dried oregano
2 tsp ground cumin
1 tsp sweet smoked paprika
1 tsp white peppercorns, lightly crushed
2 tsp fennel seeds, lightly crushed
¼ tsp ground cinnamon

To serve
soft white bread rolls and coleslaw

Preheat the oven to 150°C/fan 130°C/300°F/ gas mark 3. Heat the oil in a large casserole. Loosen the bone from around the chicken thighs a little with a sharp knife, to help them cook more evenly. Brown the chicken pieces on all sides, then remove to a plate.

Put all the paste ingredients into a blender and blitz until fairly smooth. Don't worry if the whole spices aren't completely ground, it really doesn't matter here. Add the paste ingredients to the casserole and fry for a couple of minutes. Add the tomatoes and beer or water, then either season with salt or add the smoked hickory salt. Return the chicken pieces to the casserole and bring to the boil. Cover, then transfer to the oven.

After an hour, remove from the oven. You should find the chicken is tender and falling off the bone. Remove the chicken from the casserole. Put the casserole back over a flame and reduce the sauce, it needs to remain quite wet, but should not be watery. Shred the chicken with two forks, discarding the bones, then return it to the casserole.

To serve, pile into soft rolls with the coleslaw. The chicken will store well in the fridge for a week, or in the freezer for three months. To reheat, simply decant spoonfuls to a frying pan with a splash of water and fry until heated through and starting to go a bit crisp round the edges.

A coleslaw for pulled chicken

This will work well with anything very savoury or smoky as it has a lot of fresh sweetness, as well as a hint of savoury from the nigella seeds. You could also add mint if you like. Try serving it in a sandwich with some shredded *Classic Southern-fried chicken* (see pages 149–151) with some hot sauce.

½ white cabbage, shredded
1 fennel bulb, shredded
4 spring onions, finely sliced into rounds
1 green apple, peeled and grated
finely grated zest and juice of 1 lime
1 tbsp fennel seeds, ground
1 tsp nigella seeds
2 tbsp finely chopped coriander stems
2 tbsp crème fraîche or natural yogurt
1 tbsp mayonnaise
1 tsp cider vinegar
large pinch of caster sugar
sea salt and freshly ground black pepper

Put the cabbage, fennel, spring onions and apple in a bowl. Toss with over lime zest and half the lime juice immediately, to help the apple stop turning brown. Add the spices and coriander stems.

Mix the crème fraîche or yogurt with the mayonnaise, then whisk in the vinegar, sugar and remaining lime juice. Combine this with the contents of the bowl, then season with salt and pepper.

The shawarma sandwich

You can use any type of bread for this, but I like round, fluffy naans best. You can use shop-bought, but here is my recipe for a quick version. Zhug and tahini are brilliant together, but you could replace the tahini with yogurt instead, if you like.

Makes 4
For the flatbreads
225g plain or wholemeal flour, plus more if needed, plus more to dust
2 tsp baking powder
½ tsp sea salt
200g Greek-style natural yogurt

1 tbsp olive oil
semolina, to dust (optional)

For the tahini dressing
1 garlic clove, crushed
½ tsp sea salt
100ml tahini
1 tsp ground cumin
1 tsp sweet smoked paprika
juice of 1 lemon
2 tbsp olive oil

To serve
1 quantity Chicken schawarma (see pages 215–216) or other grilled chicken
2 tomatoes, finely chopped
1 small red onion, finely chopped
1 quantity Zhug, if you have it (see page 224)
100g cooked chickpeas (optional)

To make the flatbreads, whisk together the flour, baking powder and salt. Mix in the yogurt and olive oil until you have a dough. If it seems too sticky, add a little more flour. Knead into a smooth dough on a floured surface. Wrap in cling film and leave to rest in the fridge. You can leave it there for a couple of days, if you like.

Divide the dough into four and tease each out into a round of around 18cm. It will be quite thin, but will puff up when cooking. To cook, either heat your oven to its highest setting and put in a baking tray to heat up, or simply grill on a tawa or frying pan. Dust with semolina or flour and add the rounds of dough, a couple at time. Bake or grill for just a few minutes until puffed up and brown.

To make the tahini dressing, put the garlic in a bowl and mash with the salt. Whisk in the tahini, then sprinkle in the cumin and paprika. Gradually add 100ml of water, the lemon juice and oil. This can be stored in the fridge, but will probably separate – just give it a good stir every time you want to use it.

To assemble, take a portion of the chicken shawarma or other grilled chicken and pile into a warmed naan. Add finely chopped tomato, chickpeas if using, and red onion, then drizzle over zhug and the tahini dressing.

The roti

A Caribbean-style roti is slightly different from the sort found in South Asia. It's usually thinner and much wider in diameter, because rather than being torn up as a way of picking up food, it is folded into a parcel. If it's too thick, it won't work.

So if you don't want to make your own roti breads, buy a thin tortilla or sandwich wrap rather than a smaller chapati. I use a chapati tawa for my flatbreads; they're brilliant for cooking and heating up all kinds of flatbreads including tortillas. You can pick one up very cheaply in any South Asian supermarket.

The best chicken filling for this is *A dry Caribbean chicken curry* (see pages 141–142). You could also add some diced potato or some chickpeas to this during the reduction stage. I like to eat it with coriander, but that is very inauthentic!

For the roti/chapati
250g plain flour, plus more to dust
½ tsp baking powder
1 tsp sea salt
1 tbsp vegetable or coconut oil, or ghee
up to 150ml water

For the filling
1 portion of Caribbean chicken curry *(see page 141)*
coriander leaves
mango chutney (optional)

To make the roti, sift together the flour, baking powder and salt. Add the oil or ghee and rub it into the flour, then gradually add the water, around 50ml at a time, working it in each time. Work it together with your hands and knead lightly before judging whether you need slightly more water; you want a fairly dry dough here, not sticky. Turn the dough on to a floured work surface and knead until smooth. Cover and leave for around 30 minutes.

Knead the dough for a few more minutes, then divide into four pieces. Knead and shape each piece into a smooth ball. Flour the work surface and roll each piece out to a diameter of at least 25cm. When you start rolling, you'll feel as though you won't get it this wide, but persevere and apply as much pressure as you can, you will get there.

Heat a large frying pan or, if you have one, a chapati tawa, over a medium heat. You will know it is hot enough if, when you sprinkle a drop of water on it, it will immediately splutter and evaporate. Cook, turning frequently, until the roti is cooked through, but still soft, you don't want it to get too brown. Wrap up in a tea towel to keep warm and pliable.

To assemble the roti, reheat the filling, pile some into the middle of the bread and sprinkle with coriander leaves and any condiments you might fancy. Turn in the top and bottom edges and press round the filling, then turn the right edge over and roll up, leaving the edges facing down. Serve immediately. Bizarrely, I have seen people unwrap these and eat with a knife and fork in Caribbean restaurants, but I think it should be a hands-only affair, wrapped in paper.

The kathi (or kati) roll

This is a very traditional street food snack from Calcutta, made with paratha (a flaky, enriched chapati) and an omelette. You can use the same curry as with the roti, or any of the other curries for that matter, but it's frequently made with chicken tandoori served with a chutney. This roll is of my own devising, so not remotely authentic.

The traditional method of making paratha involves folding rolled-out roti dough into quarters so it's triangular shaped, then rolling it back out into a round. I never manage this to my own satisfaction, despite hours practising with my mother-in-law to hand, so I've devised this method, which still results in lovely, flaky paratha.

Makes 4
For the roti
1 quantity Roti dough, made with half wholemeal, half white plain flour
50g melted unsalted butter or ghee
1 tbsp oil or ghee
1 egg, lightly beaten
sea salt and freshly ground black pepper
1 quantity tandoori Butter chicken (see page 133), or any minced chicken kebabs or chicken curry

For the chutney
1 large or 2 small red onions, sliced into crescents
1 large bunch of coriander
2 green chillies, roughly chopped
2 garlic cloves, peeled and roughly chopped

2cm piece of ginger, peeled and chopped
2 tbsp tamarind paste (not concentrate)
finely grated zest and juice of 1 lime
1 tsp caster sugar
a little yogurt (optional)

Follow the recipe for the roti bread opposite to the point when you divide the dough into four. Take each ball and roll into a 20cm diameter round. Brush the round generously with the melted butter or ghee. Tightly roll up the round until you have a roll, then roll this with the palm of your hands so it becomes longer and thinner. Coil this round and tuck the outside end into the centre. Flatten slightly, then roll out into another 20cm diameter round. Coat with more melted butter, then repeat the whole process. Don't worry if, when you roll it into a round, it seems too slick with butter, or if your paratha has holes in it, it will all come together by the time you've finished.

Heat a frying pan or chapati tawa over a medium heat, then cook the parathas for a few minutes on each side, turning frequently, so as to not to get them too brown. Keep warm and pliable in a tea towel.

To make the chutney, blanch the onions in boiling water for two minutes, then drain and refresh in cold water. Put all the other ingredients in a food processor with a drop of water and purée until smooth. Mix the onions with the coriander purée. Temper with a little yogurt, if you like.

To make the omelette, heat the oil or ghee in a frying pan the same size as your parathas. Season the egg with salt and pepper, then pour it on to the pan and swirl it around, making sure the whole is covered with a thin layer. When you can see the base is set, top with a warmed paratha.

As soon as the egg has just set and the omelette and paratha look glued together, remove from the heat. Reheat the chicken, pile it in a strip along the centre of the omelette side, then add chutney.

Roll up as tidily as you can and eat immediately.

VARIATION: MURTABAK

My husband told me about this one. He spent a summer visiting Malaysian student friends and remembers this as being one of his favourite street foods there. It's not the easiest of things to perfect, I never feel I manage to get the dough quite thin enough, but it still tastes good. Since struggling away with this, a friend told me I should just use the largest spring roll wrappers I can find. It isn't quite the same but it does make life easier.

Make the Roti dough (see opposite) and rest it, preferably overnight. Divide into four balls. Make the *Larb* or *Laab* (see page 172), adding 1 tsp *Garam masala* (see page 136) to the mixture and replacing the beans with peas. Beat 2 eggs.

Heat a non-stick frying pan or tawa and rub over a little oil. Roll the roti out as thinly as possible, you need to get them to around 25cm in diameter. This isn't the easiest thing to do; in Malaysia, they spin it round and slap it down on the counter and it gets larger and thinner each time. I have to resort to a rolling pin. What does help is oiling your hands, rolling pin and work surface instead of flouring everything. When you feel you've got it about as thin as you can manage, add a couple of tbsp of egg to the middle, then top with one-quarter of the Larb mix. Fold into a parcel. Put on the heated tawa or frying pan and cook for several minutes on each side, flattening with a spatula, until the dough is cooked through and browned.

The bokit

Returning to the Caribbean here, but this time to the French West Indies. The bokit is a split bread roll similar to, but skinnier than, our English muffin (which is what I use here). It's stuffed with all kinds of things, the chicken version is either stew or curry chicken. I use *Chicken colombo* (see pages 139–140) and shred it, then pile up the accompaniments.

For the bokit
1 tsp lard
4 English muffins, split
½ quantity Chicken colombo (see pages 139–140), shredded
1 tomato, sliced
a few crisp lettuce leaves

For the avocado cream
1 large avocado, peeled, destoned and finely chopped
juice of 2 limes
2 garlic cloves, crushed
½ tsp ground cumin
handful of coriander (optional)
½ tsp hot sauce (optional)
25ml olive oil

To assemble, heat a frying pan or griddle. Melt over the lard, then lightly brown the muffins on both sides.

Blitz the avocado cream ingredients together until smooth. Spread it on one of sides of the muffins, then reheat the chicken and pile it in. Top with a slice of tomato and some lettuce. Eat immediately while still warm.

SOME OTHER LEFTOVER SANDWICHES

There are many recipes in this book which lend themselves to stuffing between two slices of bread or some other kind of flour-based wrapper. Here are a few of my favourites:

Coronation chicken

Use the recipe on pages 122–124 for the chicken filling. Slice some rounds of cucumber very thinly and put these in a pickling liquid the same as the one in the Coronation chicken recipe. Marinate the cucumber for a few minutes, then drain thoroughly. Butter your bread, pile up the chicken filling and lay a blanket of cucumber on top. The cucumber is an excellent foil for the creamy, slightly curried chicken.

The chicken Veronique wrap

Take a light sandwich wrap. Put a pile of lettuce in a strip down the middle, then follow with some just warmed, leftover *Chicken Veronique* (see page 125) with a little of its sauce. (You could whisk in some buttermilk to this, if you like.) Add some fresh, uncooked grapes and season with salt and freshly ground black pepper. Wrap up tightly, cut in half and eat.

The chicken wing baguette

This is inspired by a recipe by Nigel Slater, which took chicken tandoori wings and turned them into a sublime sandwich. Take any leftover wings, or at least do your best to save some for this recipe. Strip the wings and put the skin and meat into a bowl. Heat some butter in a frying pan and add a splash of water. Add your pickings from the chicken wings and cook gently so the flesh softens and the skin re-crisps. Slice a baguette lengthways and rub half a garlic clove over the cut sides. Butter, then pile in shredded lettuce (Cos or Iceberg is best). Top with the chicken wings. You can add mayonnaise to this if you like, but I don't think it needs it.

Grilled chicken, three ways

Any barbecued chicken is good between two slices of bread (preferably a sturdy ciabatta roll or similar), but these are the three combinations I like the most:

Use smoky marinated chicken and serve with *Peach ketchup* (see pages 225–226) or some mayonnaise with some chipotle paste stirred through it, with tomato, slices of red onion and some pickles.

Use blackened chicken and serve with slices of avocado and a mayonnaise you've doctored with the juice and finely grated zest of a lime. Lots of fresh cucumber and lettuce is good here.

Use *Chicken diavolo* (see page 215) or chicken that has marinated in lemon and herbs and serve with rocket and a drizzle of yogurt. You could add grilled slices of chorizo to this one, too.

The slider or burger

Here you need soft baps and the works: pickles, slices of onion and tomato. You can cook the sliders or burgers as described on pages 164–165 or you can grill or fry them, with a bit of steaming at the end if you are using cheese. For the latter, rub a little oil onto a griddle or frying pan.

When smoking hot, add the sliders or burgers and cook for two minutes on each side, then continue to cook for a minute on each side until done. These need to cook through and the best way to know whether they are done is by using a thermometer; their internal temperature should be 75°C/167°F.

If you want to add cheese, put a slice on top of the burger when it is almost done and cover with a domed lid or cloche until it has completely melted.

Pile into burger buns with lettuce, tomatoes, pickles and any relishes you fancy. I like *A good multipurpose barbecue sauce* (see page 214) with a little mayonnaise and lots of cucumber pickle.

The leftover herb butter sandwich

If you make the *Freekeh-stuffed chicken with a herb butter* (see pages 69–70), it is worth making slightly more butter than you need, as you can keep it in the fridge or freezer and use it for this sandwich.

Take two slices of bread, preferably sourdough, and toast them. Slather in herb butter, it will melt through the holes in your bread on to the plate but never mind, you can mop up later.

Cover with chicken, slices of tomato and avocado and a drizzle of hot sauce (or a sprinkling of hot smoked paprika). Cover with the remaining slice of toast and eat.

The chicken toastie

There are two things that are mandatory in a chicken toastie. The first – a no brainer – is chicken. The second is cheese, lots of it. Apart from that anything goes, but I don't think I'd put dry chicken in, it needs sauce. Some of the recipes in this book are sublime when given this treatment. Try *A dry Caribbean chicken curry* (see page 141), *Red mole chicken* (see pages 143–145), or even *A sweet, smoky chilli* (see pages 145–146).

You also need something to freshen it up. I favour lots of chopped coriander with any of the above, some finely chopped onion and perhaps a finely chopped tomato, too.

If you don't have a toastie maker, you can make this in a lightly oiled frying pan or griddle. You need it over a medium heat, hot enough to melt the insides, but not so hot that it will burn the bread before the cheese has melted. Press down with a spatula as you go. Or weight it down with a small frying pan that has a can in it.

And finally, a quick tostada

This is also a kind of open sandwich. Take small corn tortillas and fry them in groundnut oil for a few moments on each side to crisp them up. Make a black bean salsa with 100g cooked black beans, 2 finely chopped tomatoes (or I also like watermelon as an alternative), finely chopped red onion and lots of chopped mint and coriander leaves. Season well with salt and freshly ground black pepper and squeeze over lime juice. Dollop this in the centre of the fried tortillas, add some of the A very fast *Mexican stir-fry* (see page 156), then add sour cream and grated cheese. You could put this under the grill, if you like.

16. THE OFFALLY BITS

When I was growing up, we either bought our chickens from farmers we knew, or from the market, and it was inconceivable that a whole chicken might be sold without its giblets. I'm not sure when this practice died out; I certainly remember, when I first started buying chickens for myself, I would always find the little bag of giblets in the cavity.

At home, we never did anything very adventurous with them. The livers were usually separated from the rest and either added to stuffing or hidden in something made with minced meat. The rest were used to enrich stock, a gravy made from a chicken stock and giblets was quite common. It never tasted offally, just slightly stronger than the darkest chicken meat.

These days the bag of giblets is rare and isn't supplied with most oven-ready chickens. This is a shame; they might not amount to much, but if you bought one chicken a week it would not be long before you had enough of each type of offal to make a proper meal out of them. However, we can buy them separately. I can find free-range or organic livers, hearts and necks quite easily. If you manage to buy birds which come with the giblets – and you don't want to use them for stock – separate them out. Put the gizzard (a digestive organ) with the hearts, as they have a similar texture and can be cooked in the same way.

There's a lot going for livers and hearts in particular. They're very cheap and very nutritious, loaded as they are with iron, folate and a host of vitamins, particularly vitamins A and B12. So it's useful to have a few recipes for them in your repertoire.

CHICKEN LIVERS

When buying chicken livers, look for those that are deeply coloured and glossy and avoid any that are a bit grey. To prepare, separate them out and pull out the connecting tendons. Cut out any green-tinged flesh, as this may have been tainted by bile from the gall bladder and will make the liver bitter.

The adults in my household adore chicken livers, a large plate of them would probably be in my husband's top 10 dishes and I'm quite partial, too. The biggest problem I've had is getting the children used to them, I think that, as they are high in iron, they can taste a little too metallic for them. I solve this by mincing them up with other meats to get them used to the taste, then gradually decreasing the amount of other meat. (I've now got this down to a 50:50 split.)

Chicken liver and porcini ragu

When I was growing up it was normal to add just one chicken liver to a ragu, I think Delia Smith always did this and I followed suit. However, a chicken liver ragu is very good in its own right or, as here, with dried mushrooms. You don't have to serve this with pasta, it would also be good with a large bowl of green or brown lentils.

handful of dried porcini, soaked in warm water for 20 minutes
1 tbsp olive oil
slice of unsalted butter
1 onion, finely chopped
1 celery stick, finely chopped
1 garlic clove, finely chopped
200g chicken livers, trimmed and finely chopped
1 tbsp tomato purée
150ml marsala
100ml vermouth
100ml chicken stock
1 tbsp rosemary leaves, very finely chopped
sea salt and freshly ground black pepper
2 tbsp double cream

To serve
4 portions of pasta, such as pappardelle
finely chopped parsley leaves
finely grated parmesan

Drain the porcini, reserving the soaking liquid. Chop them as finely as you can. Heat the olive oil and butter in a large casserole. Fry the onion and celery over a gentle heat until softened and starting to colour. Add the garlic and cook for another minute. Push everything to one side then increase the heat. Add the chicken livers and cook briskly, stirring constantly, until seared on all sides. Mix with the onion and celery, then add the porcini. Stir in the tomato purée, then add the marsala and vermouth. Let it bubble fiercely for a minute. Pour in the reserved mushroom liquid and the chicken stock and add the rosemary. Season with salt and pepper.

Simmer gently until the sauce has reduced and thickened, at least 15 minutes. Stir in the cream.

Serve with a wide, flat pasta such as pappardelle, sprinkled with parsley and parmesan.

Chicken livers with a lemon, parsley and caper gremolata

This is a very fast way of cooking chicken livers. I like to eat this piled on to crusty bread with lots of butter, so it's a good one for crostini, but I think it would probably be good with some boiled potatoes and a green salad, too.

1 tbsp olive oil
slice of unsalted butter
1 onion, finely chopped
400g chicken livers, trimmed and finely chopped
1 large tomato, finely chopped
1 tbsp sherry vinegar
2 tbsp chicken stock
sea salt and freshly ground black pepper
finely grated zest of 1 unwaxed lemon
2 garlic cloves, finely chopped
2 tbsp salted capers, rinsed, drained and chopped
leaves from a small bunch of parsley, finely chopped

Heat the olive oil and butter in a frying pan. Add the onion and sauté until well softened.

Add the chicken livers and cook for two minutes on each side. Add the tomato and pour over the sherry vinegar and chicken stock. Season with salt and pepper. Cook for a further three or four minutes.

Combine together the lemon zest, garlic, capers and parsley. Sprinkle this over the chicken livers when serving.

Chicken livers with peas, broad beans and ham

This is really a version of liver and bacon. I like it with some very crisp sautéed potatoes, although I believe mash is the usual accompaniment. If you have any savory – winter or summer – it is the perfect herb to serve with broad beans. If not, add some thyme instead.

1 tbsp olive oil
slice of unsalted butter
100g thick lardons of any Spanish or Italian ham
1 shallot, finely chopped
200g chicken livers, trimmed
50ml madeira or ruby port
100ml chicken stock
100g peas
100g broad beans
sea salt and freshly ground black pepper

Heat the olive oil and butter in a large, shallow, lidded frying pan or casserole. Add the ham and shallot and fry over a medium heat for a few minutes to get some colour, then push to one side, increase the heat and add the chicken livers. Fry on each side for a minute, then pour over the madeira or port. Bubble for a minute or two, then pour in the chicken stock. Add the peas and broad beans and season with salt and pepper. Cover. Simmer for a few minutes until the vegetables are tender and the livers are just cooked, a little pinkness in the centre is fine.

Chicken liver keema peas

This dish evolved over time to lead the children into eating chicken livers, as they were suspicious. It started off mainly as minced chicken or pork enriched with finely chopped livers and hidden by lots of vegetables. Over time, the mince was reduced until it is now just half-liver half-mince along with vegetables, lentils and lots of aromatic spices. You can still mess around with the proportions if you like; I would start with 100g chicken livers to 4–500g mince and build up from there.

1 tbsp vegetable oil
250g chicken livers, trimmed and finely chopped
250g minced chicken or pork
1 onion, finely chopped
1 courgette, coarsely grated
1 large carrot, coarsely grated
2 garlic cloves, finely chopped
2cm piece of root ginger, grated
small bunch of coriander, leaves and stems separated and finely chopped
2 tsp mild garam masala
½ tsp turmeric
¼ tsp ground cinnamon
1 tsp nigella seeds
1 tomato, finely chopped
75g red lentils
300ml chicken stock
sea salt and freshly ground black pepper
250g peas

Heat the oil in a large casserole or saucepan.

Fry the chicken livers briskly, then remove. Add the minced meat and brown this too, then add all the vegetables, garlic, ginger and coriander stalks. Cook for a couple of minutes, then add the spices, tomato, lentils and stock. Season with salt and pepper and return the livers to the pan. Add the peas.

Bring to the boil, then reduce the heat, cover and simmer for around 45 minutes, until everything is tender.

Serve with the coriander leaves stirred through, with fluffy naan on the side.

(To pressure-cook this, cook for 15 minutes at high pressure, then release the pressure slowly.)

Chicken liver parfait

The intention with this is to make a smooth, rich, spreadable pâté. I am firmly in the camp that thinks a layer of jelly on top is a good thing here; it helps preserve the parfait and I love the combination of earthy, slightly spiced livers and a fruity sweetness. So much so that I find it impossible to decide what kind of jelly to use. Usually, I have a collection of savoury apple jellies that I have flavoured with different spices or herbs. I simply melt some of these down, pour on top of the parfait and they reset nicely.

Favourite combinations have included an apple and blackberry jelly flavoured with bay leaves and crème de mûre, and a quince jelly given a hint of *quatre epices* (see pages 139–140). Here, I use apple and ginger wine jelly.

Incidentally, the other thing to serve with this parfait is a sweet onion jam, toasted, buttered brioche and a sweet dessert wine.

For the parfait
100g unsalted butter
1 small onion or shallot, very finely chopped
1 tsp thyme leaves
½ tsp ground allspice
1 mace blade, ground (or a grating of nutmeg)
¼ tsp ground ginger
400g chicken livers, trimmed and finely chopped
sea salt and freshly ground white pepper
75ml madeira or marsala
25g bone marrow, finely chopped (optional)
75ml double cream

For the jelly
300ml apple juice
sprig of thyme or lemon thyme
2 tbsp ginger wine
3 leaves of gelatine

Melt a small piece of the butter in a frying pan. When it starts to foam, add the onion and sauté over a gentle heat until it is very soft and translucent. This will take a while. Add the thyme leaves, allspice and mace and ground ginger. Increase the heat and add the chicken livers. Season with salt and white pepper. Fry for a minute to brown the chicken livers, then pour over the madeira. Add the chopped bone marrow, if using, at this point.

Simmer until the bone marrow has melted and the madeira has reduced to just 2–3 tbsp. Allow to cool a bit, then tip into a food processor and blitz. Add the remaining butter and the cream and blitz again. You want this as smooth as possible with absolutely no tendons to spoil it, so at this point it is a good idea to push it through a sieve. Put into earthenware pots and smooth over evenly.

To make the jelly, heat the apple juice in a saucepan with the thyme or lemon thyme and reduce by half. Add the ginger wine and simmer for another couple of minutes. Soak the gelatine leaves in cold water until soft, then wring out and add to the contents of the saucepan. Stir over a gentle heat until the gelatine has dissolved, then strain. Pour this over the pâté. Put in the fridge to set.

Chopped liver

This is the Jewish version of pâté, slightly coarser, with more robust flavours than the smoother parfait. It's best made with schmaltz – and gribenes – but if you don't have these, you can use butter or olive oil instead.

Chopped is a slight misnomer, as these days the mixture is puréed rather than finely minced.

To make this completely kosher, the livers are usually salted to remove blood and any green spots must be cut out.

2 tbsp butter, oil or schmaltz
1 large onion, finely chopped
400g chicken livers, trimmed
sea salt and freshly ground white pepper
handful of gribenes, if you have any
2 hard-boiled eggs, finely chopped
1 tsp brandy or Calvados
finely chopped parsley leaves

Heat the butter, oil or schmaltz in a frying pan and add the onion. Sauté until very soft and golden. This will take a while, so deal with the chicken livers now. Rinse them thoroughly, drain and pat dry on kitchen paper. Sprinkle with salt. Heat a griddle or grill and, when very hot, grill the chicken livers until well browned on both sides.

Add the livers to the onions and stir for a minute, then allow to cool and put in a food processor. Blitz until smooth, adding a handful of gribenes, if you have some, and seasoning with salt and white pepper.

Mix in most of the eggs, reserving a spoonful for sprinkling on top, then add the brandy and parsley. Put into an earthenware pot and smooth over. Sprinkle with the remaining egg. Serve with crackers and perhaps some gherkins and/or caperberries.

CHICKEN HEARTS

If you like a slightly firm, dense texture, chicken hearts are actually more palatable to a lot of people who need convincing about offal, as they don't taste too gamey, they just taste like very well-flavoured thigh meat.

They do need careful preparation and cooking though. First, make sure they don't have a membrane covering them; this is sometimes already removed, sometimes not, but peels off very easily. Next, you can trim off any of the top layer of fat, although really you shouldn't as it will keep the meat tender. Chicken hearts need very fast or very slow cooking, anything in between and they'll be as tough as old boots. So I am giving an example of each.

A quick note about gizzards, too, as you can cook them alongside the heart. They are quite small, but need cutting in half to remove a little sac of grit which will be found inside.

Grilled chicken hearts

You can cook these on a barbecue or on a griddle pan. They can be glazed with anything. I like a Japanese teriyaki sauce, or this one which is inspired by Peruvian *anticuchos*, which usually use ox hearts. Serve as part of a barbecue, or simply with some salad and fried potatoes. You can also slice them up and put them in a sandwich.

3 garlic cloves, crushed
2cm piece of root ginger, grated
2 tbsp olive oil
2 tbsp soy sauce
2 tbsp red wine vinegar
1 tbsp honey
1 tsp chilli flakes or powder
1 tbsp ground cumin
500g chicken hearts

Mix all the marinade ingredients (everything except the chicken) together. Add the chicken hearts and leave to marinate for at least a couple of hours. Heat your griddle as hot as you can get it. If using bamboo skewers, soak them for at least 30 minutes, then thread the hearts on to them; I reckon six to eight per skewer is plenty.

Grill for just a few minutes on each side – I think two or three should be ample – basting with the marinade as you do so. Allow to rest for a few minutes, then eat.

Braised chicken hearts

This was a bit of an experiment, as I wanted a rich, slightly spiced sauce with elements of sweet and sour. I've cut these in half, so they go better with pasta. Serve with a wide pasta such as pappardelle, or mashed potatoes.

1 tbsp olive oil
500g chicken hearts, halved
1 onion, finely chopped
2 garlic cloves, crushed
1 red chilli, finely chopped
1 tsp sweet smoked paprika
pinch of ground cinnamon
sprig of thyme
200ml red wine
200ml chicken stock
2 tomatoes, finely chopped
2 tbsp pomegranate molasses
1 tbsp capers, rinsed and drained (optional)
squeeze of lemon juice
handful of parsley, finely chopped

Heat the olive oil in a casserole until it is on the verge of smoking, then fry the chicken hearts on all sides very quickly. As soon as they are brown, remove them from the casserole and reduce the heat. Add the onion and sauté for several minutes until softening, then stir in the garlic, chilli and spices. Tuck in the thyme, then pour over the red wine. Allow this to bubble up for a minute or two, then add the chicken stock, tomatoes and pomegranate molasses.

Return the chicken hearts to the casserole.

Bring to the boil, then reduce the heat to a slow simmer and cover. Simmer for around one hour, or until the hearts are tender. Add the capers, if using, and the lemon juice and serve with a good sprinkling of parsley.

This is one of the times when I would normally use a pressure cooker, as it does get hearts tender very quickly: cook for 10 minutes on high pressure, then release the pressure slowly.

Braised chicken necks

There are a surprising number of recipes around for chicken necks. They are seasoned and deep-fried or roasted, curried and stewed. I even found a Tuscan recipe that I just didn't feel equal to. It involved boning the neck and stuffing it with minced pork and beef. I'm sure this would taste great, but I'm not sure where to start with this.

If you don't want to braise the necks on their own, you can replace some of them with wings and, if you have them, the gizzard. You could also add some bacon.

1 tbsp plain flour
2 tsp English mustard powder
1 tsp freshly ground black pepper
¼ tsp ground cinnamon
1 tsp fine sea salt
1kg chicken necks
groundnut oil
1 large onion, chopped
2 celery stalks, sliced
1 large green pepper, finely chopped
1 large carrot, finely chopped
3 garlic cloves, finely chopped
2 bay leaves
2 tomatoes, finely chopped
500ml chicken stock
handfuls of parsley, chopped

Mix the flour with the spices and salt. Dust the chicken necks with the seasoned flour.

Heat 1 tbsp of the oil in a large casserole or saucepan. Fry the chicken necks on all sides until well browned. Remove, then add a little more oil and sauté all the vegetables for 10 minutes, until softening and browning around the edges. Add the garlic and cook for a further two minutes. Add the bay leaves and tomatoes, stir to combine and pour in the chicken stock. Simmer very slowly for around 30 minutes. Serve with lots of chopped parsley, with either a large pile of mashed potato or some rice.

Chicken feet

I debated long and hard about whether to include a recipe for chicken feet. In the end, I decided against it. They're just not my thing.

My first experience of them was in a dim sum joint. The basement restaurant was full to bursting and ringing with the sound of clattering plates and shrieking children and, being a bit deaf anyway, I couldn't really hear the waitress. I peered into a bamboo steamer, saw the contents were a deep orange and thought the waitress said they were 'chilli beef'. They were of course 'chicken feet'. I nibbled around the edges a bit, but got quite confounded by both the lack of meat and the number of tiny bones. Later, I looked up recipes and felt quite nauseous about an instruction to 'first cut off the toenails'. This is slightly illogical of me, because I am quite happy dealing with pig's head or calf's foot.

The other clincher was the quality of the meat. I just couldn't find ethically reared chicken feet and didn't want to buy the large bags from the Oriental supermarket, even though they are cleaned. Sorry.

Further Reading

For a very illuminating read and brilliant analysis on the ethics of chicken production:

Ellis, Hattie, *Planet Chicken*, Sceptre, 2007

A very readable and practical guide to keeping layers and meat birds with recipes:

Diacono, Mark, *Chicken and Eggs*,
River Cottage Handbook No.11, Bloomsbury, 2013

Some Useful Chicken Cookery Books
(Mainly, but not exclusively, about chicken)

Cole, Janice, *Chicken and Egg*,
Chronicle Books, 2011
McLagan, Jennifer, *Fat*, Ten Speed Press
Ruhlman, Michael, *The Book of Schmaltz*,
LittleBrown, 2013
Schrager, Brian Lee and Sussman, Adeen,
Fried and True, Clarkson Potter, 2014
Sheraton, Mimi, *The Whole World Loves
Chicken Soup*, Warner Books, 1995

Stockists

As mentioned earlier, I don't want to recommend specific producers, but the following have lovely birds and are occasional providers of parts such as hearts and necks.

www.pipersfarm.co.uk
www.laverstock.co.uk
http://www.suttonhoochicken.co.uk

The only place I have found that supplies chicken oysters is Hugh Grierson:

http://the-organic-farm.co.uk

For some of the harder to find ingredients:

www.thespiceshop.co.uk stocks the largest range of spices I have ever come across and the quality is superb.

www.seasonedpioneers.co.uk are just about the only stockists of filé powder in the UK and do some decent blends.

For superb quality chillies, dried and fresh:

http://www.capsicana.co.uk
http://www.coolchile.co.uk/
http://www.southdevonchillifarm.co.uk/

For everything Oriental from fresh produce, every type of noodle imaginable, gyoza wraps and even kimchi and coconut water:

http://www.japancentre.com
http://www.japan-foods.co.uk
https://www.orientalmart.co.uk
http://www.spicesofindia.co.uk
http://www.waiyeehong.com

Acknowledgements

Thanks to ...

Everyone at Ebury, especially Sarah Lavelle for commissioning the book and to Laura Higginson for taking such good care of it.

Lucy Bannell for such clear sighted, sensitive editing and for being so patient over my woollier thoughts.

Will Webb for a design I adore.

Everyone the photoshoot, especially the very talented Andy Sewell, the equally talented and also unflappable Ellie Jarvis and Stephanie Dellner.

Clare Hulton, agent sans pareil, I thank my lucky stars I have you to support me.

Tim Hayward, Jinny Johnson and the beneficent Thane Prince for many helpful thoughts and brainstorms, and to everyone else who offered recipes and advice, especially Rachel McCormack and Grant Hawthorne.

My butcher, Hook and Cleaver, especially Martin Kirrane, for all the invaluable advice, demonstrations and general help throughout the writing of this book.

Maria Murtagh for beautiful and inspiring pots, I use them daily.

Finally, my family: my parents for setting me on my way in terms of both food and writing. And Shariq, Adam and Lilly, who never tired of chicken and who made me laugh with frequent renditions of a chickeny 'Dreadlock Holiday'. Love you all.

Index

T

V

W

Y

Z